# Georgia Quilts

THE UNIVERSITY OF GEORGIA PRESS  ATHENS AND LONDON

# Georgia Quilts

## PIECING TOGETHER A HISTORY

----------------------

Edited by Anita Zaleski Weinraub for the Georgia Quilt Project

A  W O R M S L O E
F O U N D A T I O N
P U B L I C A T I O N

Quilt photography by William C. L. Weinraub unless otherwise noted.

© 2006 by The University of Georgia Press
Athens, Georgia 30602
All rights reserved
Designed by Louise OFarrell
Set in 10.8/15 Garamond Premier Pro
Printed and bound by Kings Time Printing Press
The paper in this book meets the guidelines for permanence
and durability of the Committee on Production Guidelines
for Book Longevity of the Council on Library Resources.

Printed in China

10   09   08   07   06   P   5   4   3   2   1

10   09   08   07   06   C   5   4   3   2   1

Library of Congress Cataloging-in-Publication Data
Georgia quilts : piecing together a history / edited by Anita
Zaleski Weinraub for the Georgia Quilt Project ;
[quilt photography by William C. L. Weinraub].
p. cm. — (A Wormsloe Foundation publication)
Includes bibliographical references and index.
ISBN-13: 978-0-8203-2899-7 (hardcover : alk. paper)
ISBN-10: 0-8203-2899-5 (hardcover : alk. paper)
ISBN-13: 978-0-8203-2850-8 (pbk. : alk. paper)
ISBN-10: 0-8203-2850-2 (pbk. : alk. paper)
1. Quilts—Georgia—Themes, motives. I. Weinraub,
Anita Zaleski. II. Weinraub, William C. L.
NK9112.G46 2006
746.4609758—dc22          2006021615

British Library Cataloging-in-Publication Data available

This book is dedicated to the quiltmakers of Georgia, past and present, and to those who were determined and devoted enough to record their stories and preserve our quilt heritage for future generations—the unpaid, overworked volunteers of the Georgia Quilt Project. Working together, we have accomplished a great deal; we have certainly achieved our goals and then some. Although at the outset we all anticipated seeing lots of wonderful quilts, we never realized how much greater the rewards of quilt documentation would be—meeting so many fellow Georgians, hearing hundreds of stories, making unlikely friendships, and sharing dozens of documentation experiences ourselves, to the enrichment of our experience and understanding of Georgia's quilts and quiltmakers and of our fellow Georgians.

*This is history coming together when we see the*
*kaleidoscopes of colors that stretch across a yard*
*piece: the Double Wedding Ring, Jacob's Coat*
*. . . the patterns are endless. We become aware*
*that each one of us is uniquely different. Then,*
*we realize this is what makes quilting so special;*
*none of us is alike. When we come together with*
*all our family histories and express ourselves in*
*quilts, we are sharing a part of what God gave us*
*and the heritage He gave us to live.*

—Honorary Chairwoman Elizabeth C. Harris,
Georgia Quilt Project, GQP Kickoff Ceremony,
February 22, 1990

# Contents

- - - - - - - - - - - - - - - - - - - - - - - - - - - - -

# *Acknowledgments*

- - - - - - - - - - - - - - - - - - - - - - - - - - - - - - - - -

Like the quilt documentation project itself, this book has been a collaborative effort, a result of the work of many individuals. Though it is not possible to name them all here, a few deserve special recognition: In addition to the authors, the Georgia Quilt Project (GQP) board members contributed much time and advice from the planning stages in the early 1990s through publication of this book. Bill Weinraub, until his untimely death in 1997, provided computer assistance, as well as office space and equipment, in addition to photography, often giving of his time and expertise over and above what could reasonably be expected of one person. Liv Grønli and Carolyn Kyle put in many long hours in the early stages, preparing documentation forms for distribution to the authors. Judie Glaze spent many days at the keyboard computerizing selected data for the appendix. The University of Georgia Press staff, especially Jennifer Reichlin, expertly advised, mentored, and shepherded the manuscript through the editing and publishing processes. Many thanks, too, to Nicole Mitchell of the press for her strong support of and belief in this book project from the very beginning. All of the authors were generous with their time when asked to review manuscripts.

Finally, neither the GQP nor this book would have been possible without the continuing interest in our activities of Georgia's quilt guilds, which have provided volunteers and supported the project financially since 1989.

# Georgia Quilts

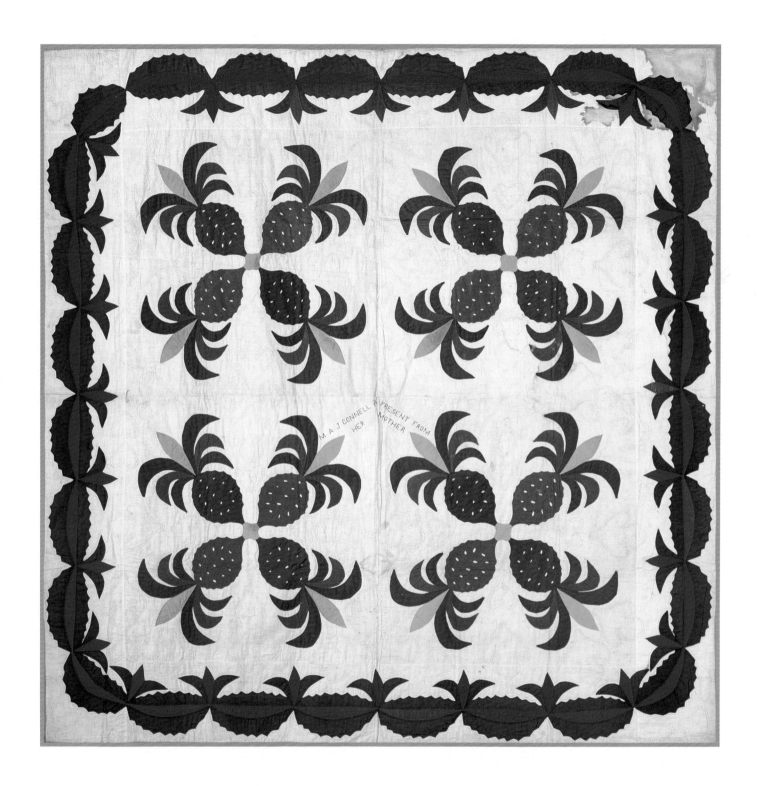

# Introduction

ANITA ZALESKI WEINRAUB

--------------------------------------------------

Ask any Georgian if someone in his or her family made quilts, and the answer will be yes almost every time. What is it about quilts that caused thousands of Georgians to take the time to share theirs with the Georgia Quilt Project (GQP)? For many, the desire to have their family's quilt recorded somewhere for posterity, the need to acknowledge their forebears, and the reassurance that part of their family's history would be preserved were enough to bring large crowds to the GQP's Quilt History Days. Quilts represent families, memories of the past, the loved one who is no longer here, and the nostalgia that most of us feel about things being somehow simpler and better "back then."

Rich or poor, black or white, urban dweller or rural farmwife, all kinds of Georgians made and continue to make quilts. Quilting in Georgia cuts across racial, economic, geographic, and other lines.

When the GQP undertook to document the state's quilts, the organizers sought to create a written and photographic record of Georgia's quilts as they existed at the end of the twentieth century. This body of research would be useful to historians, genealogists, and quilt researchers. To that end, seventy-six Quilt History Days were held around the state between 1990 and 1993. Georgians were asked to share their quilts and allow the GQP to photograph and record information about them. The project volunteers were overwhelmed at almost every site—hundreds of people brought in many more quilts than could be processed in a day, sometimes forcing the staff to limit the number of quilts one person could register to five or, at busy venues, three. Nearly ten thousand quilts were documented, yet this is only a fraction of the quilts that exist in Georgia.

Quilts, taken collectively, along with the stories told by owners of a grandmother long gone, of life on the family farm, of trying times or good times or ordinary day-to-day living, can be invaluable vehicles for learning about life in the past. Not only can one learn what kinds of fabrics were used in clothing in the past by examining a scrap-bag quilt, but through interviews with the owners of quilts, a picture of Georgia never before seen emerges—a picture of rural and small town life, of community interaction and mutual support, of getting by and making do on the farm, of war times, and of those other times when life was good and sweet and simple. This is the kind of information GQP volunteers gathered, to be preserved along with the images of the quilts as part of the historical record.

*Anita Zaleski Weinraub*

2

## *The Evolution of the GQP*

The GQP was formed in 1988 as an outgrowth of the North Georgia Quilt Council (NGQC, now Georgia Quilt Council), an umbrella organization representing individual quiltmakers and quilt guilds throughout North and Central Georgia. After conducting a feasibility study, the NGQC determined that there was sufficient interest in documenting the state's quilts and offered the GQP some seed money.

When the project incorporated in 1989 as a non-profit Georgia corporation, it was decided that the GQP would be an all-volunteer group; no one would receive payment to participate in the documentation effort. Goals of the project were simply stated:

✧ to create an archive of information about the quilts and quiltmakers of Georgia;

✧ to encourage appreciation and preservation of Georgia's quilts; and

✧ to promote and encourage the art of quiltmaking and the appreciation of quilts through education.

All quilts in Georgia were eligible for registry, regardless of provenance. Both newly made and older quilts were welcome. Quilt tops, quilt blocks, and a few items of quilted clothing—in addition to quilts—were documented when they appeared at a Quilt History Day. Woven coverlets were not documented. A public Quilt History Day format was chosen: volunteers would travel throughout the state and hold quilt history events, inviting Georgians to share their quilts with us. Local and regional coordinators were appointed to enlist volunteer involvement at the local level. We took care to ensure that all regions of the state were represented, as well as both rural and urban areas of each region. We made special efforts to encourage participation by quiltmakers from all racial, ethnic, and cultural groups. Whenever possible we held a two-day (Friday and Saturday) documentation so both working people and others would have an opportunity to bring their quilts.

### Planning for and Format of Quilt History Days

Networking, fund-raising, and planning for the Quilt History Days took place during 1989; we contacted thirty-five states then conducting or having previously conducted such surveys for assistance and advice. Project representatives attended quilt documentation events in Alabama, Florida, Nebraska, New York, and North Carolina. Within Georgia the GQP sought advice from the Georgia Folklife Program, the Georgia Department of Archives and History, museum personnel, and academicians. Professor John Burrison of Georgia State University was particularly helpful in providing contacts and leads. In preparation for the

Figure I.1. Family Memories Crazy Quilt. Nellie Taylor Giddens (b. 1929), Macon (Bibb County), 1992. 23" x 52". Hand-pieced and -appliquéd cotton, polyester, silk, and satin. Collection of the maker. [GQP 2247]

Nellie created a family heirloom in the crazy patch style by utilizing scraps of her children's bibs and gowns, hankies, her late husband's World War II army uniform, and many other fabrics with sentimental value to her. Some of the lace and tatting are more than 125 years old. The piece is heavily embellished with embroidery, as well as with one of her late husband's Boy Scout medals (he was an eagle scout), a pin she wore when dating her husband, a lock of her son's hair, and one of the GQP's pins. A flower from a hat of her mother's is a particular favorite of Nellie's. Nellie served on the GQP board as data entry coordinator from 1989 to 1999. She is an extraordinarily skilled quiltmaker and has won many ribbons for her work. An enthusiastic member of the Heart of Georgia Quilt Guild in Macon, Nellie is known for her talent, generosity, and energy.

Nellie Giddens, ca. 1995.

Elizabeth C. Harris

At the kickoff of the GQP, Michele Rodgers (Bartow History Center), Elizabeth C. Harris, and Barbara Fennell (Etowah Art Gallery) stand in front of Hurricane Hugo, made by South Carolina schoolchildren in appreciation for supplies sent them by Georgia schoolchildren after Hurricane Hugo.

## Kickoff of the GQP

The GQP arrested the attention of Georgians at its kickoff ceremony in the State Capitol Rotunda on February 22, 1990, during the busy legislative session. Eight quilts were suspended from rotunda railings, and three more were displayed on the floor. Quilters set up a frame and quilted to one side. An information table and a refreshment table completed the tableau. Speakers included then First Lady Elizabeth C. Harris (honorary chairwoman of the project); Annie Archbold, director of the Georgia Folklife Program; Fred Fussell, chief curator of the Columbus Museum of Art; Stephanie Swanston, program coordinator of the APEX (African American Panoramic Experience) Museum in Atlanta; and Anita Zaleski Weinraub, chairwoman of the GQP. More than two hundred people were on hand to celebrate with us. Then governor Joe Frank Harris declared the week of February 20–24, 1990, Quilt History Week in Georgia. This was the first time a quilt exhibit had hung in the state capitol; it was not, however, the last. The GQP mounted another in Governor Zell Miller's office during the autumn of 1992, in collaboration with the Georgia Council for the Arts.

first scheduled Quilt History Day in March, nationally known quilt experts Barbara Brackman of Kansas, Laurel Horton of South Carolina, and Bets Ramsey of Tennessee conducted training workshops in January 1990 in Atlanta on fabric and quilt dating for ninety core volunteers.

We raised additional funds by a variety of means—raffling quilts, selling donated doll quilts, and during the Quilt History Days selling photographs of quilts to their owners. Pins, T-shirts, tote bags, aprons, and other items with the project's pine tree logo were also sold. Georgia's quilt guilds made generous financial donations, as did individual quilters and quilt lovers.

After some practice documentations were held with the help of the Chamblee Star and Heart of Georgia Quilt Guilds and the fanfare of the kickoff ceremony (see sidebar) was behind us, the first public Quilt History Days were held in March 1990. Press releases were issued to the local media of the documentation dates and hours. The Quilt History Day format was similar to that used in many other states: owners were interviewed for family and social history relevant to the quilt and its maker and were encouraged to relate any stories associated with them. A technical and physical examination was performed to determine dimensions, pattern, age, fiber, and other details, and photographs were taken of all quilts. A numbered label was sewn to the back of each documented quilt.

The Georgia Quilt Project documented more than eight thousand quilts between 1990 and 1993, and

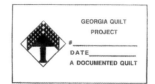

Figure 1.2. A label like this one was stitched onto the reverse of every quilt the GQP documented.

Figure I.3. Sumter County, Ga., ca. 1910. A rural family displays its quilts on the fence. SUM136B, Vanishing Georgia Collection, Georgia Archives.

more than a thousand additional quilts have been documented since then. Although not all of them came with a family story, everyone who brought a quilt to one of our seventy-six Quilt History Days (see appendix B) had a reason for doing so and was viewed as a valuable historical informant and welcome participant. Some people brought their quilts down from attics or up from basements, from cedar chests or closet shelves, in order to see what we could reveal about them. Perhaps details of the quilt's history had been lost. Perhaps a quilt had been purchased and the new owners wanted to know how old the quilt was or if they had paid a fair price. (We did not appraise quilts or put monetary values on them, and we encouraged people to keep quilts in their families.) With pattern-identification

and quilt-dating books in hand, we attempted to give owners some information about their quilt or quilts. In addition, we gave owners written information about the care and conservation of quilts so that they might better preserve them for their descendants.

We saw all kinds—exquisite heirlooms, threadbare survivors, masterful, plain, crude, new, and old—but regardless of its condition or cleanliness, or whatever it might lack in workmanship or aesthetic appeal, we always found some positive quality to observe and record, for it was obviously valued and held in some regard by the owner.

The desire to share quilts and the owner's need to tell about the ancestor, mother, grandmother, or loved one who made them were remarkable discoveries for us. Often, when Quilt History Days coordinator Mary Ross arrived at the site at 8:15 to begin setup, she found a line of people with quilts in their arms, already patiently waiting their turn. The first thing Mary did many mornings was put out some folding chairs on which people could rest their heavy armloads of quilts. Owners would often wait many hours for us to complete the documentation process.

Since our procedure almost always funneled down to a single photography area, we could process quilts only as quickly as we could photograph them. With an experienced crew, we could achieve a pace of photographing sixteen quilts per hour. This meant that—and this was in the days before autofocus and digital cameras—we had fewer than four minutes to hang the quilt (sometimes with special handling); verify the quilt identification number; place a number plaque below the image; take overall photographs in color transparency, black-and-white print, and color print film; take closeup and detail shots as needed (a minimum of five exposures per quilt, each individually composed and focused); and take the quilt down, refold it, and reunite it with its paperwork.

This was a fast-paced station, yet sixteen per hour, when there might be literally a hundred or more quilts (and their owners) waiting, was a grueling but ultimately unsatisfactory pace. The inexorable arithmetic of quilts per hour and hours per day required that we limit the number of quilts per owner and quilts per day. In many instances we simply had to turn people away, to our mutual disappointment. In such cases we supplied owners with a list of upcoming Quilt History Days and encouraged them to bring their quilts to another location. Although more than eight thousand quilts were documented, we could have easily logged twice that number had the means been available.

The photography area naturally drew spectators

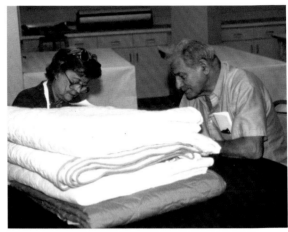

Figure I.4. A quilt owner is interviewed by a volunteer. Columbus (Muscogee County), 1990. All photos on this spread by Anita Z. Weinraub.

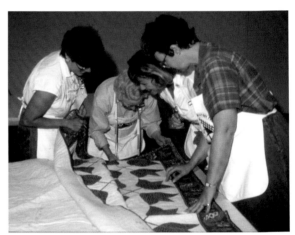

Figure I.5. Trained volunteers perform a physical examination of a quilt, Columbus, August 1990. From left: Stephanie Moses, Fran Burns, Vista Mahan, Margie Rogers.

from among the quilt owners and the other volunteers. For its portrait, each quilt was raised above the floor against a black backdrop and lit with floods (the actual pictures were made with flash) for all to see. This created a visual parade in which each quilt, in turn, was given star billing; we called it our "private quilt show." We always provided a waiting area with chairs within view of the photography area, where owners, after be-

Figure 1.6. A mechanical engineer, photographer Bill Weinraub constructed a flexible tripod mount to hold three identical cameras—one with color transparency film, one with color print film, and one with black-and-white film—to streamline the photography of each quilt brought to Georgia's Quilt History Days.

Figure 1.7. Each quilt took center stage for its "portrait." Columbus, 1990.

ing interviewed, could wait for their quilts and comfortably enjoy the show. The black backdrop and studio lighting, and the care taken to handle, hang, and record each quilt properly, allowed the public to see quilts in a whole new way. First, owners were struck by the very premise—scholarly interest in *their* family quilts. Then, too, quilts look quite different hanging and viewed from a distance than they do folded up at

home or spread out on a bed. Not only were the owners treated to a new view of their quilts, they were also able to hear oohs and aahs as others present admired them. This would frequently lead to chatting among the owners: "Is that quilt yours? It's just beautiful. Who made it? How old did they tell you it is?" And the stories of the quilts would once more be told—the sharing and transmission of information continued at an informal level.

## Memorable Quilt History Days

Many stories about the quilts and quiltmakers of Georgia past and present, first heard at our Quilt History Days, are recounted in the pages of this book. Some of the stories about the Quilt History Days themselves, too, have become part of Georgia's quilt history, a body of shared lore to be told and retold again and again. Although space constraints prohibit our including an anecdote from each of our seventy-six Quilt History Days, several come to mind readily. The hundreds of volunteers who helped us around the state will recognize many of them, smile or chuckle knowingly, and thus recall what we look back upon as a unique time for all of us—for quilt project volunteers and quilt owners alike, a period during which we all took time from our busy lives and stopped to take a closer look at the quilts, those silent, inanimate objects that seem always to have been (yet will not always be) there, each with its own story, each waiting for a chance to tell it and have it recorded.

Our first public Quilt History Days were held in Tifton March 17 and 18, 1990. The Georgia Agrirama, the state's official museum of agriculture, was our sponsor, and the event was planned by the capable Pat Phillips, then coordinator of Curatorial and Research Services at the Agrirama and a GQP regional coordinator. (Pat, now Pat Phillips Marshall, is at present curator of Furnishings and Decorative Arts at the North Carolina Museum of History.) The site chosen was the spacious Rural Development Center (RDC), where we would have several rooms in which to work, an ample lobby to receive owners, and an auditorium in which to photograph the quilts, with plenty of seating for owners. The only stipulation was that we vacate the lobby and auditorium by five each afternoon—on Friday evening (the seventeenth) the local charm school was holding a rehearsal for its annual recital, to take place Saturday evening. No problem! After all, how many quilts could there be in Tift County, Georgia, a fairly rural county whose only large town is Tifton, the county seat (population 14,200)? In any case, we would be careful not to accept more quilts than we could comfortably process by about four o'clock in order to vacate the lobby and auditorium by five. Were we in for a surprise! Not only did we have to turn people away on Friday and encourage them to return Saturday, but at four o'clock we were not even close to processing the hundred-plus quilts we did accept. Both the charm school and administration of the RDC generously allowed us to use the lobby, which was the only place large enough to continue the photography. Setting up in the lobby took upward of an hour, and the documentation process went fairly slowly from then on, due to the reduced space, the need to stay out of the way of the rightful occupants (the charm school), and the somewhat reduced volunteer force—many were unable to stay past the dinner hour. We didn't finish that first day in Tifton until well past nine that night. We all felt quite satisfied with our job well done and well deserving of supper at the local Chinese restaurant, but slowly the realization sank in that in a few short hours we would have to do it all again. We had worked for more than twelve hours and had to begin

Figure 1.8. Volunteer Marion Nicholson stitches an identifying label with its documentation number onto the back of each quilt documented. Stone Mountain (DeKalb County), 1993. Photo by Anita Z. Weinraub.

again in the morning after only a few hours' rest. Luckily for our weary bodies, Saturday brought heavy rain (and a tornado watch), fewer quilts were brought in, and we carefully monitored the progress of the quilts so as to finish by our 4:00 p.m. deadline; not only was our task completed but we, too, were "finished" by then.

We learned a lot from that first experience, and based on this and several other early efforts, we began to joke that running the Quilt History Days was a process that would be perfected only after the last Quilt History Day had come and gone. As it turned out, this proved to be quite true—we were learning and perfecting until the very last day. Space, space, space, and adequate ceiling height were our watchwords (and lack of same our bane) until the very end. Our sites varied from the extremely cramped to the spacious and commodious, from the sweltering to the cold and drafty to the slightly comical. In May 1991 we shared the Lowndes County Fairgrounds with a dog show (separate buildings). In January 1991 we documented quilts at the Thronateeska Heritage Foundation in

Albany. Except for the photography, all phases of the documentation process were conducted on the chilly, canopied but open-air railroad platform at the rear of the building (a converted train station). The strong draft from opening and closing the door blew over our photography light stands and backdrop during a lunch break!

At the opposite end of the climatological spectrum was a steamy experience in Thomasville. We were scheduled to be in a vacant storefront on the town square. This would provide us with a good view of the annual heritage celebration the same day, Saturday, May 18, 1991. A severe thunderstorm the night before the Quilt History Day caused the roof of the building to leak, resulting in a flood in the storefront and loss of electricity. Local coordinator Cheryl Walters Watson speedily arranged for us to use the lobby, dining room, and lounges of a nearby residential hotel for the elderly. Unfortunately, the same thunderstorm had also shorted out the air-conditioning system of the Peartree Park facility. May in Southwest Georgia can be torrid, and to round out our trio of bad luck, Saturday dawned hot, sunny, and humid due to the previous night's rain. We dripped and dragged all day, although everyone tried to make the best of it, and the personnel at the hotel were accommodating. The residents were understanding about not being able to eat in their dining room. Cheryl was also able to recruit people performing community service that weekend to spell our volunteer force, which had to take more frequent breaks to have a drink and to step *outside* to cool off on that steamy day. That was also the day many of us saw our first bed race, which went right past the corner of the hotel. It would have been entirely appropriate if the beds had sported quilts, but none of them did.

In Moultrie, on May 17, 1991, prison parolees were assigned to help us—they told us ours was the most agreeable assignment they had been given, especially since we had treated them to a McDonald's meal by way of a thank-you. Although initially puzzled at the premise of making such a fuss over quilts, by the end of the day the parolees had become converts to the cause.

In all of Social Circle there was no building large enough to host a Quilt History Day, although there was much local interest in our work and many, many quilts to be documented. The original solution to the dilemma was put forth by coordinator Alice Hughes: we would use two sites and ferry the quilts in between. The First United Methodist Church hosted most of the documentation activities, but the photography was set up in the library—across town and too far to walk. Will any of us ever forget the sight of Alice in her minivan making *endless* trips back and forth taking a shortcut through the cemetery? Unfortunately, one of the Social Circle days was rainy. This had been anticipated and wrapping stations were set up at each end to protect the quilts—no such special treatment for poor Alice, however!

Certainly the most elegant site where we documented quilts was the governor's mansion in Atlanta. GQP honorary chairwoman and then Georgia First Lady Elizabeth Harris invited us to document the Harris family quilts. We were served tea and duly humbled by our surroundings. Another period setting was the Taylor-Grady House in Athens. The Cotton Patch Quilt Guild sponsored those Quilt History Days, and the Junior League of Athens generously opened this historic home to us. Opening the pocket doors between the parlor and living room provided plenty of depth and width for photography. There was just

## Maxine Thomas

Maxine Thomas was assistant dean of the University of Georgia Law School when she brought her quilts in to be documented. She submitted the following account of her quilting experiences in Japan and with the GQP:

"Few experiences have been more rewarding than the year I spent in Sendai, Japan. While I was there ostensibly to teach law, one of the many side benefits was the chance to participate with a small group of women quilters.

"Afraid that I might be bored over the course of a long year, I arrived in Japan loaded down with fabric, batting, needles and thread to fill my anticipated empty hours. But very soon I made friends and when they found out I quilted (I had made one small wall hanging and one quilt), they immediately presented me to Keiko Gouke, quilting *sensei* (teacher). Keiko had been a painter before she was introduced to quilting and her quilts were paintings in fabric and thread. She is now a renowned quilter in Japan with many award-winning books and articles about her quilts.

"The quilters (a small band of four to six of us) met weekly in the upstairs of Keiko's small house and talked of families and hopes and dreams while needles spun through fabric and the smell of small sweets and tea wafted through the room. Unlike my brief experience in quilting groups in the United States, at each of these meetings we worked on our individual quilts stretched out over our laps with no frame or even a hoop; to this day that is the way I quilt. The only time we worked together on any one woman's quilt was when someone reached the point of basting quilt top to batting and back. The floor was then our platform and long basting stitches provided a spider web–like skeleton that the owner then had for her quilting.

"When I returned to Athens, Georgia, I was delighted to hear about the GQP's quilt documentation effort. None of us could have imagined how many people would respond. I recall telephoning the number from the news article about the Project to ask whether they were going to have more than one documenting session in Athens. Leadership Georgia was meeting in Dalton the weekend scheduled for the documentation and I was not certain I would get back in time. I was assured that if I made it back I could bring my Japanese quilt and have it documented. Something told me that morning to leave Dalton early and head back to Athens. When I got to the Taylor-Grady House, there were very few cars. I assumed there had been very few quilts brought until I saw signs stating that they had been swamped and that no more quilts could be accepted. I turned around to go back to the car, then decided I would go and ask why mine could not be documented as promised. There was a small note on the door which read, 'Maxine Thomas, please knock.'

"This quilt depicts the children's story of a young maiden found in a bamboo plot who was the most beautiful young woman in the village and, it eventually turns out, was a princess who had come from the moon to bring joy to the lives of an old man and an old woman. The quilt is pieced in Japanese silk fabric scraps from a kimono maker's shop. The princess's name is written in Japanese characters. There are many things that we do in our lives that bring great joy. For me, quilting and having my quilt selected as part of this book are surely among those joys."

Maxine Thomas, 2006.

Kaguyahimay. Original design, Maxine Thomas (b. 1948), Watkinsville (Oconee County), now of Jamestown, Ohio, made while maker lived in Sendai, Japan, 1989. 67½" x 65¾". Hand-appliquéd and -quilted cotton, silks, and synthetics. Collection of the maker. [GQP 2480]

enough space between two low-hanging crystal chandeliers in the living room to photograph the quilts, with the hanging-up and taking-down tables in the parlor behind our backdrop. The technical examination of the quilts took place in the upstairs hall and bedrooms; fortunately, we had a couple of young student volunteers in good shape who nimbly carried quilts up and down the stairs all day long.

Especially meaningful to us were those occasions when children observed us at work or even participated in the documentation effort. Of course, many quilt owners brought their children with them, but there were a few occasions when our educational goal was directly in our sights as we proceeded through the day. In Louisville, English teacher Jane Donahue recruited English students at what was then Louisville High School as our volunteers for the day. We were given use of the school gym, and our student volunteer crews were rotated with the change of every class period. Much work was done by the students in preparation for the Quilt History Day: the interview and technical examination forms were studied; students practiced interviewing each other about their family histories; tips on manners, directing crowds, and handling quilts were imparted. Students were encouraged to ask questions at home about family quilts and to bring them to the Quilt History Day for documentation. When the day finally came, women from the local senior center set up a quilt in a frame in the center of the gym and spent the day quilting with us. Many of the children had never seen quilting in a frame. As we so frequently heard throughout the state, quilting seemed to have skipped a generation in Louisville—it was something the grandmothers did but not the mothers. We felt good about having instilled a sense of pride of family heritage in some of those youngsters,

Figure 1.9. A volunteer in Louisville reunites documented quilts with their owners and makes sure they receive a handout regarding the care and conservation of quilts. Photo by Anita Z. Weinraub.

and we also learned that the generations are not always so far apart and that common ground can be found, especially when chatting informally as we could in the setting of a Quilt History Day.

In Toccoa we documented quilts in the auditorium of the elementary school. Throughout the day, classes would visit and learn a little about what we were doing. Similarly, when our last Quilt History Days were held at the Smokerise Baptist Church in Stone Mountain, the nursery school classes there were brought in to visit and see some of the quilts being photographed. On occasion, as in Carrollton, Athens, and Dahlonega, college students comprised part of the volunteer force.

Friendships were formed and reinforced, and even a lost relative discovered during our Quilt History Days. Volunteer Alice Hughes of Walnut Grove (Walton County) learned that she and the husband of volunteer Ollie Wright of Carrollton (Carroll County) have a common ancestor. Several quilt owners brought quilts to several Quilt History Days; seeing their familiar faces at yet another place new to us was a pleasure indeed.

*Anita Zaleski Weinraub*

12

Mrs. Meldra Panchelli expressed interest in our photography setup one day in Milledgeville. She was referred to our photographer when he was taking a short break. Mrs. Panchelli's first husband, Dr. William Harris, had been a dentist by profession and a photographer by avocation. The couple used to spend their vacations doing the poultry show circuit taking pictures of, yes, prize chickens. None of us had ever heard of a chicken photographer. Mrs. Panchelli also brought several quilts to be documented (see one in fig. 2.6), which have been passed down through her family.

As was inevitable with a project that stretched over three years and involved a specific, repetitive process enlivened by changes in venue, weather, and personnel, Georgia's Quilt History Days developed something of their own culture. Lunch and snacks were something we all looked forward to—an opportunity to get off our feet for a few minutes of rest from the pressures of the day—and there was almost always a great deal of pressure due to the number of quilts brought in. The midday meal was usually quite brief and in shifts, since we were always conscious that many owners were waiting patiently for their quilts. Some lunches were veritable gustatory delights, others a mere brown bag. Bretta Perkins's Unrepeatable Soup, served at the Jarrell Plantation in Juliette, became a GQP legend. One of the great mainstays of Quilt History Day lunches was pimiento cheese, which appeared regularly (see "Tribute to Bill Weinraub"). Lunch settings were as varied as the menus, with the sole common ingredient being great care to keep food and drink separate from the area where the quilts were. Sometimes we ended up outdoors, once in a storage closet (Statesboro), and at the Savannah Visitors Center we ate in a railroad dining car parked alongside the museum.

## Overview of Georgia's Quilts

At Quilt History Days we saw everything from whole-cloth quilts whose tops were made from one or two pieces of fabric to a quilt made from more than 35,000 tiny patches. Some quilts were made of the finest silks, satins, and velvets. We also saw quilts made from sacks that had once held tobacco, guano, rice, sugar, or feed, from Crown Royal Whisky bags, from scraps from women's bras, from tobacco premium flags, funeral ribbons, used trousers, old mailman uniforms (made by a thirteen-year-old boy recovering from scarlet fever in 1912), prize ribbons from dog shows, and even milk filters. In addition to the usual cotton (in the earlier quilts) and polyester batting, we also saw a quilt with an inner layer of used pantyhose, and one tied quilt stuffed with chicken feathers. Many quilts were cared for reverently, always kept on the "best bed" or folded and wrapped and then laid in a closet or chest. Others were found in the trash, on a back porch, in a corn crib, discarded in the woods, or even wrapped around an auto engine.

The stories that were told about the quiltmakers ran the gamut as well. We saw a signature quilt that was made for a bachelor by the young women of his town, a quilt made by a woman born without fingers on her right hand, and a quilt made for a deaf woman so she could show people in the nursing home where she lived about her life. There was a quilt made by the youngest of three sisters, all of whom had married the same man in succession. Another quilt was made by a woman who accidentally swallowed her thimble and died. Several quilts were made as parting gifts for a pastor, friend, or family member. An African American quilting group in North Carolina made such a quilt for a member in 1958 when she moved to Georgia—mem-

## A Grandson Remembers His Childhood

Our Quilt History Days awakened an interest in family and in history among the participants. Several people wrote the project to thank us for caring about their quilts, to amplify or correct information they had provided, and to compliment us on our undertaking. Carl E. Butler, then of Brunswick (Glynn County), brought in the quilt made for him by his grandmother, Maggie Lee Webb Butler. In 1993 he wrote the GQP the following nostalgic account of his other grandmother, Vacie Mae Bradford Andrews:

"This whole [documentation] episode has brought back some very pleasant memories for me. I was very close to my 'Grandma' Andrews. I spent quite a few summers with her in rural Wilkes County. (I grew up in adjacent Elbert County.) I can remember going with her to gather straw to make brooms or to gather small tree limbs to make 'brush brooms' that she used to sweep her yards. She never let a blade of grass grow

A brush broom was used to keep sand yards free of growth. Here a woman identified only as Lillian sweeps her yard in Baldwin County, ca. 1940. BAL155, Vanishing Georgia Collection, Georgia Archives.

in her yards. They were covered with a pretty white sand and she kept them swept clean with the brush broom which made intricate patterns in the sand.

"I do remember quilting being done by her at her home. Sometimes in the 1950s—for I had not yet started school at that time—I went with my aunt to my grandmother's. She had four large hooks in the ceiling of the living room. They hung the quilt frame from these hooks and my grandmother, aunt, great aunt, and a few other ladies quilted while I played on the floor in front of a coal burning heater. I remember the room quite well, with a large old pump organ, a hall tree, and a framed picture of Governor Eugene Talmadge displayed very prominently.

"I learned to eat (and even enjoy) pig feet while staying with my grandmother! My uncle had a small country store about a quarter of a mile up the road. I loved to walk up there and get ice cream in the small round paper cartons with a flat wooden spoon to eat it with. I could only go get the ice cream after I had eaten a pig foot with vinegar, which I had refused to do. I learned to eat them and many other items just to get that cup of ice cream. After walking to my uncle's store, one of the favorite stops on the way back was at Sue's, an aging black lady who lived in a very small shack. Sue's house, like my grandmother's, had no running water or plumbing (although my grandmother did have electricity and Sue didn't). Her house was very dark, there were no windows and all the walls were covered with newspaper. I think this was for insulation, but I'm also told that 'haints' [ghosts], which Sue talked about a lot, had to read all those words on those papers when they came into a house. Anyway, Sue entertained me with all sorts of stories and even let me play with her numerous cats that were always present.

"Although I'm only 42, this all seems like a completely other era. [It's] hard to imagine the progress we have made over the course of these years. I know I'm a richer person for having experienced life back in *those* days—and it saddens me that most children now will never experience those things. Most children today would probably say 'Quilt? What's a quilt?' Thank you for the memories you helped bring back. And thank you for your efforts to preserve a part of our culture and our past."

Maggie Lee Webb Butler, 1949. Photo courtesy of Carl Butler.

String Quilt. Maggie Lee Webb Butler (1879–1965), Elbert County, ca. 1940. 63½" x 83". Hand-pieced and -quilted cotton. Collection of Carl Butler. [GQP 5431]

bers of the Dorcas Society, as they called themselves, signed blocks as a farewell. Another quilt, of album blocks, was made in the nineteenth century for a young woman to take to college and collect the signatures of new friends. A retired schoolteacher made a quilt from the dozens of handkerchiefs she had received from students over the years. Several quilts were pieced by children and teens recuperating from illnesses such as the previously mentioned scarlet fever. More than one quilt was made from scraps from the trousseaux of women whose fiancés never returned from the Civil War. And then there were quilts whose makers claimed some connection to famous people: we documented quilts made by Senator Sam Nunn's grandmother, former governor Joe Frank Harris's grandmother (see fig. 8.8), ancestors of the mayors of Valdosta and Milledgeville, and descendants of Zachary Taylor, Jefferson Davis, James Madison, Roger Williams, Mary Todd Lincoln, William Penn, and John Adams—or so the stories went. One owner told us that the ancestor who made the quilt she brought in was a descendant of the man who held the Bible for George Washington at his inauguration. We documented a quilt made in honor of Barbra Streisand, and one made of the same pattern and colors as the interior hangings of one of Muammar al-Qaddafi's tents. We also documented a Possum Quilt (see fig 1.7) and a Pimiento Cheese Quilt (see "Tribute to Bill Weinraub").

Quilt owners loved to be drawn out about their quilts and about their families, and the volunteers of the GQP loved to listen to their stories. Many a tale was told of hard times during the Great Depression, wearing feed sack clothing, hand carding batts from cotton picked on the family farm, and mama or grandma making quilts so the family had something to use as cover to keep them warm. Some owners were as proud of the plainest, most poorly made, lovingly used quilts

as others were of exquisite heirlooms clearly made by an expert needlewoman—as they rightly should be, since the quilt has become a personal symbol of hardship endured, a grandmother remembered, or a childhood long ago.

Some of the more poignant moments during our Quilt History Days occurred during the interview portion of our documentation process. One woman brought a quilt made by a great-aunt around the turn of the century (fig. 1.10). It was a green and white crib quilt in the Robbing Peter to Pay Paul pattern, made with hope and expectation for the ancestor's first child. This firstborn child died shortly after birth, as did all subsequent babies. As the story spread through the volunteer force that day at the Columbus Museum of Art, people would drift over just to gaze thoughtfully for a few moments at the green and white quilt, empathizing with the unfortunate quiltmaker long gone from our world but whose story and whose quilt are lovingly preserved in her family.

We once noticed a woman crying in the audience at a Quilt History Day. People would occasionally get teary-eyed when speaking of a loved one during the interview, but we had not seen tears in the photography audience. A volunteer approached her and asked gently if she was all right. The woman sniffled and said, "Oh yes, I was just thinking about how proud my grandmother would be if she could be here to see everyone admiring her quilts."

These stories have already become part of the GQP story. Like the quilts, they have become pieces of our past, pieces of our history, part of our shared experiences. Any of these terms will suffice, and at the same time no term could possibly be adequate to describe the uniqueness of the documentation experience as it enriched our lives and made us humbly aware of the greatness and scope of Georgia's history and the his-

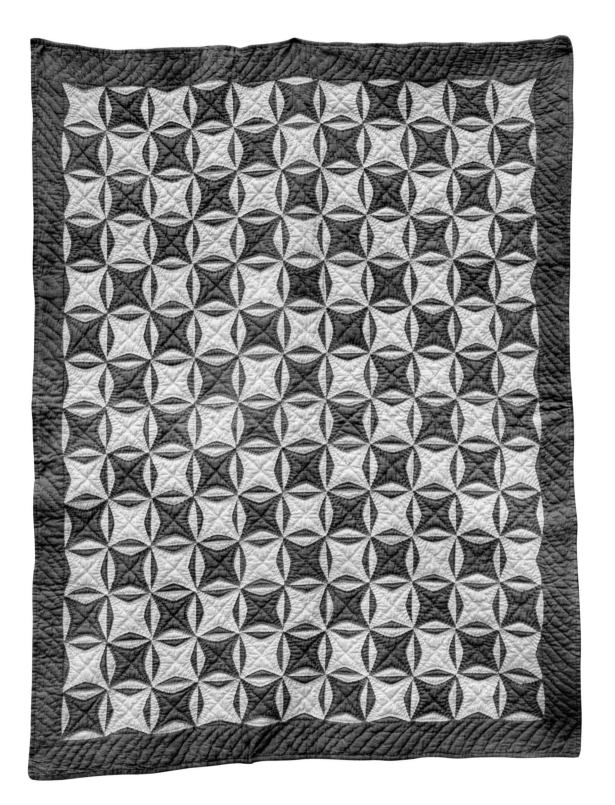

Lilla Owens Thrash with her brother and nephews, ca. 1910. Photo courtesy of Mary Davis.

Figure I.10, Robbing Peter to Pay Paul. Lilla Owens Thrash (1876–1964), La-Grange (Troup County), ca. 1897. 38 ¾" x 48 ¾". Hand-pieced and -quilted cotton. Collection of Mary Davis, grand-niece of Lilla Owens Thrash. Photo by Anita Z. Weinraub. [GQP 2194]

## The Quilts of Nannie Gilbert Dickson

Perhaps the best documented southern quiltmaker of all time is Talula Gilbert Bottoms, born in Georgia in 1862. She was a prolific quiltmaker who wrote a memoir of her life and her quilts in 1943. The memoir, written in secret, came into the possession of her granddaughter, Nancilu B. Burdick, after Talula's death in 1946, and it sent her upon an absorbing journey of discovery of her grandmother's quilts and of her family's history, culminating in the publication of *Legacy: The Story of Talula Gilbert Bottoms and Her Quilts* (Nashville: Rutledge Hill Press, 1988). Although the story of Talula Bottoms's life and quilts is told in *Legacy*, there is a subsequent Georgia "twist" to the story to relate here.

Wooden box in which Alice Lynch stored her quilts. Collection of John and Brenda Lynch.

Nancilu spoke at the Fayette County Historical Society in April 1989 while on tour to promote her book. It is there that board members of the GQP first met her. Nancilu, who lives near Buffalo, New York, was a regional coordinator for the New York Quilt Project and provided valuable advice to the GQP, which was then in its organizing stage.

In researching her book, Nancilu Burdick had made several trips to Georgia, where she met cousins she had never known before. One of these was John Lynch of Senoia, whose great-grandmother was Nannie Gilbert Dickson, Talula's sister. Another was George Hugh Stell, whose grandmother was Talula's half sister (see chapter 3, "Tattered Veterans and Genteel Beauties").

John Lynch attended several Quilt History Days to document some of his family quilts. As part of his interviews he related a wonderful story of coincidence and discovery.

Alice Dorman Lynch, John's mother, was the granddaughter of Talula's sister, Nannie. When Nancilu Burdick's book was published, John's wife, Brenda, took it to show her mother-in-law one February Sunday in 1989. While looking through the book, Alice Lynch said, "Well, I've got a quilt that looks just like this one." She went to an old pine box that had stood in the front hallway for more than twenty years. It was covered with fabric, and Brenda and John had walked past it every time they had been at the house, never wondering what it might contain.

The box revealed a treasure trove of thirty-five quilts and quilt tops, some of them of the same patterns as quilts that appear in *Legacy*. John was called over the same afternoon, and Alice Lynch told her son and daughter-in-law what she knew about the makers of the quilts.

Alice Lynch related that Nannie Gilbert had made some of them; Talula and Nannie's mother, Holly, was

Nannie Gilbert Dickson, ca. 1876. Photo courtesy of John and Brenda Lynch.

Pear Basket. Nancy (Nannie) T. Gilbert Dickson (1854–1929), Fayette County, ca. 1870. 77¾" x 91". Hand-pieced, -appliquèd, and -quilted cotton. Collection of John and Brenda Lynch. [GQP 4993]

credited with making at least one. On Nancilu Burdick's next trip south, she examined the quilts and recognized the familiar Grecian Star, one of the dozen or more in that pattern that her grandmother, Talula, had made for gifts to nieces and grandchildren. Another, the Oak Leaf and Reel, like Talula's Magnolia Leaf (Legacy, 72) and with the same "hearts" quilting design, suggested the two sisters exchanged patterns and quilted together.

It was fortuitous for the family and for Georgia quilting history that Brenda Lynch visited her mother-in-law that day in February, for Alice Lynch died within a month.

Thanks to Nancilu Burdick's research, and the happenstance of a woman stopping by to look in on her mother-in-law, not only the family but the Georgia Quilt Project is fortunate to have information to preserve about several quilts that are connected to a broader family of well-documented ones.

tory of its people as represented by its quilts. As we examine other aspects of Georgia's quilt history in the pages of this book, relating them back to our documentation experience and placing them in historic perspective, we urge you to remember that this history is alive and was related to us by the quilt owners themselves, in most cases family members of the quiltmakers. There are so many more stories than we were able to document or to relate in this book—please keep your ears open for more quilt stories wherever *you* live and encourage the teller to record them somewhere *now*. The sidebar about the quilts of Nannie Gilbert Dickson illustrates the fragility of the oral history as an information source.

## The Book and Exhibits

Although it is not possible to include photos of all the nearly ten thousand quilts documented, the text and photos in this book highlight and illustrate characteristic aspects of Georgia quilts. A brief reader orientation to the state's geography, history, and development leading to Atlanta's present stature as the powerhouse of the South, by Darlene R. Roth (chapter 1), is followed by Irene McLaren's study of the earliest quilts documented, those made prior to the Civil War (chapter 2). The Civil War was fought partly on Georgia soil, and at Quilt History Days many people shared stories about their families' wartime experiences, capably retold by Julia Anderson Bush in chapter 3, "Tattered Veterans and Genteel Beauties." Cotton was king in Georgia, and Patricia Phillips Marshall's chapter examining this all-important crop (chapter 4) is followed by Vista Anne Mahan's chapter on what happened to the cotton after it was harvested—spinning that cotton and weaving it into cloth at Georgia's textile mills add to the Georgia quilt story (chapter 5).

African Americans have always quilted in Georgia, have always quietly made their contributions to the body of quilts in the state, and thus take their rightful place throughout this book as well as in my chapter, "African American Quiltmaking in Georgia" (chapter 6). Arguably the most famous quiltmaker of all time was Harriett Powers, a black woman from Athens, Georgia. Catherine Holmes brings this extraordinary woman's story to life in chapter 7, "Sermons in Patchwork."

Although you will see some fabulously and exquisitely crafted quilts in the following pages, many of the quilts documented were everyday quilts made to be used as cover for the family. Martha Mulinix addresses the topic of "cover" quilts and provides the reader with a look at the quilt-making traditions of her family (chapter 8).

Hundreds of quilts made from feed sacks were documented across the state, and my "There's Something about Feed Sacks..." (chapter 9) covers the topic from its early days to the reproduction feed sack fabric popular among quilters today, with a focus on the colorful feed sacks of the 1930s and 1940s and the stories Georgians recounted about their use in clothing and quiltmaking.

Many Georgians have participated in group quilting activities. From the proverbial quilting bee to church quilting groups to the modern-day quilting guild, many forms of group quilting existed and still exist in Georgia. Folklorist Janice Morrill's analysis of these groups gives new insight into the reasons women frequently chose to quilt together (chapter 10).

In the 1990s, Georgia quiltmakers celebrated and commemorated a global event—the Olympic Games being held in the South for the first time. The last chapter of this book records the story of the Olympic quilts; our Georgia quilts, given as gestures of wel-

Figure I.11. Pat's Backyard. Original design, Lora D. Pasco (b. 1927), Decatur (DeKalb County), 1998. 27¾" x 39½". Hand-pieced, -appliquéd, and -quilted cotton. Lora, a prize-winning quiltmaker known for her exquisite appliqué work, made and donated this cheerful wall hanging to the Birdhouse Artfest Silent Auction to benefit Habitat for Humanity. Photo by Holly Anderson.

come and friendship to people from all 197 countries participating in Atlanta's 1996 Centennial Olympic Games, are now in every corner of the earth.

By the time the Quilt History Days were behind us, the GQP was already deeply involved in the Olympic gift of quilts. The project also coordinated sales of hundreds of wall hangings and small quilts to benefit Habitat for Humanity in 1995, 1996, and 1997 in conjunction with the Birdhouse Artfest annual fund-raiser.

The information gathered by the GQP enabled the Atlanta History Center to develop two major exhibitions exploring quilting as a labor of love and an aesthetic achievement. Georgia Quilts: Piecing Together History (November 1998–September 1999) showcased eighty quilts dating from 1800 to 1920. Designs of the Times: Twentieth-Century Georgia Quilts (September 2006–April 2007) presented seventy quilts that celebrate the vibrant, artistic, and diverse traditions of quilting in Georgia during the twentieth century.

In 2006 the board of directors of the GQP selected the James G. Kenan Research Center at the Atlanta History Center as the repository for all the data and images gathered from around the state. This collection is a significant addition to the Kenan Research Center, which collects primary and secondary source materials in all formats relating to the history of Atlanta and the culture of the American South.

## The Future of Quiltmaking in Georgia

Where quilting will go in the twenty-first century and beyond is anyone's guess. The enthusiasm and passion of today's quiltmakers all but guarantee the survival and evolution of this form of handwork. As Tess Thorsberg of the Heart of Georgia Quilters in Macon says, "In my former life (before quilting), I have done crochet, knitting, clothing construction, tole and decorative painting, landscape painting in oils, crewel and other needlework—but *nothing* has ever captivated me, thrilled me, satisfied me, frustrated me, driven me, *completed* me the way quilting has—I can't wait to see where it takes me next!" Today, traditional methods, patterns, and colors have been given a personal and technological twist. Many quiltmakers today use computers to design quilts, try out color combinations, or-

Figure 1.12. Smiles. Marjorie Annette Walger Claybrook (b. 1940), Augusta (Richmond County), now a resident of Richmond, Virginia. This quilt was made in 1986, when Marjorie lived in Toledo, Ohio. 40" x 44". Cotton and blends. Machine-pieced, hand-appliquéd including reverse appliqué, hand-quilted. Collection of the maker. [GQP 5734]

In 1977, Marjorie took a quilting class at the Toledo Museum of Art and found her medium; she has worked in textiles ever since. Her work is shown primarily in galleries and fine art exhibits rather than quilt exhibits. Two of Marjorie's pieces were purchased by the City of Atlanta and are part of a permanent installation in the International Terminal of Atlanta's Hartsfield-Jackson International Airport. Marjorie helped organize the Augusta Quilt History Days.

der supplies, and communicate with other quilters on the Internet. Other than the requirement of two layers of fabric with some batting between, almost anything goes in quiltmaking today. The wall hanging, which came into prominence in Georgia in the 1980s, continues to thrive today as more and more people quilt from a desire not only to make something beautiful but also to express their creativity, experiment with a pattern, and not be limited to a bed-size format. Quilts have come out of the bedroom, onto the walls, into every room of the house, and into museums and other public buildings for all to appreciate.

*Anita Zaleski Weinraub*

The real story of the GQP lies in the shared experiences; the public's overwhelming desire to record something about a departed loved one or ancestor lest their history be forgotten by future generations; the great willingness of Georgians to seek us out, to wait patiently and without complaint for hours for a chance to tell us the stories of their families and to show us the quilts that remain as tangible evidence of those who have gone before. Sadly, in many cases, their names have already been lost, but their quilts persist as a reminder that this family, too, has a history and has carefully preserved something precious and dear from its past.

The information gathered by the GQP has helped place Georgia quilts within the regional and national contexts. Once this information is computerized, it will be a powerful tool for historians and quilt researchers alike. Further analysis of the data should re-

Figure I.14 Although the quiltmaker did not sign or date this nineteenth-century pineapple appliqué quilt, the prominent dedication in the center makes very clear for whom it was made. Detail from GQP 413, made by Jane Elizabeth Hancock Morris in Berrien County ca. 1875.

veal much about quilting trends, regional differences, and perhaps topics not yet discovered. When joined with information from other state documentation projects, a complete picture of Georgia's place along the quilting continuum will emerge.

As we piece together a history in the following pages, one quilt at a time, you will begin to see an aspect of Georgia's history that has been preserved collectively in the minds and hearts of the owners of Georgia's quilts. Closeness of family, a sense of community, and a desire to leave something tangible behind in the form of a quilt are themes recurring throughout our story. We hope you enjoy your journey through the past and present of Georgia's quiltmakers as much as we have enjoyed our own journey around the state in order to share it with you.

Figure I.13. The GQP Board, at Mary Jo's Fabric Store, Gastonia, North Carolina, 1993. From left: Patricia Phillips Marshall (regional coordinator), Anita Zaleski Weinraub (chairwoman), Holly Anderson (vice chairwoman), Margie Rogers (former secretary), Ann Gravelle (treasurer), Mary Ross (Quilt History Days coordinator), Nellie Giddens (data entry coordinator), and Carolyn Kyle (secretary). Not pictured: former board members Marybelle Recker, Sarah Leidel, Liv Grønli, Ruth Ganeles, and Judie Glaze. Photo by Mary Jo Cloninger.

# 1. A Background for Quilting in Georgia

### DARLENE R. ROTH

--------------------------------------------------

Quiltmaking is defined and influenced by local circumstances. Born in its particular geography, affected by a succession of different peoples, and influenced by southern and American politics and economics, Georgia has been especially supportive, often protective, of quilting as a traditional craft. This chapter explores those parts of Georgia's history—including the Civil War and the state's cotton and textile industries—that have affected quilting. Elsewhere in this book there is more to read about those influences. This chapter also describes how railroads, woman suffrage, the world wars, and the Great Depression, as well as Atlanta's exuberant personality, have played roles in quiltmaking in the state.

Jan Curran Vincent, 2006. Photo courtesy of Charlie Vincent.

Figure 1.1. Atlanta Welcomes the World. Original design, Jan Curran Vincent (b. 1939), Big Canoe (Dawson County), 1995. 51" x 67". Hand-pieced, -appliquéd, and -quilted cotton. Private collection in Switzerland. [GQP 9278]

An artist in porcelain, textiles, and other media, Jan created a picture of her home state with the Atlanta skyline in the center surrounded by images of Georgia's heritage and natural beauty. One of the gift quilts from the Georgia Quilt Project (GQP) to the 1996 Centennial Olympic Games.

## Geography

Georgia's three distinct physiographic regions—the coast (including the coastal plains), the piedmont plateau, and the mountains—were settled from east to west by European immigrants. From James Oglethorpe's colony at Savannah in 1733, settlement moved inland along the rivers until it stopped at the natural fall line (see more about Oglethorpe in the next chapter, "Early Quilts"). Beyond that point in all of the rivers, steamboats could no longer navigate the water, which became rocky and shallow. This first phase of interior development led to the settlement of the lower piedmont and the creation of the important fall-line towns: Columbus, Macon, and Augusta. It took almost a century to fill in the rest of Georgia's political borders; the upper piedmont and the mountains were the last places that Euro-Americans and African Americans reached. The primary city in the northwest section of the state, Atlanta, was founded in 1837, more than a hundred years after Savannah.

The differences among the state's regions and the lag time in their respective settlement, especially between the coast and the northwest interior, contribute to Georgia's quilt story. For one thing, Georgians draw a social and cultural line between the colonial coast and the pioneer interior—notably between Savannah as the epitome of antebellum mores and Atlanta as the upstart urban center and the epitome of Yankee boosterism. A line also runs between rural, pre–Civil War Georgia (Athens and Columbus) and industrial centers in the urbanized and suburbanized post–Civil War Georgia (LaGrange and Atlanta). In a largely agricultural state, Georgians draw distinctions based on core crops as well: tobacco, peaches, cotton, and subsistence crops define different areas of the state.

Quilts follow suit. Slave-made quilts dating before the 1860s are more likely to have originated in central and southern Georgia, in the old cotton counties, although today, through inheritance, they may be found wherever their owners live. Utilitarian quilts will have emanated from anywhere but will be concentrated in rural areas, in small towns, and in mill villages attached to industrial centers. And "fancy-work" quilts of some styles (white work, Broderie Perse) would more likely have been done where imported fabrics were available and where white cloth could be kept clean easily—primarily through the availability of a large slave class that would tend to not only the laundering but some of the quilting.

## Non-European Peoples

Georgia's European colonists did not settle an unpopulated land: Native Americans had been living for thousands of years in what was to become Georgia. Because Georgia was the last British colony to be formed on the American continent, its period of contact with the Native Americans was relatively short compared to that of other American territories (see the next chapter for more on early English settlement). Relations between Indians and Euro-Americans varied from cordial to hostile depending on the vicissitudes of trade and political agreements.

The Creek Indians, whom the English encountered first, chose not to mix much with the foreigners. From the time of Oglethorpe's arrival, the Creeks, who came north from Florida to inhabit the southern portions of Georgia, ceded land to the State of Georgia, moving ever westward until they were displaced from Georgia entirely into Alabama.

The second important Indian group, the Cherokees, moved south and west into Georgia and Tennessee from the Carolinas. Contained by the Creeks to the northwest corner of Georgia, the Cherokees tried to assimilate by adopting American ways of farming, governing, living, and dressing. Their efforts failed to protect them from further white invasion. Despite the establishment of a democratic state of their own, headquartered at New Echota in northwest Georgia, the Cherokees were forcibly removed from Georgia in 1838 and taken to Oklahoma, where the tribe still lives. North Carolina is home to remnants of the original eastern band of Cherokees who escaped the Trail of Tears in the 1830s, but the Cherokees who live in Georgia today are twentieth-century immigrants from other states.

As a result of the brevity of native–white settler contact and the complete displacement of Native Americans from the state, few if any Native American quilts survived the removal of the Indians. Furthermore, there is little documented or confirmable evidence of Cherokee and Creek influence on historic Georgia quilts. And today's quilts made by Georgia Cherokees have no known historical linkage to the earlier tribes.

Such was not the quilt history of African Americans brought to Georgia in the eighteenth century. The Georgia colony was established in 1733 with indentured servitude of European settlers but without African slavery. Because of pressure from the Carolinas and elsewhere, the local prohibition against slavery ended shortly after Georgia's founding. By 1752 there were 500 blacks in colonial Georgia, compared to 3,500 whites—who were a mix of English, Irish, Scots-Irish, and German immigrants. During slavery times Georgia had nearly as many blacks as whites; in some of the southern and coastal counties, in fact, African Americans made up 60 percent or more of the local population. By 1860, just prior to the Civil War, the two populations were nearly even in size (591,550 whites and 465,698 blacks) and blacks could be found through-

out the state. Their numbers were lowest in the northern mountain counties, highest in the coastal counties. African Americans now constitute approximately 29 percent of the total state population of 9 million. More are to be found in Georgia's urban centers than in the rural areas, though counties in the old coastal plains plantation belt still retain black majorities.

African Americans in Georgia have had profound impacts on quilting in the state. They have created endemic styles and used unusual varieties of materials. They probably did some of the fine quilting in historic quilts, and remain some of the state's most respected folk artisans. The state's most famous historic quilter, Harriett Powers (born a slave), whose two surviving quilts reside at the Boston Museum of Fine Arts and the Smithsonian Institution, represents the best of the eclectic and traditional approaches to quilting that Georgia's African Americans have combined.

## Cotton: The Essence of Quilts

Cotton is important in Georgia history, and its story is told at length in the "King Cotton" chapter. But it's helpful to take a moment here to consider how textile mills influenced the availability of yard goods to the women of Georgia.

Cotton growing, while a feature of the coastal regions from the 1780s on, did not dominate Georgia agriculture until the 1820s, when it began to replace other crops in the piedmont and upland sections of the state. In the 1830s, large-scale gins and steam-powered textile mills made their appearance alongside older grist and saw mills in each of Georgia's urban areas: Macon, Columbus, Savannah, Augusta. By 1860 Georgia was the textile industry leader in the South. For the most part, Georgia mills wove not fine cot-

Annie Amelia Brewer Ray, ca. 1935. Photo courtesy of Agnes Floyd.

Figure 1.2. Tree Quilt. Annie Amelia Brewer Ray (1877–1947), Glynn County, early 1900s. 64¼" x 88". Hand-pieced and hand-quilted cotton and flannel. Collection of Agnes M. Floyd. [GQP 5391]

Annie Amelia Ray was part Cherokee Indian. Although no quilts were documented that were made by full-blooded Native Americans, many Georgians, both black and white, have affirmed that a quilt-making ancestor had Indian blood.

Figure 1.3. Cotton defined the Georgia economy until 1920, when its production dwindled to almost nothing. After a half century, cotton started making a comeback as a viable field crop. Today the back-breaking work of picking cotton, seen here being performed by African American field hands, is done by machinery. Photo courtesy of the Atlanta History Center.

By the postbellum period, the textile industry and ease of transportation of finished goods made weaving homespun less necessary in most parts of Georgia. Therefore, a well-made quilt with a homespun backing and arrayed with precious detail is not only a rare thing today but an illuminating thing, ready to tell the story of "from field to finery" that rural quilts could tell. Such quilts are characteristic of Georgia's quilting heritage, as are those made with found mill products, like flour sacks, and those made from the most delicate, imported English cottons.

## Women during and after the Civil War

The "Tattered Veterans and Genteel Beauties" chapter addresses more fully the Civil War and its impact, but women's condition and the overall disruption of wartime warrant mention here.

During the war, women's efforts in Georgia as in other southern states were directed to supplying military needs: blankets, uniforms, socks, scarves, mittens, personal linens. Records survive of work sessions in which black and white women together produced items required for the war effort. In factories that made the tools of war, Georgia women rolled cartridges, bagged gunpowder, or packed supplies. Other women worked as nurses in hospitals, primarily tending to the personal hygiene of the wounded; if literate, the women wrote letters for them and read aloud the Bible and literature appropriate for mixed company.

Quilting during this time of deprivation reflects the hardships and the sorrows of the period. Many a quilt, stitched lovingly by a mother, was sent to war with a beloved son. Few quilts survive: most wore out from hard use at home and in battle; others were recycled into use as burial cloths, hospital sheets, and blan-

tons but thread, cording, hucking, toweling, sheeting, sacks, bags, and canvas.

Women who lived in or near Georgia's cities and largest towns had the most accessibility to finished yard goods and to mill seconds and overruns, since most of the mills were located on rivers in or near the large cities (Columbus, LaGrange, Augusta, Athens, and Atlanta). Despite their access to quilt resources, city women and those who could easily get to the cities to shop probably had the lowest need for quiltmaking: they could often afford to have quilts made for them by others if needed, and when they did quilt for themselves, it was often out of a desire for ornamentation and self-expression.

*Darlene R. Roth*

kets. Quilts sewn to commemorate courage and heroism were more likely to survive, as were those made as fund-raisers.

With so many men drawn into the war, women at home were pulled into unfamiliar and uncomfortable roles: some ran plantations and farms; some joined the numbers migrating to the cities, often moving in with relatives. At war's end, economic necessity drove many to work, using traditional women's skills to support themselves: they set up boarding houses and eating rooms; they became seamstresses, cooks, laundresses, and hat makers.

The number of white women working in the textile mills rose after the war. Beginning in the 1880s, cotton mills nearly doubled in number and quadrupled in productivity in the decades before the turn of the century. Most of the cloth produced was still of the rougher kinds manufactured before the war, but Georgia also produced fine-quality threads. The textile mills continued to be concentrated in the piedmont but spread into the upper piedmont, with mills established in Atlanta, Canton, Gainesville, and other points at the foot of the mountains.

## The Imprint of Railroads

Georgia's armament industry, especially at Atlanta and Augusta, made the state an important Union objective during the Civil War, as did the railroad system that tied the major cities together. Railroads connected the coastal region with the interior of the South (all the way to the Mississippi River) and had their major intersection in Atlanta.

Railroads were already essential in the economy of the state and the region, so they were the first element of Georgia industry to be rebuilt. Within two years after the war ended, the railroads connecting Atlanta with major points to the south, east, and north were running at full schedule. Between 1880 and 1920, the number of rail lines more than doubled in Georgia.

Trains provided the primary form of intercity transportation and dominated economic life. At least a third of Georgia's small towns started as stops along one railroad line or another. Today many of the railroads that preceded these "strip" towns—towns laid out along each side of the railroad tracks— are gone, but the towns' origins are revealed by their shapes. As the hub of the railroad lines, Atlanta was the largest railroad town and prospered the most during this time. In 1900, 150 passenger trains a day were passing through Atlanta on their way to other destinations.

The late nineteenth century saw vigorous growth for the state, which enjoyed improved transportation attributable to the rise of the railroads. Except in the far northeast section of the state, where the terrain was too hilly and impenetrable to iron rails, one side of Georgia was now accessible to the rest of the state in a matter of a few hours rather than a few days. Railroads increased the availability of products made in the U.S. North, Midwest, and West Coast. And they made it possible for Georgia products to reach these spots as well. Georgia's most famous product, Coca-Cola, took bold advantage of the state's rail connections. Coca-Cola's ability to create and exploit new approaches to marketing was matched by its ability to penetrate the most isolated areas with its product.

Because of differentials in railroad rates (it cost more to ship something out of Georgia than into Georgia), Georgia's prewar dependency on nonnative products held until the mid–twentieth century. Georgians bought supplies, furniture, clothes, sometimes even houses from catalogs, magazines, almanacs, newspapers, and other periodicals when local stores could not fill their needs or the items could not be made lo-

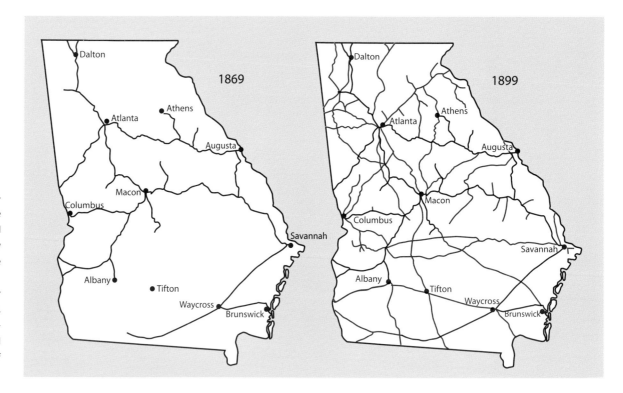

Map 1.1. A great expansion in Georgia railroads in the decades after the Civil War brought both commerce and easier transportation. Dozens of new small towns were founded along the rail lines.

Redrawn by David Wasserboehr from *The Atlas of Georgia* by Thomas W. Hodler and Howard A. Schretter (Athens: The Institute of Community and Area Development, The University of Georgia, 1986).

*Darlene R. Roth*

cally. People who could do so traveled to Atlanta and other cities to do quality shopping; when they could not, they depended on local railroad deliveries for the latest fashions, inventions, and technologies.

Railroads blurred some of the cultural differences between coastal residents and interior communities. Once the state was connected by rail, quilts in one part of Georgia began to resemble quilts in other parts of the state. Patterns were created, shared, or borrowed from elsewhere in the nation, published in women's magazines circulated in the South, renamed if they were Yankee in origin, and adapted to suit the needs of the occasion and family. The railroad even inspired quilt patterns: it is not uncommon to see an appliquéd locomotive in quilts commemorating a town where the railroad was instrumental in its founding. And few if any quilters would now make a quilt that did not

have some imported or borrowed aspect to it—either in pattern inspiration, technique, or materials. Likewise, southern patterns found their way to other parts of the country, offering inspiration and technique to quilters in Oregon, Illinois, and Kansas.

## The New Woman Comes to Georgia

The woman suffrage movement came to Georgia in 1890 with the founding of the Georgia Equal Suffrage Association, bringing with it probably the greatest challenge yet to southern female identity. Women in Georgia and across the South had survived the deprivations of war, the dislocations of Reconstruction, and the depressions of the 1870s. They had expanded their roles, willingly or unwillingly; they had taken ad-

Evie Connell Russell on her wedding day with her husband Abram and her mother-in-law, 1890. Photo courtesy of Molly Kimler.

Figure 1.4. Pieced Tulips. Hand-pieced and -appliquéd cotton by Evie Connell Russell (1875–1962), Wrens (Jefferson County), ca. 1900. 88" x 90". Hand quilted by granddaughter Molly Kimler (b. 1953) in Social Circle (Walton County), 1984. Collection of Molly Kimler. [GQP 3084]

This pattern, also called Crossed Tulips, was one of the most common nineteenth-century patterns documented. It was found in all parts of the state, attesting to the mobility of quilt designs with the advent of the railroad.

vantage of the opportunities of education, increasing charity roles in church and community in the 1880s; and they were poised on the brink of sharing in something called "the New Woman" in the 1890s.

In 1890 a Georgia woman could own property, open a business, and buy and sell real estate and personal belongings, yet most women, because of private choice and cultural practice, preferred not to do any of those things unless they had a compelling need. White women tended to rely on male family members to conduct any business affairs they might encounter. Black women were not exempt from social prescriptions, but more of them had economic necessity to work. More black women than white women worked for pay in Georgia, and more owned business establishments, usually small enterprises providing some kind of service.

Excluded from male enterprise by culture, women nevertheless found ways to influence public policy without suffrage, by petitioning the state legislature on issues of education, health, and welfare, and to improve their communities, by raising monies for pet charity projects. As the state's population urbanized, women found themselves becoming "municipal housekeepers," establishing women's committees, auxiliaries, clubs, and other organizations through which to exercise their influence. The associations provided broader contexts for sociability and gave women opportunities to train themselves in new skills: running a meeting, writing a budget, publicizing issues, communicating with authorities, getting people to work together for a common cause. Despite hiding behind the doctrines of "true womanhood" and the "cult of domesticity," whereby women's activities were restricted to the kitchen, to the church, and to the raising of children, women in Georgia—like their sisters across the nation—were becoming leaders among their own sex.

The woman suffrage movement divided women of the state into two camps: those few who favored woman suffrage as the next indicator of freedom, and those who opposed it as an unnecessary burden on femininity, at the very least, or as the curse of the devil, at the very worst. The suffrage issue, no matter how strongly or weakly any single woman identified with it, called into question the separation of the sexes that had enabled women of all ranks to find communal self-expression in single-sex activities. It dared to suggest that the Old Woman—the one who went to quilting bees and tended home fires—was being replaced by the New Woman, who participated in community activities and bought commercially made clothes and bed linens.

By 1920, woman suffrage had not attained unequivocal support from the women of the state, let alone the men. Given the opportunity to ratify the Nineteenth Amendment to the U.S. Constitution giving women the vote, Georgia assemblymen rushed to be the first to refuse to do so—but despite their haste, they came in second. Women in Georgia voted in their first elections thanks largely to the federal amendment ratified in August 1920. Georgia's general assembly symbolically ratified the amendment in honor of its fiftieth anniversary in 1970.

Woman suffrage and the changes in women's roles that preceded it in the late nineteenth and early twentieth centuries had an impact on traditional women's activities, including quilting. Women were now divided along political lines as well as economic, social, racial, and occupational ones. Chances were that quilters preferred at least some traditional ways. Financial circumstances dictated that some quiltmakers had no choice but to make their own bed covers. Others were still part of the isolated populations in the northwest part of the state. Some were black and servants to the

Figure 1.5. Quilt of Words. Original design, Elizabeth Grace Jones Dunn (ca. 1820–ca. 1890), Arkansas, ca. 1890. 76" x 93". Hand-appliquéd cotton; hand-quilted by Bessie McGuirt in 1991. Collection of Carol A. Gould, great-great-granddaughter of Elizabeth Dunn. [GQP 7992]

The family speaks of Dunn's piety, suggesting that this quilt represents her thoughts on human frailty and divine goodness at the end of her life.

white community. Some did quilting that was overtly ornamental as an object of conspicuous consumption or an act of commemoration. Crazy quilts made from expensive fabrics were the rage among well-to-do Victorians. They fit the times: they were purely self-expressive, often self-indulgent, and however ordinary, they were hardly utilitarian.

In Georgia's mountain schools (most of them established in the 1890s and early 1900s by women), traditional crafts were fostered and preserved as ap-propriate avenues to self-sufficiency for the female residents of North Georgia. Yet quilting had to be passed on from family member to family member, friend to friend. Women were no longer learning to sew as a matter of course; they sewed only if their economic situation required it. Quilting was transformed from a mainstay of female occupation to one of any number of optional pastimes. Further, through the technological advances of the nineteenth century (especially electrification and mass production), women

Figure 1.6. (*facing and above*) Crazy Quilt. Tresie White Miller (1860s–ca. 1950), Jefferson (Jackson County), 1870s. 69¾" x 71". Hand-embroidered silks and velvets, unquilted, no batting. Collection of Miller Dial, grandson of maker. [GPC 3182]

Elaborately embroidered with many decorative stitches, the quilt is also adorned with embroidered flowers, an eagle, a ship, and a silk label from Paris.

Crazy quilts gave women the opportunity to display elaborate embroidery stitches, which usually outlined each of the crazy "patches" in the quilt. Wife of a farmer and mother of five, Tresie Miller was known to have held quiltings with friends. Although it is not quilted, the family thinks that friends contributed to the making of this quilt.

now had access to reasonably priced goods. Both the art and the utility of quiltmaking, like other crafts, survived in certain restricted circumstances: by personal choice for leisure-time entertainment and out of necessity and custom in undeveloped areas of the state. The movement to expand women's horizons had done its part to both depress quilting activities in the economic mainstream and to preserve them among the economically depressed.

## The Great Depression and World War II

President Franklin Delano Roosevelt declared the South to be the nation's number one problem in the 1930s. Though from upstate New York, he knew Georgia intimately. Georgia was a second home for him, where he established the Little White House at Warm Springs and enjoyed the therapeutic powers of the local mineral waters. He knew that despite the success of certain southern products and places (Coca-Cola and Atlanta among them), the South as a whole was poorer, sicker, more illiterate, and more void of economic development than the rest of the country. Cotton cultivation had collapsed through two developments: prices dropped after World War I due to successful competitive cotton cultivation elsewhere in the world, and the boll weevil devastated crops in the decade following 1913. People left farming; many left the state. Thousands of blacks especially, caught between political segregation and economic degradation, made their way to northern cities. Long before the Great Depression in 1929, Georgia and her sister southern states were already economically depressed.

Change came about with Roosevelt's New Deal of the 1930s. Money began to flow into the South instead of out. Roosevelt's governmental alphabet soup gave

Figure 1.7. Possum Quilt. Original design, Mary Elizabeth Moore Sorrells (1842–1897) and others, Pocataligo Community near Ila (Madison County), ca. 1885. 78" x 85". Hand-appliquéd and hand-quilted cotton with restoration work in polyester doubleknit and blends. Collection of Jennifer Debord, great-granddaughter of maker. Photo by France Dorman. [GQP 2834]

Made for a possum hunter by his wife and her friends, this quilt exemplifies both a peculiarly southern tradition (possum hunting) as well as the informal community of women that flourished in rural Georgia in the latter part of the nineteenth century. Its 1970s-era patches add to the folksy charm of this piece.

nourishment to a failing state, filling voids, building new infrastructures. The REA (Rural Electrification Administration) brought electricity to rural areas; the WPA (Works Progress Administration) brought roads, sewers, and telephone lines; the FSA (Farm Security Administration) brought new crops, new technologies, erosion control (using kudzu, which soon brought its own problems), and pest management. The CCC (Civilian Conservation Corps) brought jobs to places where none had been before. And the NRA (National Recovery Act) delivered items of necessity and hope.

Quilting experienced a revival, as an economical and creative means of providing comfortable and warm bed coverings. Born of necessity, quilts crafted during the Depression were often made of inexpensive cloth and found materials—used clothes, blankets, flour sacks, and even earlier quilts (see also chapter 8, "Cover," and chapter 9, "There's Something about Feed Sacks," for more on quilts made from such materials). Quilting was again considered a valuable and utilitarian thing to do.

Some of the WPA's cultural projects in other southeastern states documented traditional southern crafts and artisans. Records of the Tennessee Valley Authority in Tennessee and North Georgia noted quiltmakers among the relocated citizens along the Tennessee River. Americans outside the South began to discover the folk arts that had been part of the cultural fabric of the South for the past several centuries, and they began purchasing quilts as one way to support indigent crafters. In the process, appreciation for quilts and their dollar value rose.

World War II ended the Depression and revived the southern economy by shifting its base from cotton. The war years meant women were called tempo-

Figure 1.8. More women went to work during World War II than ever before. The Bell Bomber Plant in Marietta, Georgia, seen here, was the largest employer in the state at the time, with more than 30,000 workers. White women especially were shaken out of their traditional roles as homemakers to perform unusual occupations, such as setting rivets. Photo courtesy of the Atlanta History Center.

rarily into factory work, as they had been in the Civil War, and the war maintained, at least for a while, the kind of conditions that were conducive to crafting quilts. And after the war the South, newly air-conditioned and thrust into the modern age, pursued new paths to prosperity. Haltingly at first, boldly and backwardly during the civil rights movement, then rapidly headlong into the Sunbelt phenomenon, Georgia has often led the way, providing leadership as different and variously courageous as that of human rights activists the Reverend Martin Luther King Jr., President Jimmy Carter, and communications mogul and environmentalist Ted Turner.

## Atlanta as the Sunbelt Capital

Despite Savannah's hundred-year head start and the burning of Atlanta in 1864, Atlanta emerged from the Civil War as the largest city in Georgia; it emerged from World War II as the largest city in the Southeast, a status it has maintained since then. Called the Big A by some and the Big Peach by others, Atlanta lies in Georgia's northwest quadrant. So large a metropolis is Atlanta that fully half the state's population lives within an hour's drive of the state capitol building. Atlanta's long reign as the Sunbelt Capital is attributable to its success at business, politics, and self-promotion.

Some of the more remarkable of Atlanta's efforts at self-promotion are all the more important here because they often offered opportunities for local quiltmakers to display their handiwork amid the communal visions of grandeur, prosperity, and achievement. In the last quarter of the nineteenth century, beginning a few years after Atlanta wrested the state capital from Milledgeville, the city hosted a series of large-scale celebratory expositions.

Figure 1.9. The Woman's Building at the Cotton States and International Exposition in Atlanta in 1895. Photo courtesy of the Atlanta History Center.

The first two, held in 1881 and 1887, honored the cultures of the piedmont, the growth of the cotton economy, and the emergence of the South as an industrial competitor after the Civil War. The largest of these fairs, the 1895 Cotton States and International Exposition, celebrated interregional harmony and Atlanta's role in rebuilding the South. The 1895 Exposition added an unprecedented exhibit gallery with its Negro Building and otherwise imitated much that had been done in Chicago's Columbian World Exposition in 1893. The Woman's Building at the Atlanta 1895 Exposition (fig. 1.9) held displays of feminine artwork, inventions by women, crafts, and new technologies affecting women's lives. Conferences honored writers, club leaders, philanthropists, entrepreneurs, and educators among women; local women's organizations hosted their annual national conventions in the building. The building itself had been designed by a female architect (not from Georgia, where there were none) and was managed by a group of accomplished Atlanta and Georgia society leaders. Despite its elaborate buildings and exhibits, the 1895 Expo was at heart an overgrown county fair, with contests for cooking, sewing, canning, and quilting. A blue ribbon awarded at the 1895 fair was a coveted prize, a once-in-a-lifetime acknowledgment of feminine arts.

The next great Atlanta promotion was the Forward Atlanta campaign of the 1920s, purely a business affair: the Atlanta Chamber of Commerce sought to increase the number of businesses in the city and to encourage, especially, the establishment of branch offices of national firms in Atlanta. The campaign succeeded in fostering an infusion of new capital and entrepreneurship into the Atlanta economy. Similar promotions at the state level during the same decade also netted economic advancement. Attracted by cheap labor costs and savings in transportation costs through locating

Figure 1.10. Postage Stamp Log Cabin. Margaret "Maggie" Dora Brice Vaughters (1872–1946), Dawsonville (Dawson County), 1910. 68" x 79". Hand-pieced and hand-quilted cotton. Collection of Charles E. Burt Sr., grandson of the maker. [GQP 1716]

This exquisite quilt was made from one-half-inch squares—15,540 of them! Maggie Vaughters's quilt won the grand prize at the Ninth District Fair in Gainesville in 1910. The grand prize was a pump organ that is still in the family home.

nearer to the source of cotton, many textile mills relocated from the Northeast to the Southeast. Areas of Georgia definitely benefited from this trend, especially mountain counties and some of the established textile centers—LaGrange, Columbus, and Atlanta in particular. Sheets, bedspreads, and carpets issued forth from Dalton as Georgia products and big national sellers. The tufted chenille business, from which the Dalton product lines grew, originated in women's work in the county and represented a great leap forward from flour sacking, cords, and canvas.

Since the success of the 1920s, Atlanta has increased its participation in national and international events, all of which the city has used to its own advantages—economic expansion, commercial advertisement, cultural outreach. In a series of successes, Atlanta hosted the 1988 Democratic National Convention, won the bid for the Super Bowl in 1993, and hosted the 1996 Centennial Olympic Games (see chapter 11, "Olympic Gift Quilts: Georgia Quiltmakers Welcome the World" later in this book).

Georgia's history—from its earliest inhabitants through the developments engendered by the coming of the railroad to the devastation of the Civil War, followed by the wrenching experiences after the war and the momentous changes brought by the twentieth century—offers a rich and varied platform from which to create the state's future. Now, in this third millennium, new populations from around the country and around the world, and new technologies for communicating and for manufacturing, challenge Georgians to continue to value their quilt-making traditions and to foster as many variations on the piecework theme as the past has produced.

*Darlene R. Roth*

## Darlyne Dandridge

Some contemporary African American quiltmakers use African themes in their work. Darlyne Dandridge sought out the GQP soon after moving to Georgia from her native California in 1991. A dynamic, innovative quiltmaker who departs from traditional patterns to create contemporary, abstract wall quilts through her use of color and design, Darlyne views each quilt as a jumping-off place for the next, since her ideas never stop flowing. Her African heritage and her identity as a woman are favorite themes as she explores her creative boundaries.

With a degree in journalism and a background in public television, Darlyne enjoys sharing her quiltmaking and her African heritage in presentations to school groups and quilting groups. She participated in a collaborative team of quilt artists who designed a permanent installation in the quilt tradition for the Corporation for Olympic Development in Atlanta for the 1996 Centennial Olympic Games. Mother, community activist, and former Artist in Residence for the City of Atlanta, Darlyne still finds time to quilt and to volunteer with the GQP. Darlyne is a charter member of both the Afro-American Quilters of Los Angeles and the Women of Color Quilters Network.

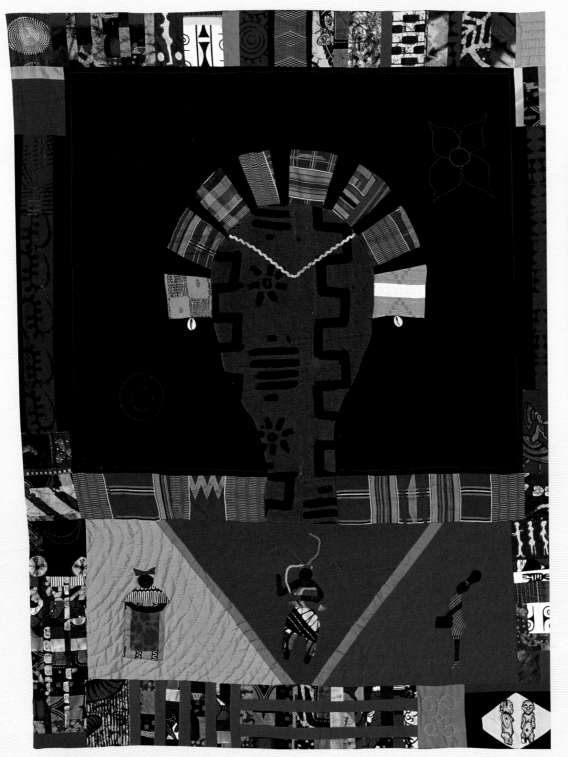

Darlyne Dandridge, ca. 1990.

Womanhood. Original design, Darlyne Dandridge (b. 1955), Atlanta (Fulton County), 1993. 24" x 37". Hand-appliquéd and hand-quilted cotton. Collection of the maker. [GQP 7884]

# 2. Early Quilts

**IRENE MCLAREN**

- - - - - - - - - - - - - - - - - - - - - - - - - - - - - - - - - - - - - - - - - - -

The Georgia Quilt Project was fortunate to document 244 quilts that were estimated to have been made prior to 1861, which the GQP had defined as the early period. Relatively few of those quilts were both dated and signed, and with the passage of so many years, tracing the origins of undated and unsigned quilts is difficult and often impossible.[1] This chapter gives an overview of the conditions that shaped quilts made in the early period. Specific quilts and their makers' stories are highlighted as representative of the various quilt types that existed before 1861.

The loveliest objects often receive the tenderest care; thus the oldest quilts brought to Quilt History Days were the finest of their type: chintz quilts, elaborate appliqués, or intricately pieced patterns. Surviving early quilts generally contain very thin batting and are artistically quilted. The thin cotton battings allowed for fine quilting in patterns of flowers, vines, and leaves, and close background quilting of tiny clamshells, closely spaced fans, double parallel lines, or diamonds.

Just over half of the 244 pre–Civil War quilts documented were pieced; the remainder were appliquéd, a combination of piecing and appliqué, whole cloth, or other. Stars were by far the most common identified pieced pattern, but also represented were Irish Chain, Tulip, Sunburst, Mariner's Compass, New York Beauty, Log Cabin, and One-Patch. The most popular appliqué patterns were rose or other floral, followed by album or wreath and original design.[2] Descriptions and examples of some of these pieced and appliquéd patterns are found later in this chapter.

Many of the 244 early quilts were made from materials either partly or wholly produced on the family farm. Cotton, flax, and wool could be grown in the southern climate, and a multitude of natural dyestuffs was available. Other quilts were made of fine chintz, hinting at the affluence of the maker's family. But even the finest chintz quilts frequently had a backing made of strips of homespun cloth.

## The First Europeans in Georgia

Firmly established in the New World in twelve colonies from New England to the Carolinas, the British decided in 1730 to provide some protection from the presence of the Spanish in Florida by establishing a buffer zone south of the Savannah River. Colonization of a new territory would offer a solution to other problems plaguing the British: English prisons were overflowing with citizens jailed, essentially, for being unable to pay their debts. In addition, the government wanted English-controlled sources for imported flax, wine, rice, and silk.

Member of Parliament James Oglethorpe proposed a plan that would satisfy these needs. Indebted families would be taken under the protection of a group of trustees and brought expense-free to the new colony along the coast of Georgia. The trustees would provide each charity family with fifty acres of land, cattle, basic tools, and provisions to last the first year of settlement. In return, settlers were expected to plant mulberry trees for the feeding of silkworms on their land, work at communal labor for a year, remain in Georgia for an additional two years, and be available for military duty as needed.

England's King George II gave all the land between the Savannah and Altamaha Rivers to James Oglethorpe and the trustees. In November 1732 they sailed with the first group of colonists to establish the city of Savannah. By then, over a hundred years had passed since the Pilgrims had landed in New England. Supplies arrived regularly to the Georgia colony, and there was brisk trade with England.

Each charity family was given five acres in town for a house and garden and forty-five acres to farm in the woods; a settler arriving at the colony at his own expense could be granted up to five hundred acres, depending on the number of servants he brought.

Several restrictions were imposed to encourage an industrious and orderly society in the colony. Rum was forbidden because it might lead to indolence. Slavery was banned because the possession of slaves would cause inequality among the colonists, and the supervision of slaves would reduce the attention that the settlers could give to the development of the colony.

A third restriction, also for security reasons, controlled disposition of the land. Land could be passed on through inheritance but could not be sold. This kept the population concentrated and therefore safer than if scattered. It also prevented the accumulation of large land holdings by the more ambitious or successful.

In order to colonize rapidly, the trustees also offered a haven to groups fleeing religious persecution in other European countries.

Perhaps six thousand people came to Georgia by sea in the 1730s, and two-thirds of them eventually left the colony. As poor farming practices used up the soil, debtor families, also unhappy with the restrictions, moved to fresh areas when their time of servitude was over.

Protests led to the lifting of the regulations concerning the sale of property, and in 1750 the ban against slavery was also lifted. These two changes allowed the plantation system to develop and resulted in an improvement in the economy of the area. Silk production never prospered, however. By 1761 indigo and wheat had become important crops, along with rice, in the coastal areas.

Migration from the western parts of Virginia and North Carolina had increased the population in the mountainous area of the colony by the end of the eighteenth century.

The cultural background of the early quiltmakers was primarily Scottish, Irish, and English: they were mostly rural Protestant housewives, along with a few teachers and businesswomen. In spite of the demands and loneliness of rural life, women found the time and energy to use the resources at hand to make not only utility bedcovers for warmth but appliquéd and pieced quilts of great beauty. Some quilts said to have been made by African American slave labor were also documented by the GQP.

No quilts survive from the initial years of the Georgia colony; it is presumed that any quilts made at that time have since been used up or lost as people moved from place to place. Among the 244 documented pre–Civil War quilts, surprisingly few were of coastal origin, despite the fact that Georgia colonial history had its beginnings in Savannah. One explanation for such scarcity may be the fires that periodically ravaged the city. Two major fires in 1796 and 1865 together destroyed about five hundred homes. Other major fires occurred in 1820, 1883, and 1889, though lesser fires were so frequent that a Savannah newspaper commented when several months passed without one. Newspapers of the time wrote of householders throwing their possessions into the streets in an effort to save them. This was not always successful, however: after the 1796 fire, John Pooler published a list of such items with a request for their return; among these was "a large India print chintz bedcover."

## Early Fabric Printing Techniques

Early printing of patterns on fabric was done with the use of wooden blocks on which patterns were carved. Dyes were applied to the block, which was then carefully positioned on the fabric in order to transfer the patterns. If additional colors were to be included in the print, additional carved blocks were needed for each color. This was a time-consuming technique, and the beauty and accuracy of the finished fabric depended on the skill of the printer. No fabric in any of the early

Figure 2.1. Detail from whole-cloth quilt. Maker unknown, probably made ca. 1800–1825. Possibly made in South Carolina; brought to Georgia in 1916. 67" x 76". All hand-stitched cotton. Collection of Louise and Martin Smith, descendants of the maker. [GQP 2878]

This is one of the earliest quilts documented by the GQP. In addition to the floral print, one can discern a woodland scene with horses and a wagon, similar to the toile fabrics enjoying a resurgence of popularity among quiltmakers today.

quilts documented was noted to have been made by this technique.

By the mid–eighteenth century, fabric printers in Ireland had discovered that using copper plates allowed much finer detail than the wooden blocks. Within a few decades, however, the plating had evolved into a roller, which accelerated the printing process and resulted in more accurate printing. The earliest prints involved only one color on a ground, but within a century printers could roller print six or eight colors in one process.

Possibly the earliest quilt brought to a Quilt History Day is one of whole cloth made of a pink and white cotton that was positively identified as being roller printed. The quilt's owner believes the fabric was brought from England. Although we do not know when this was written or by whom, a note with the following information was found pinned to the quilt:

> Hand made quilt. Quilted in 1790. Handed down through 7 generations.

Given that the roller printing method was invented in 1783 and in Scotland, the likelihood of this quilt being made in 1790 is slim. However, it probably does date to the first quarter of the nineteenth century.

## Chintz Quilts

Chintz was a popular fabric for quiltmakers in the eighteenth and nineteenth centuries because of the richness of color and design provided by these printed and glazed cottons—the same attributes that still entice modern quiltmakers. The earliest chintzes in America were probably of the type from India known as palampores, which were imported via England and France from the seventeenth century and into the eighteenth. By 1700 chintz was being manufactured in England as well as in India. In 1774 John Hewson of Philadelphia opened a bleaching yard and printworks, producing popular chintzes and other printed textiles. Chintz was readily available throughout Georgia (except the mountains) by 1850, and chintz quilts remained popular in the South until nearly the 1860s. The chintz used in Georgia's early quilts might have been produced anywhere from Philadelphia to India.

Early quiltmakers often simply incorporated blocks of the printed chintzes into their quilts. Others reproduced the Tree of Life design of the old palampores by creating tree trunks and branches from pieces of chintz and other fabrics and adorning them with an array of flowers, leaves, birds, and other animals. This had the practical advantage of using only small pieces of an expensive fabric arranged across a less costly background. Chintz also found its way into sampler-styled blocks of wreaths and flower-filled baskets, common in friendship and presentation quilts.

One method sometimes used to secure the cut-out chintz pieces to the main fabric was a buttonhole stitch. The technique of using a tiny buttonhole stitch to sew shaped pieces onto a background was known as Broderie Perse (literally, Persian embroidery). This style was popular in Georgia and the Carolinas long after it lost favor in northern states.

### Mary Elizabeth Taylor's Tree of Life

"William Taylor From his Grand Mother 1824" reads the cross-stitched inscription on an exquisite chintz quilt owned by the Telfair Academy of Arts and Sciences at the Owens-Thomas House in Savannah, making it the earliest dated quilt documented. In her version of the Tree of Life design, the maker, Mary Elizabeth Clayton Miller Taylor (1774–1846), chose a clump of hollyhocks as the central motif.

The chintz flowers and leaves of the appliquéd hollyhocks dominating the center of the quilt are a fine ex-

Detail of Tree of Life, GQP 8150.

ample of Broderie Perse. Three pieced zigzag borders of chintz set against a neutral background surround the central figure before a final border of a printed swag. The background quilting in the central area is a closely spaced grid of double lines. Diagonal lines secure the border. The edge is bound with striped tape.

We luckily know a bit about Mary Elizabeth Taylor and her family. She was born in Halifax, North Carolina. She was the daughter of Andrew Miller (1734–1784), a Scottish immigrant and businessman with loyalist ties during the American Revolution. Her mother was Elizabeth Blount (1747–1831), born in Chowan County, North Carolina, and the daughter of a wealthy Edenton planter who was a colonel in the American Revolution. After the war, the U.S. government seized the property of the now-widowed Mrs. Miller due to her late husband's ties to the British; she sued to recover it.

In 1799 in Stateburg, South Carolina, Mary Elizabeth Clayton Miller married William Taylor (1769–1840), who had immigrated to South Carolina from Scotland. Mr. Taylor's business interests brought the family to Savannah; he was a merchant, the partner of Mary Elizabeth's brother and also of Andrew Low, and owned much property in Savannah, including a wharf that still stands today. He was also a cotton factor, owned stock in a steamboat company, and was president of the St. Andrew's Society, an organization that aided Scottish immigrants to America. After her husband's death, Mary Elizabeth presented his cross back to the society. One of the executors of his will was William Gordon, the father of Girl Scouts founder Juliette Gordon Low. William Taylor's name appears frequently in midcentury Savannah newspapers. The family owned slaves. Thus it can be assumed that the Taylor family was prominent and quite affluent.

Although also engaged in charity work, Mary Eliza-

Mary Elizabeth Clayton Miller Taylor (1774–1846), ca. 1830. Painting by John Wesley Jarvis. Photo courtesy of the Andrew Low House, Savannah, owned by The National Society of The Colonial Dames of America in the State of Georgia.

Figure 2.2. Tree of Life. Mary Elizabeth Clayton Miller Taylor (1774–1846), Savannah (Chatham County), 1824. 103" x 104¾". Hand-pieced, Broderie Perse hand-appliquéd, hand-quilted cotton. In the collection of the Telfair Museum of Art, museum purchase. [GQP 8150]

beth had the leisure to create exquisite quilts from imported fabrics almost certainly purchased for the purpose. She was interested in the Bethesda Orphan House (for boys) and in 1801 founded the Savannah Female Orphan Asylum. After the death of her husband, she lived with her daughter at the corner of Montgomery and Broughton streets. She died in Savannah in 1846 and is buried in the Laurel Grove Cemetery.

Mary Elizabeth and William had several children, but only two survived, Alexander Miller Taylor (1800–1829) and Elizabeth Ann Taylor Goodwin (1802–1882).

Their son, Alexander, married Julia Clark (1799–1846) of Newark, New Jersey, an heiress. Only two of their four children survived: William Taylor (1822–1893) and Alexander Clark Taylor (1825–1911), both born in Newark. The quilt shown here was made for this first grandson, William, and is dated two years after his birth. He became a physician and in 1873 established a drugstore in Vineland. He never married. Living in the North during the Civil War, neither William nor Alexander Clark served in the Civil War.

The Taylor family ties to Savannah ended with Mary Elizabeth, although it is known that her grandsons visited her there. Only her exquisite quilt and her portrait returned to Georgia, a gift of Elizabeth Ann Taylor Goodwin's children.

Two additional quilts made by Mary Elizabeth Clayton Miller Taylor are both of chintz and in the same central medallion style. Inscriptions on the three quilts suggest that Mary Elizabeth made all three to commemorate the births of the recipients, her son Alexander and his sons William and Alexander. The quilts inscribed to the two Alexanders are in the collection of the Museum of Early Southern Decorative Arts in Winston-Salem, North Carolina, and were not documented by the GQP. The earlier quilt is inscribed in cross stitch as follows: "Alex. dr M. Taylor. July 1803." It is believed that this quilt was made for Mrs. Taylor's son, Alexander Miller Taylor. The other was made for Alexander's son, Alexander Clark Taylor, and is inscribed "A. C. Taylor from his grandmother 1832." They were given to the museum as gifts of Alexander Clark Taylor's great-granddaughter Julia Taylor Scholz.

Although the dates inscribed on the quilts do not coincide with the birth dates (they are two or more years after the events), quilts this large and elaborate, if made by a single individual, could easily have taken that long to complete. It is also possible that Mary Elizabeth waited to assure herself that the recipients would survive infancy before beginning their elaborate quilts.

## Hannah Miller's Tree of Life

In the days before mass-produced goods, people might bequeath at their deaths individual articles of clothing and bed linens. In one such bequest in 1826, Johanna Christiana ("Hannah") Miller left nine quilts and one "counterpane" (a woven spread) to various family members, including an appliquéd quilt to her niece Dorcas Dow. Passed down through the family along with a little record book of family births, deaths, and marriages, the niece's quilt and a "summer spread" (a quilt with no batting or quilting) not mentioned in the will are now owned by a descendant; both contain pieces from the same bolt of chintz.

Born in 1762, Hannah Miller lived in Chatham County with her husband Peter and their two sons. Her chintz appliquéd quilt is an outstanding example of the Broderie Perse Tree of Life style found in the first quarter of the nineteenth century (fig. 2.3). The quilt is well preserved for its age. Although the brown fabrics have succumbed to the corrosive dyes used in

Figure 2.3. Tree of Life chintz appliqué. Johanna Christiana "Hannah" Miller (1762–1826?), Savannah (Chatham County), date made unknown. 88½" x 92¾". Hand-appliquéd and -quilted cotton. Collection of Anne Whelchel. [GQP 8164]

Figure 2.4. (*facing*) Summer Spread. Johanna Christiana "Hannah" Miller (1762–1826?), Savannah (Chatham County), date made unknown. 84½" x 84½". Hand-appliquéd cotton, no batting, unquilted. Collection of Anne Whelchel. [GQP 8163]

the printing process, the quilt is otherwise in good condition. The unusual multicolor feathery-printed chintz of the carefully mitered border is still bright. Fine, even quilting stitches outline the design of the appliqué, with the entire background quilted in a crosshatch spaced one-half inch apart throughout the body of the quilt, increasing to one-inch spacing in the border. The summer spread is composed sampler-style by appliquéing leftover motifs from the chintz onto a background fabric (fig. 2.4).

## Plantation Life

Life for the rural southern woman prior to the Civil War was far from the romanticized version seen on the silver screen. Very few holdings comprised thousands of acres; in fact, in Georgia the term "plantation" could refer to a land holding of as little as four hundred acres. However large or small the family holding of land and slaves, the plantation mistress took full responsibility for the domestic activities of the household, such as cooking, cleaning, canning, textile production, and sewing.

Women often married at fifteen or sixteen, sometimes younger, in nineteenth-century Georgia. Large families were the norm: by age twenty, a woman might already have four or five children. Her husband might have had many slaves to produce the cash crops and an overseer to direct their activities.

Although house servants did the housecleaning, laundry (including the making of soap), and food preparation, the plantation mistress assigned duties, trained and oversaw the household workers, and dispensed supplies. She supervised or participated in everything relating to food production. This included the kitchen garden, dairy, canning and preserving, butchering, and meat processing. She was responsible for the

health care of the slaves and often acted as intermediary between the slaves and the overseer. Although she had no legal authority to conduct business, she managed money for the household and oversaw the plantation operation when her husband was absent.

Each slave received a clothing and bedding allotment; typically, at least two sets of clothing a year and a new blanket every two to three years were issued. Although on some plantations the housewife might buy cheap cloth for the slave women to sew their families' clothing, on others the cloth would be produced by home industry. To accomplish this, some slaves were trained as spinners, weavers, dyers, and seamstresses, with the mistress supervising the activities.

### The Kirkland Estate

An examination of the inventory of the estate of Timothy Kirkland (1799–1864) offers additional insight into life on a rural plantation or large farm prior to the Civil War. Kirkland was born in Bulloch County in 1799. He married Anna Holloway in 1824, and they settled in Appling County with other family members.[3]

The Kirklands raised eleven children on a large farm where cotton was grown with the labor of twenty-eight slaves. The 1860 census records Timothy's real estate at $2,000 and his personal property at $28,482. Anna and their three youngest children, two girls and a boy, were living in the household. At the time of his death on September 19, 1864, the bulk of his personal property was the twenty-eight slaves listed by name in his inventory; their total value was $18,550 (individual values for the slaves ranged from $300 to $1,200). At the time, at least three other slaveholders in the county owned more than fifty slaves. The inventory lists the usual farm and blacksmithing tools, a cotton gin, seed cotton, and livestock. No numbers are given for the

Detail of Star Quilt, GQP 4734.

cattle, hogs, and sheep, which were probably grazing on wiregrass among the pine trees when the inventory was taken. It does list "8 head of fat hogs," which refers to hogs held in pens for winter butchering.

Kirkland's personal property lists four "bed an sted"—beds with mattress and bedding—valued at twenty dollars each. It also lists an unspecified number of quilts worth twenty dollars, which was the value of one mule. Two spinning wheels and one loom were noted in the inventory, as well. The women in the household and some of the female slaves were involved in both textile production and quiltmaking.[4]

### Sarah Simmons's Star Quilt

The fabrics of a quilt made by Sarah Simmons (1840–1899) have been positioned so that the stars seem to spin (fig. 2.5). Sarah and Willis Simmons made their home on a plantation in Webster County. It is likely that the battings and backings of some of the family's quilts were made of cotton grown there.

According to her descendants, Sarah sometimes quilted from necessity. Five of the bedcovers attributed to her were whole-cloth quilts of plain white cotton or simple striped fabric. A beautiful floral print of white on a red background backed with brown plaid was used for another. She secured the layers of these, and most of her other quilts, with allover quilting in diagonal lines or in a small arc.

When Sarah made quilts for the joy of making something beautiful, she seemed to favor stars. The small pieces of Sarah's scrap quilts are sewn by hand. At some point she acquired or had access to a sewing machine, which she used to piece the backs or set the blocks for some of her quilts. Only two of her quilts have applied bindings; most are finished front to back or back to front.

## *Popular Colors*

As the popularity of chintz declined, quiltmakers looked to other fabrics, both solids and prints, to make their elaborate appliquéd quilts. Turkey red was considered colorfast. Since no natural substance produced a green dye, green could be obtained only by overdyeing yellow over blue or blue over yellow. With time, the green tended to fade toward whichever primary dye was the stronger.

A combination mineral-vegetable dye was introduced about 1840 that produced a dark green, called chrome green, which had a reputation for being colorfast. From this time until the end of the century, red, green, and white—the three most reliable colors—with accents of pink, yellow, or orange were the dominant colors in appliquéd quilts.

Synthetic dyes became available about 1875, though reds and greens were not as dependable. Both tended to fade to brown or tan, the greens more so than the reds. Many of what might be considered odd color choices in old quilts can be attributed to these fugitive dyes, which were unstable and tended to fade or to lose or change their color over time.

Figure 2.5. Star Quilt. Sarah Ann Elizabeth Black Simmons (1840–1899), Weston (Webster County), ca. 1860. 70" x 85". Hand-pieced and hand-quilted cotton. Collection of Ned Allen Simmons, great-grandson of the maker. [GQP 4734]

## Aunt Ollie's Quilt

Believed to have been made by slaves under the direction of the plantation mistress near Albany, the bedcover known as Aunt Ollie's Quilt alternates an album patch block with an Irish Chain block (fig. 2.6). Aunt Ollie's Quilt is finished with straight-grain binding, which was the custom of the time when a bound edge was chosen; although bias bindings are easier to turn and result in a softer, more rounded edge, they were rare because of their less economical use of cloth.

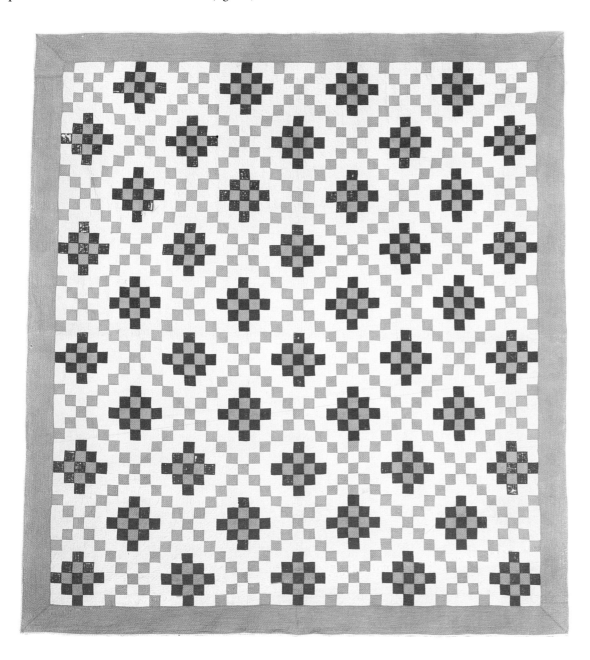

Figure 2.6. Aunt Ollie's Quilt (Irish Chain Variation). Makers said to be slaves on the Northern Glover Plantation near Albany (Dougherty County), ca. 1860. 101" x 109". Hand-pieced and hand-quilted cotton. Collection of Meldra H. Panchelli, descendant of the owners of the Northern Glover Plantation. [GQP 5577]

Although not at all uncommon in Georgia, slave-made quilts are difficult to document.

Elizabeth Anne Murphy Evans, ca. 1870.
Photo courtesy of Marion Winter.

Figure 2.7. Pomegranate and Rose. Elizabeth Anne Murphy Evans (1805–1873), Hephzibah (Richmond County), ca. 1850. 98" x 100". Hand-pieced and -appliquéd, hand-quilted cotton. Collection of Marion Winter, great-great-great-granddaughter of the maker. [GQP 5853]

## Betsy Evans's Pomegranate and Rose Quilt

Nicholas Murphy and his wife left England with James Oglethorpe on his second voyage to the new colony. Arriving in 1736, Nicholas was granted one acre of land in the village of Augusta and 250 acres on the river below town. His son Edmund, born November 24, 1745, boasted that he was the first white male born in Augusta.

Among the ten children born to Edmund and wife Nancy was Elizabeth Anne (Betsy), born in 1805 in Hepzibah in Richmond County on a section of land granted to Edmund for his service during the Revolution. Betsy married Robert Evans (both are buried in the old Murphy Cemetery on land once part of her father's plantation).

Betsy was a skilled quilter. Her midcentury Pomegranate and Rose measures 98" × 100" (fig. 2.7). Nine blocks, each measuring 25½ inches, have been appliquéd with leaves and flowers of red and green and set with a triple sashing. A wider multiple border, carefully mitered, frames the quilt. The quilting is a simple close grid of diamonds in small, even stitches.

## Martha Bumpass's Princess Feather Variation

A seamstress who never married, Martha Bumpass (1813–1906) lived in Nash County, North Carolina. Her Princess Feather Variation quilt, made in the mid–nineteenth century, features an elaborate, six-layer rose in the center of each of its four large (forty-inch) blocks (fig. 2.8). Eight feathers and eight roses radiate from these central roses. Filling out the corners of each block are four-layer roses that echo the cornerstones placed at the intersections of the triple sashing and

Figure 2.8. Princess Feather Variation. Martha Bumpass (1813–1906), Nash County, North Carolina, ca. 1840–70. 90" x 90". Hand-appliquéd and hand-quilted cotton. Collection of Henry L. Owen Jr., great-grandnephew of maker. [GQP 3338]

borders. Bumpass used white, green, and red quilting thread in outline, clamshell, and tapering circle patterns to complement this vibrant piece. Her descendants brought the quilt to Georgia in 1978.

## New York and Other Beauties

Georgia quiltmakers of the early nineteenth century quilted not only from the need to keep the family warm but also to create something of lasting beauty. Many examples survive of intricately pieced patterns, elaborately quilted.

Patterns we know today as New York Beauty, Whig's Defeat, and Sunburst were popular in the period from 1840 until after the Civil War. (The pattern now known as New York Beauty was far more popular in the southern Appalachians, where it was called Rocky Mountain, than it was in New York or other northern states.) Quiltmakers of the mid-1800s also tested their skills with Circular Saw, also sometimes known as Fortune Wheel—a difficult pattern.

Figure 2.9. Rocky Mountain Road with Pomegranates. Julianne Deloach Rogers (ca. 1822–1911), Bulloch County, ca. 1860. 84" x 88". Machine-pieced, hand-appliquéd, machine-quilted cotton. Collection of Haroldeen M. Hart, great-great-granddaughter of the maker. [GQP 7447].

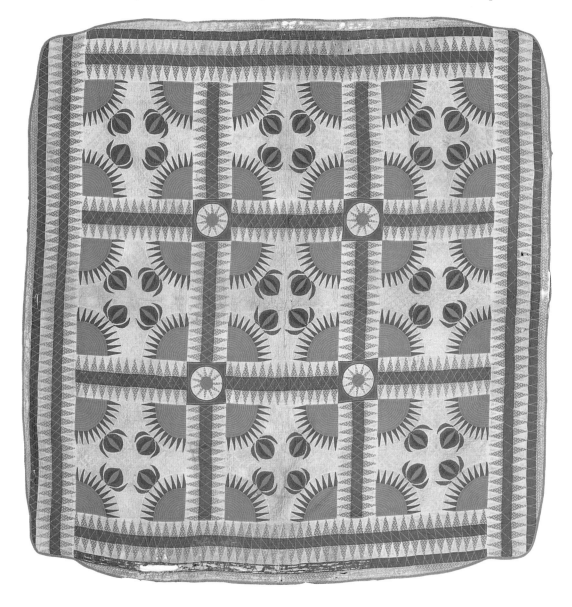

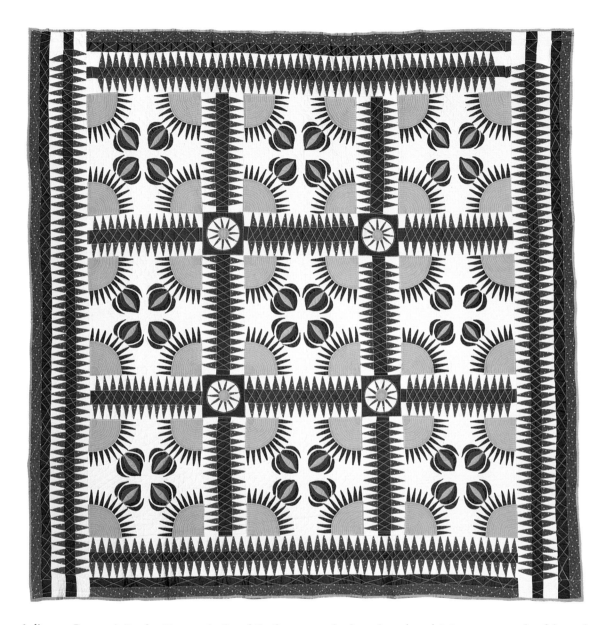

Dereta Akins McElveen, ca. 1990.

Figure 2.10. Rocky Mountain Road with Pomegranates. Dereta Akins McElveen (1916–2003), Brooklet (Bulloch County), 1982–87. 83" x 84". Machine-pieced, hand-appliquéd, machine-quilted cotton. Collection of Haroldeen M. Hart, daughter of the maker. [GQP 7446]

This quilt is a copy of the one seen in figure 2.9. Dereta McElveen "just decided to make a quilt" in the 1980s. Self-taught, she was particularly drawn to the old patterns, which she copied in fabrics resembling those in the quilts she admired. In duplicating her great-grandmother's quilt, she did the piecing by machine as her great-grandmother had, and appliquéd the pomegranates by hand. To achieve the same quality of quilting, she used an old treadle Singer sewing machine. In planning her reproduction of the nineteenth-century quilt, she compensated for the fading of the colors, to recreate the quilt as it might have looked when Julianne took the last stitch.

## Julianne Rogers's Rocky Mountain Road Quilt

Julianne Deloach Rogers, born ca. 1822 in Bulloch County, added her own creative touch of appliquéd pomegranates to the traditional sharp point of the Rocky Mountain Road pattern (fig. 2.9). According to the great-granddaughter who copied the quilt, it contains 1,444 appliquéd pieces. Expertly machine quilted in white thread, it is a rare example of the early use of the sewing machine for quilting. The sewing machine became available in most homes about 1851, when Isaac Singer developed the foot treadle machine as well as an installment buying plan to make it affordable. Family members believe the quilt was made prior to 1875.

Sarah Slaughter Hill Harp, ca. 1860. Photo courtesy of Fayette County Historical Society.

Figure 2.11. Circular Saw. Sarah Slaughter Hill Harp (1821–1909), Inman (Fayette County), 1849. 92" x 93". Hand-pieced and hand-quilted cotton. [GQP 8165]

This quilt is still owned by a family member.

.

### Sarah Harp's Circular Saw Quilt

Sarah Slaughter Hill Harp (1821–1909) lived her entire life in Fayette County. She and her husband, Mozee, a Methodist minister, had seven children. For their first child, William, she made a vibrant Circular Saw in 1849 (fig. 2.11).[5] Pieced by hand in green, orange, and tan mellowed by age, the points are set at such sharp angles that they seem to be moving. Many pieces of a fine cotton have been hand sewn together to make the backing. The edge is finished with an applied, straight-grain binding. The quilting designs in the background into which the saw is set seem to have been taken from nature—feathers, ferns, oak and maple leaves, and tulips and other recognizable flowers, different in each block.

Sarah Slaughter's granddaughter Miss May Harp (1889–1998, left) with the quilt in her home, 1989. The quilt was made for Miss Harp's father in 1849. Photo courtesy of Nancilu Burdick.

Working along with the slaves, Sarah's five daughters helped pick the cotton, spin the thread, and weave the cloth used for homemade clothing and household linens. Many quilts have been carefully preserved and passed down through the family. Sarah is said to have been the impetus for homemade uniforms for the Confederate army being sent to Atlanta from Harp's Crossing, which was named for the family.

## *Sunbursts and Stars*

Star quilts made in the late eighteenth and early nineteenth centuries often were constructed of diamonds radiating out from the center, covering the surface in a Sunburst pattern. As design concepts changed, the large sunbursts evolved into large eight-pointed stars with background space between the points, which allowed for appliquéd motifs or fancy quilting designs. In time both the large star and the overall sunburst were reduced to smaller versions that were repeated block-style and often set with sashing or decorated with appliqué where they were joined.

Figure 2.12. Sunburst. Elizabeth Rachel Bellah Riviere (1826–1888), Pike (now Lamar) County, 1849. 78" x 94". Hand-pieced and hand-quilted cotton. Collection of Mrs. William Hutchinson, great-granddaughter of the maker. [GQP 3733]

### Elizabeth Bellah's Sunburst Quilt

In 1849 Elizabeth Rachel Bellah pieced a Sunburst quilt that carried the bright red, yellow, and green calicos right to the edges of each block (fig. 2.12). The quilt consists of nine blocks, each measuring twenty-two inches. Elizabeth staggered the blocks and squared off the quilt with half and quarter blocks, allowing little empty spaces between the pieced diamond sections. Yellow diamonds set against green compose the border. The quilting, in half-inch hexagons and other designs, is exceptionally fine, twelve to fourteen even stitches to the inch in green and ecru thread.

Elizabeth's quilt is one of the few brought to be documented that had edges finished with a narrow woven tape. This was the second of two types of edge finishes considered "fancy." Tape could be imported, although it was often made at home on a handheld loom. It was such a simple weaving process that a child of seven or eight could produce a professional-looking tape. In the eighteenth and early nineteenth centuries, handmade tape was a household necessity, used for drawstrings, bonnet ties, garters, and decorative trim, as well as for finishing the edges of quilts.

Born in 1826 to parents of Irish and French ancestry and educated by tutors, Elizabeth grew up in the section of Pike County that is now Lamar.

Elizabeth was twenty-three when she made the Sunburst for her dowry. When Elizabeth neared the end of her quilting on the Sunburst, she included in double lines the date, 1849, and the inscription "When this you see—remember Lizzie." She married Francis Riviere, a plantation owner, and they had seven children.

Detail of Starburst with Mariner's Compass, GQP 5276.

### Mary Bryan's Starburst Quilt

Mary Bryan, the maker of a remarkable Starburst with Mariner's Compass quilt (fig. 2.13), lived all her life in rural Elbert County. Of English descent, she learned to quilt using fabrics that were often from cotton and dyes produced on the family farm. The colors typical of the mid-1800s are now fading, but the quilt is otherwise in good condition. A few necessary repairs have been skillfully made.

Each of the twelve large stars is pieced of two hundred small diamonds. Miniature Mariner's Compasses have been applied between the star points, and larger compasses cover the intersections of the blocks. It is closely quilted with small, even stitches. The workmanship in the quilt leaves no doubt about Mary's patience, persistence, or skill as a quiltmaker.

Figure 2.13. Starburst with Mariner's Compass. Mary Bryan (dates unknown), Elbert County, ca. 1840. 67½" x 93½". Hand-pieced and hand-quilted cotton. Collection of Laura Timmons, great-granddaughter of the maker. [GQP 5276]

## Appliqué and Reverse Appliqué

In traditional appliqué, a patch of another color is sewn to a ground fabric. In reverse appliqué, the ground material is cut away to reveal a lower layer of a different color; the raw edges of the ground or top material are then turned under and sewn to the underlying layer.

### Granny James's Princess Feather Quilt

Only occasionally were GQP researchers able to document a good early quilt with reliable provenance and dependable history. The well-preserved quilt made by a quilter known only as Granny James is one of these.

Born about 1810 in Walker County, Granny James was a Baptist and married a farmer. She had two children, Eliza Jane and Lewis, and it was for Lewis that she made the Princess Feather or Chariot Wheel quilt (fig. 2.14).

Caught up in the fever that swept the country after gold was discovered on the West Coast in 1849, Lewis went to California to make his fortune, not returning until his mother's death. Lewis's aunt Celia Catlett Smith, who lived with Granny James before her death, gave the quilt to Lewis at that time. He asked a niece, Mary Angeline Catlett, to keep it for him, telling her that it would be hers if he did not return—which is what happened. In 1912 or 1913, Mary Angeline sold the quilt for five dollars to her great-niece, Leona Lane Patty, the mother of the present-day owner and the great-granddaughter of Granny James's daughter, Eliza Jane.

Figure 2.14. Princess Feather or Chariot Wheel. "Granny James" (dates unknown), Noble (Walker County), ca. 1845. 69" x 72½". Reverse hand-appliquéd and hand-quilted cotton. Collection of Gladys Bowman, great-great-granddaughter of the maker. [GQP 4487]

## Caroline Rauscher's Reverse Appliqué Quilt

Sometime after Caroline Gohring Rauscher was born in 1823, her family left Europe and settled in Lancaster, Pennsylvania.

Caroline was living in Houston County, Tennessee, when she designed and made a quilt of scalloped sunflowers using both traditional and reverse appliqué (fig. 2.15).

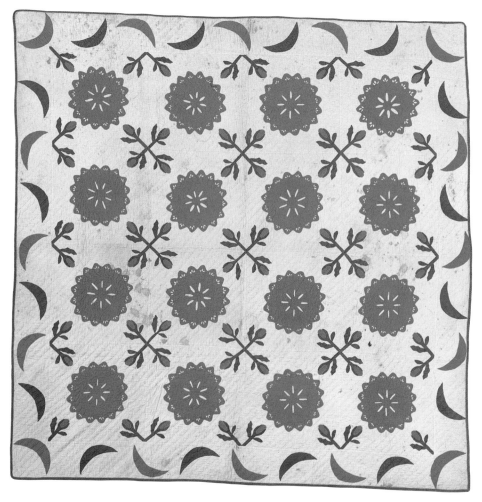

Figure 2.15. Scalloped Sunflowers. Original design, Caroline Gohring Rauscher (1823–ca. 1900), Erin (Houston County), Tennessee, ca. 1850. Reverse hand-appliquéd, hand-quilted, vegetable-dyed cotton. Collection of Frances Buskirk, great-great-granddaughter of the maker. [GQP 5275]

The colors of Caroline's quilt are still bright. If this is one of the quilts for which she is said to have dyed the fabrics using natural dyes, her expertise was considerable. The intersections of the sunflower blocks have been decorated with applied stems, leaves, and buds. Quarter-moon shapes of alternating orange and green form an airy border along the outer six inches of the quilt. The quilting is in tan thread. Caroline inserted an orange piping at the outer edge of the border before finishing the edge with a green binding.

## Granny McClintock's Whig Rose Quilt

The Whig Rose was so popular in the second quarter of the nineteenth century, when feelings ran high between the Whigs and the Democrats, that both sides tried to claim the design. It was also called Democrat Rose.

A well-preserved Whig Rose quilt made mid–nineteenth century by the quilt owner's great-grandmother McClintock is an early example of the use of the sewing machine for appliqué (fig. 2.16). Six complete blocks and three half blocks bring the top to 64" × 78". The applied pieces of red, orange, and tan (probably a fugitive green) are all secured with a small sewing machine stitch to an off-white linen background. The backing, brought over to the front and stitched by machine, is also off-white. Even hand-quilting stitches outline and echo the applied design. Family history says that the thread was spun at home from cotton and dyed with broomstraw, sassafras roots, and "some kind of red oak bark."

The owner knows that her great-grandmother McClintock was born in Ireland early in the nineteenth century. She moved with her family to Clay County, Alabama, and lived there until her death about 1908 at the age of ninety-nine, "having been blessed with good health." The quilt was brought to Georgia in 1925.

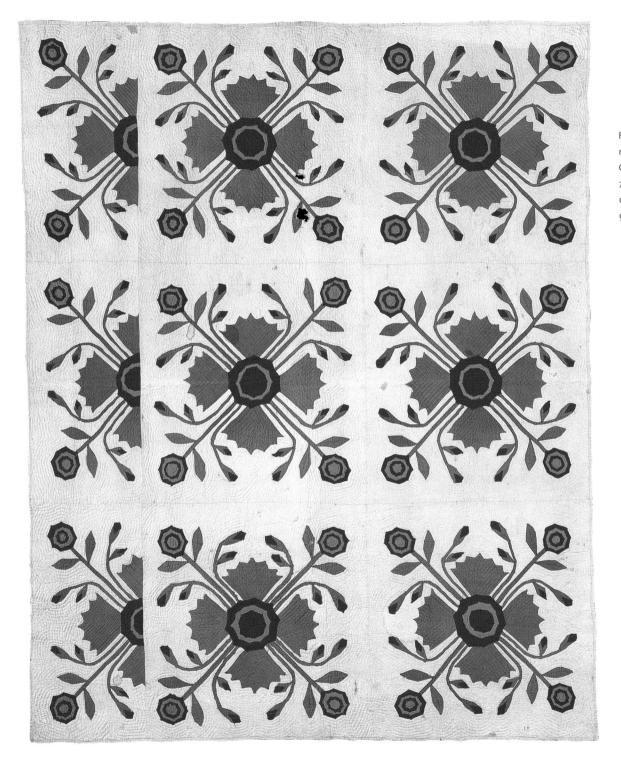

Figure 2.16. Whig Rose. Great-grand-mother McClintock (dates unknown), Clay County, Alabama, ca. 1860. 64" x 78". Machine-appliquéd, hand-quilted cotton. Collection of maker's great-granddaughter. [GQP 7643]

Figure 2.17. Star with Courthouse Steps Border or Mother's Favorite Star (Rehmel 3179). Sarah (Sallie) Summers McCloud Hutchins (ca. 1820–1900), Jones County, ca. 1860. 87" x 90". Hand-pieced and -quilted. Collection of C. Philip Comer III, great-great-grandson of the maker. [GQP 6687]

### Sarah Summers's Star Quilt

Sarah (Sallie) Summers was born ca. 1820 in Jones County and lived there until her death on October 26, 1900. An ancestor, Joseph Styles, had arrived in New Kent County, Virginia, prior to 1680. Sallie grew up a Primitive Baptist, learning to quilt at home and enjoying quilting and exchanging patterns with family and friends. She used whatever fabrics were available and taught others in the family to quilt.

Still a young girl in 1837, Sallie married Norman McCloud. Four years after Norman's death in 1855, she married again, this time to Seaborn Hutchin. She reared five daughters: Mary, Susan Elizabeth, Lillie Octavia, Sarah, and Amanda.

Her Star quilt consists of twenty-five fifteen-inch star blocks, hand pieced in bright green, orange, and brown (probably fugitive red) solids (fig. 2.17). Although the GQP documenters found no machine stitching, one fabric square on the front contains the printed words "and sewing machine," which would place the quilt at 1850 or later. The star blocks are surrounded by a five-inch pieced border in the Courthouse Steps pattern. It is bound with a green straight-grain binding. The thin cotton batting allowed small even stitches that cover the quilt with echo and outline quilting, as well as clamshells and flowers.

Figure 2.18. Circular Saw. Edie Williams (dates unknown), Calhoun County, ca. 1840–60. 80" x 87". Hand-pieced and hand-quilted cotton. Collection of her descendants. [GQP 4257]

Strikingly different from the Circular Saw pictured in figure 2.11, the painstakingly and intricately pieced teeth of Edie Williams's saw surround vibrant, flowing pinwheels of blue, cheddar orange, brown, and white. Although the brown and blue visible today may not be the original colors, the color contrast and movement of the pinwheels are as effective now as they were the day the quilt was completed.

The piece is closely quilted in outline, echo, and crosshatch patterns in blue, brown, and natural threads. Complementing the saw teeth are a diamond-pieced sashing and borders. Bound on three sides by an applied binding, the upper edge of the quilt is finished by rolling the front to the back. The upper border is shorter than the other three. One possible explanation is that through use, as the top of the quilt was pulled up nightly to cover family members, the top border wore out. To repair this and to extend the quilt's life and usefulness, someone may have trimmed away the worn portion and refinished the edge by turning the front to the back and hand stitching to secure it. This method of repair was seen frequently throughout the state. In some instances, a new piece of fabric was added to replace the worn portion, though that is not the case here

Figure 2.19. Ozark Star (origin of name not known). Top only, unknown maker, ca. 1810. 77½" x 92½". Hand-pieced cotton and silk. In the collection of the Telfair Museum of Art, bequest of Mrs. Mary Chantler Robinson. [GQP 8151]

## Hexagon Quilts

Hexagon quilts, often called Honeycomb or Mosaic quilts, were popular in England during the early period. Assembling the quilt top was most commonly done by what is today known as English piecing: each hexagon is basted over an exact-size paper piece before being whipstitched to its neighbor.

The Telfair Academy of Arts and Sciences in Savannah owns two well-preserved examples of English pieced hexagons. One, a ca. 1810 top, is a setting identified as Ozark Star by museum staff (fig. 2.19). The small hexagons of azure blue and brown fabric have been arranged into a central medallion consisting of six star points around a large hexagon pieced of eleven rows of smaller hexagons. The area between this central motif and the edge has been filled in with a mosaic of diamonds, stars, and flowers pieced from hexagons. The template was carefully positioned to ensure that the designs of the pink, blue, and brown fabrics were

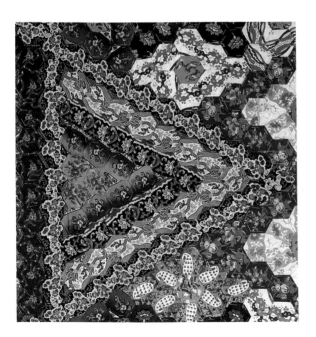

centered. Before this superbly crafted top was basted to a backing for conservation purposes, it was possible to read snatches of the paper used in its construction. The pieces are small (2⅛ inches across), but it is evident that the papers were cut from ledgers, letters, and envelope fragments (some with stamps). One of the bits of paper near the edge contains the numerals "1794" (possibly a date).

A second hexagon quilt donated to the museum has a similar central star medallion surrounded by smaller stars and "flower garden" or "rosette" sections, which have been spaced with paths of white hexagons. The templates have been just as carefully placed to pick up the design portions of the fabrics as in the 1810 top. A swatch of cotton fabric on the back of the quilt notes that the quilt was made in 1786 by the great-great-grandmother of "the Misses Phillips."

Competence with a needle was as much expected of a nineteenth-century female as competence in the kitchen. At an age when modern children are learning their ABCs, a little girl of the nineteenth century learned to thread a needle and take her first stitches. Her skills increased from simple nine-patch utility quilts to challenging pieced and appliquéd patterns intended as dowry quilts. The quilts highlighted in this chapter exemplify the exquisite needlework for which some women were known.

Today we are indebted to those who treasured and preserved these quilts as they passed from generation to generation along with family Bibles, letters, and diaries that told of life in Georgia in the first century after statehood.

# 3. Tattered Veterans and Genteel Beauties

## Survivors of the War between the States

**JULIA ANDERSON BUSH,**

**WITH INTRODUCTORY REMARKS BY DARLENE R. ROTH**

-----------------------------------------

In 1861 Georgia went to war; its young and adult men enlisted by the hundreds to go off to fight, thinking their cause was just and the battle would be short. The women of the state were left behind, for their part thinking their men would prevail and the battle would be short. By early 1862 it was clear, however, that the battle would not be short; by 1863 it was not at all clear who would prevail; and by 1864, when the war came to Georgia, the cause had lost some of its glory.

Georgia was strategically important to the Confederacy: the railroad hub at Atlanta tied the South together, while the arsenals and manufacturing centers in Columbus, Augusta, and Atlanta armed and supplied the Southern armies. For the very reasons it was important to the Confederacy, the state became the target of Federal attack—not merely to defeat Georgia but to destroy it.

Until 1864, Georgia fairly bustled with the war effort: residents manufactured armaments, produced textiles, grew food for the army. In early 1864, Federal troops, having captured Chattanooga, were poised to invade Georgia. Georgians now felt the war pressing in on them, threatening in a new way. Atlantans, keenly aware of their vulnerability, made a last-ditch effort to strengthen the city's defenses. General William Tecumseh Sherman and an army of 100,000 Federal troops left Chattanooga and launched the campaign for Atlanta. Through Chickamauga, Dalton, Resaca, and Kennesaw, Sherman used his troops as human assault waves against Confederate defenses. Suffering tremendous losses, Sherman's troops nonetheless prevailed, reaching Atlanta in July. Residents of the city, anticipating the worst and seeking refuge, fled to other parts of the state.

Sherman planned to sever transportation and communication lines in Atlanta; he did that and more, leaving behind a burned-out shell of the former industrial-rail-commercial center. From Atlanta, Sherman and his remaining troops (just over half the number who had entered the state) cut a swath seventy miles wide across Georgia from northwest to southeast, marching to Savannah and the sea in what one soldier called a "glorious tramp right through the heart of the state."[1] By their own accounts, Federal soldiers found a plenitude of livestock and crops that they appropriated, destroyed millions of dollars worth of property in the

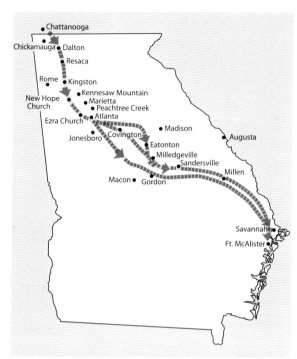

Map 3.1. Sherman's March to the Sea, 1864. Map by David Wasserboehr.

process, and foraged food and potables, clothing, and supplies from the civilians. One of General Sherman's staff officers, Capt. George Pepper, described the usual procedure when the army entered a town:

> A halt at noon beside a village, a besieging of houses by the troops, soldiers emerging from doorways and backyards, bearing quilts, plates, poultry and pigs, beehives attacked, honey in the hands and besmearing the faces of the boys, hundreds of soldiers, poking hundreds of bayonets in the corners of yards and gardens, after concealed treasure; here and there a shining prize, and shouting and scrambling, and a merry division of the spoils. In the background women with praying hands and beseeching lips unheeded.[2]

Confederate troops, fleeing ahead of the Federals or chasing behind, wrought equal havoc on the local populations. When it was done, Georgia was devastated.

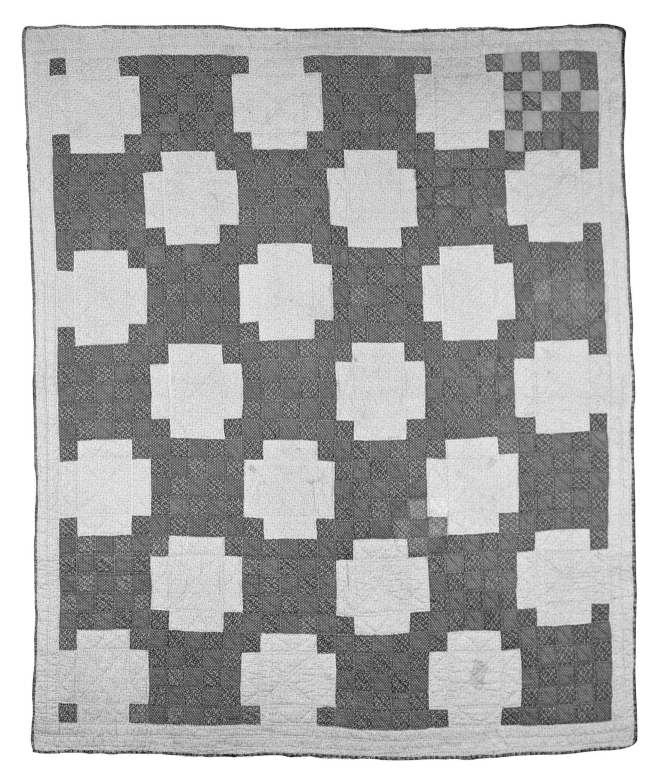

Figure 3.1. Irish Chain. Martha Richardson (dates unknown), Morgan County, ca. 1860. 67" x 78½". Hand-pieced and hand-quilted cotton. This quilt is still owned by the family. [GQP 3116]

Family legend relates that this quilt survived the war because the family's quilts were used to wrap other valuables and were hidden in the woods, covered with leaves, thus evading Sherman's army when it passed near Madison. The family speculates that stains on the quilt were a result of rainwater leaking into the hiding place. Martha Richardson's husband was a soldier in the Confederate army.

For the duration of the war, the women who had been left behind were called into service in many new capacities: they ran farms and plantations in the absence of their owners and overseers; they worked in factories; they sewed, knitted, and cooked for Confederate troops; some of them even spied for the Confederacy. They taught schools in greater numbers and took up nursing as a female profession. They formed ladies' aid societies, the first such civic organizations among women in the Southern regions, which hosted raffles and fairs and special events (like "calico balls") to raise money and gather goods for the soldiers—husbands, brothers, sons, and fiancés of the women. Through inflation, in the midst of dislocation and discomfort, despite shortages of food and imported goods, the women survived, often implementing inventive substitutes for staples no longer available—sassafras for tea, peanuts for cocoa, chicory for coffee, sorghum for sugar. Cotton was almost impossible to get since much of the cotton market had been restricted by the naval blockades of Georgia (and other Southern) ports, and cotton growing had largely been abandoned in order to raise crops for military consumption. Homespun replaced manufactured cotton goods during the war. Woven on farms and in fine mansions where weaving had not been a female occupation for decades, homespun became not only essential to the war effort but fashionable as well.

Quilts, if anyone had time to make them, were simply used up. Fabric and thread were hard to get, time was better spent on other occupations, and soldiers in the field preferred lighter weight blankets to quilts. But hospitals, refugee centers, churches, and homes used what they had or could get in the ways of bedding, and it was not uncommon for women to make quilts as raffle items or as gifts to honor returning veterans. The war years were dangerous ones for quilts—many were burned, pillaged, worn out, or donated to

the Cause. Quilts that were made during the war or that survived it are few, but stories about the families who kept, saved, or used them are numerous. From the quilt buried under the proverbial smokehouse, hidden from the invading army, to the Augusta woman who used her last pair of linen curtains to make a shirt for her husband, all families with deep Georgia roots have their own stories about the War between the States, though not all own the quilts that survived it. Following is a sampling of those quilt-related stories.[3]

## Tattered Veterans

Some quilts went to war with soldiers, and a few even returned. The Georgia Quilt Project (GQP) was able to document at least two such quilts during its Quilt History Days.

### Asbury Hargrove's Log Cabin Quilt

The Hargrove family home in Marietta, just north of Atlanta, was—unlike many other homes in the area—not burned during the war, because Brigadier General Edward M. McCook used the residence as his headquarters while recuperating from a wound. The Hargrove house was built in 1840 by the elder Asbury Hargrove (1809–1879) in much the same style as many farmhouses of that time. It had a wide hall, or dog trot, at the front door area with a large room on either side.

A Log Cabin summer quilt—so called because it has no batting—has been passed down through the Hargrove family along with the following history (fig. 3.2): The quilt had been wrapped around the body of young Asbury Hargrove at the Knoxville, Tennessee, battleground where he fell. The slave sent to retrieve the body is said to have found Asbury because he recognized the Log Cabin quilt as one made by Mrs. Hargrove. He placed the body in a buckboard wagon and

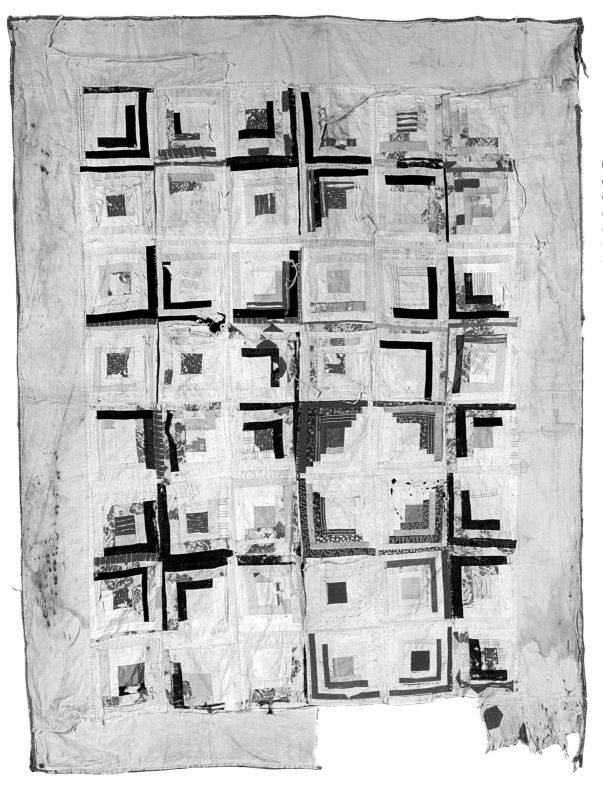

Figure 3.2. Log Cabin. Frances Mays Hargrove, dates unknown, Cobb County, ca. 1860. 68" x 89". Cotton, hand-pieced on foundation with embroidery, unquilted. Collection of Laura Belle J. Bell, granddaughter-in-law of maker. [GQP 6361]

returned home, where the son was buried in the family cemetery next to the house.

### James Elem Baugh's Lone Star Quilt

Dr. James Emory Baugh is a former mayor of Milledgeville (Baldwin County), which was the capital of Georgia during the war (mayor from 1979 to 1997, Baugh was the longest-serving mayor in Milledgeville history). He is also the grandson of the original owner of a Lone Star quilt, said to have been made by a house servant (fig. 3.3). The Baugh family home was near Shoulderbone Creek in Hancock County. The quilt is believed to date from around 1850. It was common knowledge that Confederate soldiers were frequently cold and hungry, so during the war many families sent provisions to their loved ones serving in the army. This quilt is said to have been sent to Virginia, where James Elem Baugh (1832–1902), a corporal in Company I, Forty-ninth Regiment, was fighting with Generals Stonewall Jackson and Robert E. Lee.

James Elem was first wounded at Chancellorsville but continued to serve. He was not so lucky in the Battle of the Wilderness, where he sustained such severe hip wounds that he was discharged in the fall of 1864 and sent home. All six of James Elem Baugh's brothers also served in the war, according to a letter James wrote in December 1864 requesting a transfer to Georgia. He indicates in the letter that he is no longer fit for field service and asks to be detailed home to attend to his mother's farm and to settle his father's estate: "My mother is a widow lady with all of her Sons in the Army." Peter Baugh, James's father, was a schoolteacher and farmer.

Figure 3.3. Lone Star. Maker said to be African American house servant (slave) of James Elem Baugh, Shoulderbone Creek (Hancock County), ca. 1850. 87" x 87". Hand-pieced and hand-quilted cotton. Collection of Dr. James Emory Baugh, grandson of James Elem Baugh. [GQP 5625]

James Elem Baugh brought the Lone Star quilt back to Georgia with him. Penned in ink on a front corner of the quilt is "J. E. Baugh." The stains on the binding are James's blood, according to his descendants. The family's sixty-five slaves were freed at the end of the war. Nothing is known about the maker of the quilt.

Soon after his return from the war, James married Ada Smith, daughter of Dr. W. W. Smith of Columbus (Muscogee County). Ada died in 1868 of "childbirth fever" three days after the birth of their second daughter. Prior to her death, she asked that her children be given into her sister's care if she did not survive. Mary Allen Smith arrived in Sparta (Hancock County) two weeks later to look after her dead sister's children, and in 1872 she and James married. They had three children together, and one was the father of Dr. James Emory Baugh. The quilt remains in the Baugh family.

## Genteel Beauties

Far more quilts survive from the Civil War era that never saw war; nevertheless, such quilts have war stories of their own. Levie Griffith Thompson was born in 1856 in Oconee County. As a young girl, she saw Sherman's army pass through her area and had to spend the night in a barn, according her descendants. Sherman's troops took away a cousin who was never seen again. Around 1875 she made a pinwheel-pattern quilt that was brought to the Athens Quilt History Day. Several surviving quilts were made by women who donated their time and sewing talents to the war effort by making uniforms, bedding, and bandages.

One such seamstress was Lucy Lewis Harrington. Lucy was listed in the Reverend J. L. Underwood's *Prominent Women of the Confederacy* for her efforts spent making uniforms for the troops. She was also a quiltmaker. One of her quilts, Triple Tulip in Pot, has remained in her family (fig. 3.4).

Figure 3.4. Triple Tulip in Pot. Lucy Lewis Harrington (1812–1879), Dougherty County, ca. 1850. 79" x 85". Hand-appliquéd, hand-quilted cotton. Collection of H. Neil Buzzard, great-great-great-grandson of the maker. [GQP 6318]

### Mary Elizabeth Harris Reeves and Her Soldier Husband

Along with beloved family quilts, stories about the Civil War have been passed down faithfully through succeeding generations. Mrs. Polly Stell (wife of George Hugh Stell, see introduction) of Fayetteville (Fayette County) recalls her grandfather Robert Burke Reeves (1844–1941) relating his war experience to her when she was young. Grandfather Reeves, a farmer and landowner, served in the Thirteenth Infantry Regiment, organized in June 1861, at Griffin (Spalding County), Georgia. He took three bullets in the knee and thigh at Sharpsburg (Antietam) and was reported missing. Pulled from the battlefield and set up against a tree, he remained there for ten days. He would allow medics to wash his wounds only if their water and rags were clean, and he credited this concern for hygiene with his survival.

After the battle, he was evacuated south to Savannah; from there he caught a ride on a salt wagon that took him part of the way (it is not known how far) to his home near Thomaston in Upson County. The family, of course, believed him to be dead. He walked the remainder of the way home and appeared, limping up the road on crutches, at sundown one day. A scene similar to this one is portrayed in *Gone with the Wind*, when Ashley Wilkes returns from the war. However, Mrs. Stell was told this story by her grandfather when she was a teenager, well before Margaret Mitchell wrote her famous novel. Could Mitchell have heard stories such as these while growing up, later recalling them and incorporating them into her tale?

Mr. Reeves's wife, Mary Elizabeth Harris Reeves (1848–1924), made a spectacular quilt at the age of sixteen in 1864 (fig. 3.5). Today it graces a bed in her granddaughter Polly's home. Mrs. Stell's mother told

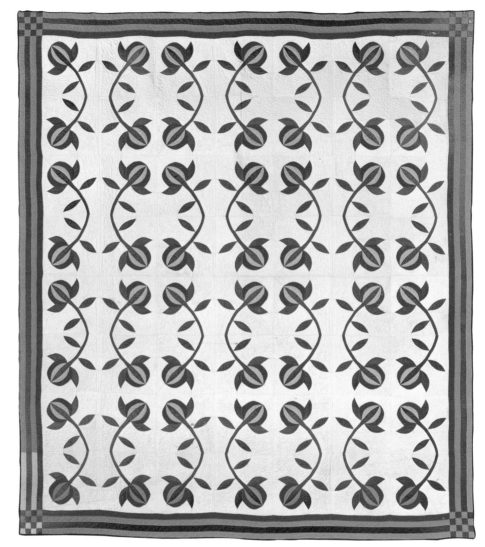

her that it took six weeks for Mary Elizabeth and Mary Elizabeth's mother, Carrie, to quilt it. The Orange Bud, as it is called, is believed to be of the same design as a quilt made by Talula Gilbert Bottoms, but that quilt has never been located. Mr. George Stell's mother was a Gilbert, and it was through Nancilu Burdick's exploration of her Georgia roots that the GQP met the Stells (see introduction).

Figure 3.5. Orange Bud. Mary Elizabeth Harris Reeves (1848–1924), Upson County, 1864. 88" x 98". Hand-appliquéd, hand-quilted cotton. Collection of Polly Stell, granddaughter. [GQP 5956]

*Survivors of the War between the States*

## Nancy Lovelace Miller and Her Soldier Sons

A collection of letters written by his Confederate soldier ancestors during the war to loved ones in Georgia was shared with the GQP by Mr. A. Stephen Johnson of West Point (Troup County). Mr. Johnson's great-great-grandparents, Jacob and Nancy Lovelace Miller (1810–1858), had eleven children. Three of their sons—John William, Nicholas Wesley, and then Alva, when he was old enough—served in the war; they were brothers of Mr. Johnson's great-grandfather, Henry W., who was too young to serve. One of Nancy Miller's quilts has the initials "N.W.M." on it, so Mr. Johnson assumes that it was made for his Uncle Wesley, who was a lawyer in Hamilton (Harris County). Just before the start of the war, Wesley wrote the following letter to his sister, Mrs. Amanda Miller Knowles, who lived in Arkansas:

Hamilton Geo
April 11th 1861

My dear Sister:

Your letter of the 26th ult. has been received. I had been looking for a letter from you for sometime. I was glad to hear that you are well &c. and hope you will do well. I am in the enjoyment of very good health at this time, and I believe I would weigh more than I ever have weighed before. I think I am doing very well in my business, and I consider my prospects fine. I think I shall make money here after a little while. My dear Sudie is now out in the country at her Father's. She has been gone nearly a week and I am very impatient to see her again. It is the first time I have been from her so long, and it goes rather hard with me . . .

Hon. Benj. H. Hill made a speech here today on the political condition of the country. He was in attendance on our Court, and consented to address the people. I hope soon to see the time when Arkansas and the other Slave States shall come out of the old Union, and unite their destinies with that of the "Confederate States." The latest news we have received up to this date, if reliable, indicates the near approach of war. I sincerely hope that our difficulties may yet be settled without bloodshed. But if war must come, our people must be prepared to meet it with brave hearts and strong arms. Write me how you are getting on.

Wesley joined the Confederate army in 1861, attaining the ranks of lieutenant and then captain in 1864. He wrote the following letter to his wife, Susan J. (Sudie) Little Miller, on July 5, 1862, from Richmond:

My own Dear Wife:

I arrived in Richmond yesterday about 12 o'clk. and was about two days longer in coming than I would have been, had the trains made all the connections and run through in their usual time. As soon as I reached the place, I came on to the Hotel, where I found your Pa and Mattie, and also Ransom and Frank. The boys had just got here from their camp, a short time before I arrived. . . . Soon after I got here, I learned from your Pa that my brother William [John William] was in town sick, and I went to see him as soon as I could. He is at a private house, and is quite weak and feeble, but is improving slowly at this time. He has been sick for some time, but he remained in camp until he was almost prostrated and could go no longer. . . .

Nearly all of the wounded are here in the city. There are several officers and men of our regiment here in town, where they have come to rest and recruit their strength. The regiment was exposed to a pretty heavy fire from the enemy for a short time. There were something near thirty men killed and about one hundred and twenty wounded in the regiment. I understand they are now at Charles City Court House unless they have left that place again very recently. It is about thirty miles from Richmond to this place. I expect to start to there

Daguerreotype of Nancy Lovelace Miller on her deathbed, 1858. Photo courtesy of A. Stephen Johnson.

Figure 3.6. Lotus Blossom Variation. Nancy Lovelace Miller (1810–1858), Longcane Community (Troup County), ca. 1850. 82½" x 90". Hand-pieced and -appliquéd, hand-quilted cotton. Collection of the Columbus Museum of Art, gift of Nancy's great-great-grandson, A. Stephen Johnson. [GQP 2126]

Another of Nancy Lovelace Miller's quilts is in the next chapter at figure 4.14.

tomorrow morning. I am glad I did not bring any more baggage with me for I cannot carry much along with me, and I do not know that I will leave some of my best clothes in Richmond and buy some coarse stout ones to wear. Lieut. Williams carried my bed clothes along with him when he left Savannah but he left them with his trunk and bed clothes at a house on the way a day or two before they got into the fight.

. . . Give my love to all the family. I am very anxious to hear from you, and I hope it will not be long before I can get a letter from you.

Your own loving and devoted husband
N. W. Miller

Lieutenant Miller was captured at Sharpsburg (Antietam), Maryland, on September 17, 1862, and released on November 11 of that year. Captain Miller's regiment fought in the Battle of Gettysburg, although from the following letter to his father, written soon after a furlough at home during June of 1863, it seems that he was recuperating from an illness and did not see action himself:

Staunton, Va.
July 12, 1863

My Dear Father:

I have been improving since I wrote to you last, and I expect to start again to my Regiment this evening. One member of my Company and several from the Regiment are going on now. Our regiment was in the battle at Gett[y]sburg, but I have not been able to get much news from it yet. I will have to write a short letter now as I have to make my arrangements to get off. I will write again soon. My love to all the family and tell all to write to me. Let me hear from you all often. Remember me in all your prayers, for I hope my trust is in the Lord, and I will pray for his protection over me.

Affectionately Your Son,
N. W. Miller

Nicholas Wesley Miller (1836–1865), ca. 1862. Photo courtesy of A. Stephen Johnson.

Captain Miller suffered his last battle wound during the Battle of Hatcher's Run in March 1865, just a few days before the surrender:

Petersburg, Va April 28th '65
Fair Grounds Hospital

My Dear Father:

. . . I was wounded on the 25th March. The Surgeons put me under the influence of chloroform on the 27th to ascertain the extent of the injury & they amputated my leg. They said it was necessary as the bone just above my knee was badly fractured & the boney joint was too badly injured to be saved. My leg sloughed off a little soon after it was amputated which threw me back some. I have suffered a great deal & still suffer some nearly all the time. I get very good attention & am attended to by our own Surgeons who staid here with our wounded. The ladies are also very kind to bring us everything they think we want to eat. . . .

Afft. Your Son
N. W. Miller

Nicholas Wesley Miller never recovered from his wound, which ultimately caused his death on June 5, 1865. The nurse who cared for him at the Fair Grounds Hospital in Petersburg, Virginia, during this last illness wrote his widow a long letter the next day, excerpted here.

My Dear Mrs. Miller:

Ere you read this letter you will have received the mortal remains of your beloved & noble husband; had prayers & efforts availed to save him, the hope held out in a previous letter to you through Lt. Grogan would have been realized; but our Father who orders all things wisely & well, has decreed it otherwise, & with bleeding but submissive hearts, we must bow to His will. . . .

My acquaintance with him commenced about the 5th of April, his wound had been received March 25. . . . I saw at once from the extreme delicacy of his appearance, that his case required the utmost care & attention, while my perception of character, also taught me that sympathy & kindness were equally necessary; greater tenderness of spirit I have never seen, "even in women," the most ordinary acts of humanity would call tears to his eyes, & every offering of friendship would be received with a beaming smile of gratitude, that seeing he so keenly appreciated the presence & attention of our sex, I carried many to his bed-side, who were invariably attracted by his lovely character, & ever made him a special object of their attention. The sufferers around him evinced the greatest interest in him, & *even the Yankee nurses* shared in the general fascination; I mention all this, that your mind may be relieved of all unnecessary fears as to his want of care; he began to rally & gain strength after the wound commenced healing, & ate the various delicacies taken to him, with a keen relish. My first care each morning was to select whatever I could command for his special benefit, to take it to him & to sit by his side to cheer & encourage him. He would often *need* this, as his thoughts would wander to her, he so dearly loved, yet who was so far distant, in this hour of trial & suffering; he often spoke of you in the *tenderest* manner, & almost the first thing he did, when I found him in the hospital was to show me your likeness, which was lying by his side. Up to the time I wrote you he was gradually gaining strength & for a week or ten days afterwards, I felt assured that he would recover, as I wrote you. After giving the letter to Lt. G. I told him of the confidence with which I had written, and he said "you ought not to have been so confident, I may yet grow worse"—but still the symptoms were too favorable, that I could not & *would* not believe otherwise, until the fatal disease attacked him, which *defied* every effort to arrest its course. . . . What a blessing it is too, that God should send his dear brother to him in his last moments to watch for, & supply every want, to soothe & nurse him with almost a mother's tenderness—he was a great comfort to him, as he was to me—for a great burden was removed from my heart when I for the first time found him at his bed-side, I knew then that he was safe both day & night in a brother's care.

On Saturday afternoon, he turned to me while his brother was absent for a short time, & said, "I must die, but I am willing. I am ready, oh! come Jesus, come now—Oh! Mrs. Wyche I dread nothing but the pangs of death." I said, "God can enable you to *bear* them or make them *light* & remember too what Jesus suffered for us—" he assented to this & seemed perfectly calm & resigned, nay, happy in the thought; the next day he said he was much better, & felt that he would recover, but we saw it was a false hope, & his brother who was weeping just out of his sight asked me to let him know the truth, that he might learn some message for you. . . . I then told him what I thought of his condition, at the same time said that all things were possible with God. He still said "I am ready at any time, but I *do* feel better." I told him that perhaps God was giving him a quiet entrance into eternity in answer to prayer—"Have you a message for your wife, if you should be mistaken in your impressions?" I said; he replied, "tell her I love her dearly, she has *ever* been a good wife to me—& she must meet me in heaven." This was the last conversation I had with him, but oh! is it not rich in comfort & hope to you—for myself it was a *privilege* to sit by his side, & note the gradual departure of a spirit so full of holy assurance & love, Oh! so different from many I have watched over in similar circumstances; & cannot you now in this sad moment of your bitter bereavement, look up with tearful yet trustful & rejoicing eyes to that *rest* into which the way-worn soldier & pilgrim has entered & whither you will one day follow him! . . . I am giving you these details, which I know will be so gratifying to you—& now with the fervent prayer that God, from his abundant fulness, will mete out to you every temporal & spiritual blessing, as well as to his dear father & other bereaved ones, I am, dear Mrs. Miller,

Your Stranger-friend,
(Mrs.) H. F. Wyche

Figure 3.7. Lily/Pineapple Variation. Frances Sarah Anne Salonon Dennard (1815–1891), Perry (Houston County), ca. 1840–1870. 99½" x 100". Hand-appliquéd and hand-quilted cotton. Collection of Tallulah Kinney Schepis. [GQP 2324]

*Julia Anderson Bush*

Nancy Lovelace Miller died of typhoid fever in 1858 having escaped the pain of seeing her sons go off to war. Both she and Nicholas Wesley are buried in the Lovelace family cemetery in Troup County. John William died in 1868. Several of Nancy's quilts survive. Mr. Johnson believes that she made at least one quilt for each of her children. They were passed down through her daughter, Ola Miller Johnson, who was Mr. Johnson's grandmother.

### Frances Dennard

Frances Dennard, wife of a captain in the Confederate army, made a Lily/Pineapple Variation quilt after her daughter, Mary Frances, returned to Magnolia Plantation (location unknown) from a trip to France (fig. 3.7). According to the family, while in France Mary Frances learned the appliqué techniques that her mother used in this quilt.

Another quilt made by Frances Dennard has also survived. It is signed H. L. Dennard, possibly her husband's initials. Both quilts are made from the same fabrics.

Frances and her daughter were well educated. They were artists and woodcarvers as well. Frances's son-in-law was Congressman Dudley Hughes (Georgia).

### Mary Ann Kelly Persons

Mary Ann Kelly (1835–1899) is said to have been only sixteen when she made a dowry quilt called Rose Album by the family (fig. 3.8). She grew up in Monticello in Jasper County.

Mary Ann married a farmer, William Pinkney Persons (1833–1919), who joined the Confederate army. He was a first lieutenant in Company A, Thirty-second Regiment, and was said to have been the tallest man in that regiment. He participated in several battles though he "never received a scratch." Named in a

Mary Ann Kelly Persons, ca. 1850. Photo courtesy of Mr. and Mrs. E. Thomas Malone.

Figure 3.8. Rose Album. Mary Ann Kelly Persons (1835–1899), Jasper County, ca. 1851. 71" x 86½". Hand-pieced and hand-quilted cotton. Collection of Mr. and Mrs. E. Thomas Malone, great-grandson of maker. [GQP 3839]

codicil to his will dated December 17, 1915, along with his "eight children," were negro servants Reubin and Cora Gilstrap "for their faithfulness to [him] in life."

Mary Ann Kelly Persons's beautiful quilt has continued its life as a gift quilt through succeeding generations. First it went to Mary Ann's granddaughter and namesake, Mary, as a gift at her birth. Mary then gave it to her nephew and his bride, Thomas and Sylvia Malone, the current owners, as a wedding gift in 1964.

### George Washington Gordon

Hidden away with other family valuables, a Chintz Friendship Quilt made in 1856 at Gordon Springs (Walker County) survived the war (fig. 3.9). It is believed that when its owner, George Washington Gordon, volunteered to serve in the Confederacy in 1862, the quilt was packed away in the attic of the family home, Boxwood, in Columbia, Tennessee. Two Bohemian crystal decanters with three dozen glasses in three sizes were wrapped in newspapers from 1861, placed in a wicker champagne basket, and hidden away in the attic with the quilt. George Washington Gordon never returned from the war; he was taken prisoner and interned at Johnson's Island (Ohio), a Federal prison camp for Confederate officers on an island in Lake Erie. In the spring of 1865, he was part of a prisoner exchange. The boat carrying him and others docked at Memphis, where Captain Gordon's sister, a nurse, begged that he be allowed to disembark since he was so ill. Her request was denied, and the day after the boat reached the site of the prisoner exchange, Vicksburg, Mississippi, George Washington Gordon died. The items hidden away so carefully remained undisturbed until the home was sold out of the family in the late 1940s or early 1950s. The items were then sent to a granddaughter, Mary Gordon Stimson, in California,

who gave them to her daughter, Diana Stimson Webb, of Waunakee, Wisconsin. Ms. Webb loaned the quilt to the Walker County Historical Society's Crown Gardens and Archives for exhibit. There, after having been alerted by then director Polly Boggess, the GQP learned of the quilt and documented it. Ms. Webb's interest in her family's history fueled her wish that the quilt be returned permanently to its state of origin. She donated it to the Atlanta Historical Society in 1990.

Thanks to Ms. Webb's genealogical research, much is known about the making of the quilt. Many of the Gordon women sewed; many references to sewing are made in letters written by family members.

George Washington Gordon was an owner of the Gordon Springs resort in Walker County. It was there that he received the quilt as a gift from family members and visitors. His oldest daughter, Mary Brown Gordon, married Dr. James Le Conte in April 1858 at the springs. He was the brother of her friend Annie Le Conte, to whom Mary wrote the following letter on September 30, 1856, and which affords us a peek at the genteel amusements of the wealthier class during the antebellum period:

Perhaps you would like to hear about the quilt. Well it is completed at last and really looks very pretty though we had a time of it the last two or three days it was in the frame. The gentlemen took a notion they must have their fun as they commenced teasing. They would hide needles and thread and make us look for them sometimes an hour then while we would be sitting around stitching away industriously the ropes would break and what a *scatteration* of thimbles, thread and everything that happened to be on top. Thus matters went on until the ladies would stand it no longer so went in early one morning and finished before they came over but we did not have the promised party there were so few here.

George Washington Gordon had promised the ladies "a ball" when the quilt was finished. The twenty-five blocks of the quilt are made from glazed chintz, delicately appliquéd in the Broderie Perse style, set on point. Several of the blocks contain dates of 1854, 1855, and 1856, and many are signed (see detail below). In the center block appears the name of Mary Gordon Stimson's great-grandmother. On other blocks are the names of numerous cousins and a great-great aunt. It seems clear that the quilt was a project for visitors and members of the family, and not turned over to slaves, if in fact there were any. It is not known where the chintz for the quilt was obtained; some of the people who signed the quilt were from larger cities in Georgia, and they might have provided it.

After Mary Brown Gordon and Dr. James Le Conte married, the rest of the family moved back to Boxwood in Tennessee. Dr. and Mrs. Le Conte remained in Georgia, and after his death in 1862, Mary remained in Georgia until the late 1860s, at which time she also returned to live at Boxwood. She kept house for her brother, George Washington Gordon Jr.

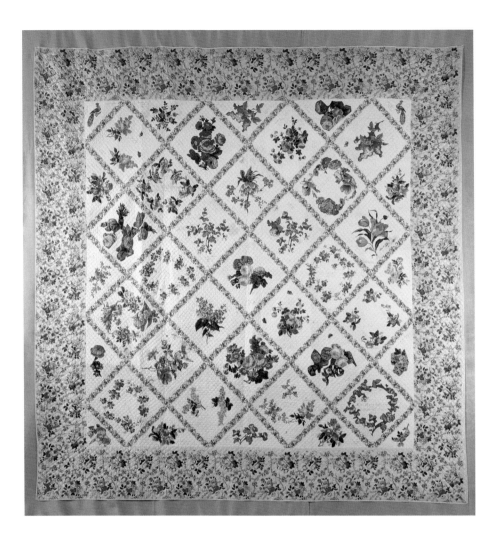

Figure 3.9. Chintz Friendship Quilt. Made by several family members of owner and visitors to the Gordon Springs resort in Walker County, 1854–1856. 106½" x 109". Hand Broderie Perse appliqué, hand-quilted cotton. Collection of the Atlanta History Center, gift of Diana Stimson Webb, great-granddaughter of George Washington Gordon, for whom the quilt was made. Photo by William Hull, courtesy of the Atlanta History Center. [GQP 420]

### The Mosteller Family

Michele Rodgers, director of the Bartow History Center in Cartersville, furnished the following account to the GQP, as told to her by Elizabeth Mosteller Parham:

> The Mosteller family lived near Adairsville, Bartow County, Georgia, for most of the nineteenth century. During the Civil War a refugee family from north of Bartow County stopped at the Mosteller home for food and shelter. Although the refugee family had no money, they wanted to pay the Mostellers for their kindness, so they gave the quilt as payment. The Mosteller family took the quilt and passed it down through succeeding generations.

Ms. Parham donated the exquisite Mariner's Compass Variation to the Bartow History Center in memory of her father, Joseph Mosteller (fig. 3.10). It is not known where the refugee family was from or how long they remained with the Mostellers.

### Mary Ann Clements

The maker of another Mariner's Compass Variation quilt is believed to be Mary Ann Seagraves Clements (1844–1910), whose husband, Charles, was a bodyguard for General Robert E. Lee on the day of the surrender at Appomattox (fig. 3.11). In 1979 when the present owner of the quilt moved into Mary Ann's grandson's house, she discovered it sandwiched between two pieces of fabric, being used as a filling for a newer bedcover. She carefully removed the outer fabrics and stitching to reveal the mid-nineteenth-century quilt inside.

Mary Ann and Charles may have been married when Charles returned from the war. The family has suggested that Mary Ann probably made the quilt top, perhaps for her hope chest, and that it may have been quilted later by her daughter, Ella (1873–1952).

Charles Clements wrote the following letter to the *Danielsville Monitor* (Madison County) on September 7, 1921.

> Allow me to say a few words to my old friends of Madison County—my native county. I represented with "Marse" Robert E. Lee in Virginia, Maryland and Pennsylvania, North Carolina, Georgia and Tennessee.
>
> I am now in my eighty-ninth year and I still work. On the seventh day of September (this month) I picked one hundred and forty-nine pounds of cotton, not withstanding the heat. I belonged to Company D 16th Ga. Regiment[4] and I am the oldest member of that company now living. I love my old county.

Charles and Mary Ann had eleven children. Their first child, Robert E., named for the general, died at birth.

Charles was quite knowledgeable about herbs, according to his descendants, and after the war he developed a cough tonic that he distributed door-to-door until the laws on such matters strengthened and prohibited such sales. His descendants are still great believers in herbal remedies.

Charles Clements cut his leg on a barbed wire fence and died of blood poisoning in 1924. His obituary begins "The last of those gallant heroes who saw Lee surrender to Grant at Appomat[t]ox 'passed over the river to rest under the shade of the trees,' when Charles James Clements, aged 91, died here Wednesday."

Mary Ann and Charles's three great-great-granddaughters will inherit this quilt with the stipulation that they take turns with its possession.

Figure 3.10. Mariner's Compass Variation. Maker unknown, quilt origin unknown, ca. 1860. 87¾" x 78¾". Collection of the Bartow History Center, gift of Elizabeth Mosteller Parham in memory of her father, Joseph Mosteller. [GQP 16]

Figure 3.11. Mariner's Compass Variation. Mary Ann Seagraves Clements (1844–1910) and her daughter Ella Dennis (1874–1952), Fulton County, ca. 1895. 70" x 79½". Hand-pieced and hand-quilted cotton. Collection of Arlene Dennis, granddaughter-in-law of maker. [GQP 1483]

*Julia Anderson Bush*

### Frances Atkins

Frances Atkins (1845–1921), or Fannie, as she was known to family and friends, made a finely executed Ladies' Fantasy quilt, also called Pineapple, around 1862 when she was a young bride-to-be making quilts for her coming marriage (fig. 3.12).

Fannie's story is sadly romantic: Fannie's fiancé was killed in the war while she waited in Henry County for his return. She never married, and lived in the homes of her sisters. Together, they made many fine quilts, several of which are owned by family members.

This exquisite quilt, with its tiny, even buttonhole stitches securing the appliqué in the Broderie Perse style, was inherited and is owned by a Henry County descendant of one of her sisters.

### Mary and Emma McCann

A quilt made in the Baltimore Album style in 1870 by Mary Phillips McCann (1822–1911) and her daughter, Emma McCann (1851–1938), is included here because of its connection to the Civil War (fig. 3.13).[5] Still owned by the family, it is said to have been inspired by a quilt brought by a Southern soldier to Augusta from Virginia during the war. Although this earlier quilt is now lost, the provenance of the Georgia-made Baltimore Album is well documented. It bears the signature of one of the makers, Emma V. McCann, as well as the date, 1870, on a banner in an eagle's beak in one of the center blocks.

Mary Phillips McCann's husband, John, was born to Irish immigrant parents in November 1819 as they sailed to America. The ship flew under an American flag, thereby making him a U.S. citizen at birth. John's parents had fallen in love and married against the wishes of his maternal grandparents. Since the bride's parents would not accept the marriage, the young couple decided to try their fortune in the "new country" across the sea. At least three other children were born to them. When he was about twelve years old, John McCann and his siblings were orphaned in Philadelphia when their parents succumbed to yellow fever within two weeks of each other. The children were placed in a Catholic orphanage. John was later apprenticed to the Baldwin Locomotive Works in Philadelphia. He met his future wife in that city while working there. They married on July 7, 1845. That same year, the family came south when Mr. McCann is said to have brought the first locomotive to Augusta. The McCanns raised four children in their house on Calhoun Street. John McCann Sr. was a master mechanic for the Central of Georgia Railroad for thirty-two years.

Mary Phillips McCann, John's wife, was remembered by one granddaughter, Irene Burges Moore Miller, as "just about the grandest woman who ever lived . . . the soul of good humor and good cheer and a wonderful 'buddy' to her many grandchildren. She could accomplish more work than any person I ever knew and more varied tasks, from the very finest needlework to whitewashing a fence. There was a contagion about her industry. . . . She never turned us away, nor did she ever seem out of patience with us or too busy to have us near her."

Toward the end of the Civil War, Mary is said to have taken down her last pair of white linen curtains to make a hand-tucked shirt for her husband. She also was fond of saying that she was "kin to two Presidents but she did not know that it did her any good." Her descendants tell us that she was a cousin of President Zachary Taylor. President Taylor's daughter married Jefferson Davis, president of the Confederacy, thus linking the two families.

Of exquisite workmanship with much embroidery

Figure 3.12. Ladies' Fantasy (Pineapple). Frances "Fannie" Atkins (1845–1921), Luella (Henry County), ca. 1850–80. 85" x 99". Hand-appliquéd and hand-quilted cotton. This quilt is still in Atkins's family. [GQP 640]

Mary Phillips McCann, ca. 1880. Photo courtesy of Ann Stalnaker.

Emma V. McCann, ca. 1875. Photo courtesy of Ann Stalnaker.

Figure 3.13. Baltimore Album. Mary Phillips McCann (1822–1911) and her daughter, Emma V. McCann (1851–1938), Augusta (Richmond County), 1870. 101" x 101". Hand-appliquéd and hand-quilted cotton. Collection of Margaret Callicott, Ann Stalnaker, Margaret Gilleland, and Bonnie Arthur, descendants of Mary Phillips McCann. [GQP 5858]

This detail from McCann's quilt (fig. 3.13, GQP 5858) shows the Georgia state seal, proving the quilt's origin and making it the earliest known example of a Baltimore Album–style quilt made in the state.

Note the exquisitely stuffed grapes and berries.

and stuffed work appliqué, the McCann quilt won at least seven first premium blue ribbons at the Georgia-Carolina Fair in Augusta in 1911–16 and 1920. Its twenty-five blocks include a railroad block, a block with Masonic symbols, one pertaining to the International Order of Odd Fellows, and one depicting the Georgia state seal. Botanical motifs abound, and an elaborate undulating flower-and-vine border frames the blocks.

Emma McCann never married. Her will bequeaths her "fancy cotton quilt" to her niece, Ruth Virginia McCann, who never married. Ruth Virginia gave it to her niece, Margaret Ann Diendorf Callicott, one of

the present owners and great-granddaughter of Mary Phillips McCann. The quilt is owned jointly by Margaret Callicott and her three daughters.

The quilts that survived the war are precious to their families, as are the memories and legends that have been passed down through the generations to the present owners. Most of the quilts have remained in their families; a few have been given to museums in order that they, as well as their stories, be preserved for future generations to remember and enjoy.

Through the vehicle of the quilt, stories more than a hundred years old have been collected and recounted in these pages. Doubtless there are many more stories associated with the War between the States and the quiltmakers who survived it. Perhaps these selected few stories will inspire readers to ask questions of elderly relatives or look through that old box of "papers and stuff" in the attic and thus learn more about their families' stories.

The makers of these quilts stitched through their "fears and tears" to provide warm covers for their families as well as comfort for themselves during the difficult times of war. The quilts are tangible objects that help to recall with pride a rich heritage and with reverence the memory of brave and honorable ancestors. This chapter is a tribute to them.

# 4. King Cotton

PATRICIA PHILLIPS MARSHALL

- - - - - - - - - - - - - - - - - - - - - - - - - - - - - - - - -

Cotton is the very foundation for the majority of quilts produced not just in Georgia but around the world. Cotton has also played an important role in the history of the state. No other crop has influenced and dominated a region as much as cotton. In Georgia, its beginnings and development reach back into the eighteenth century. Cotton was the basis of wealth for the plantation owner, providing money to purchase land and slaves. Subsistence farmers grew limited amounts of cotton to provide their families with the raw material to produce cloth. After the Civil War, the lives of landowners, tenant farmers, and sharecroppers revolved around the cotton crop. Most modern quiltmakers are unaware just how much the people of Georgia depended upon the cotton crop and how it affected their lives. In this state the crop was referred to as King Cotton, and whether it was sold for cash or used for home consumption, the people of Georgia were economically dependent on cotton for much of the past two hundred years. This chapter follows the story of King Cotton from its introduction to Georgia to its rapid spread throughout the state and into the lives of Georgians, its ultimate decline in the twentieth century, and its partial resurrection as a commercially grown natural fiber with a role once again in clothing manufacture and quiltmaking.

## Climate Compatibility and Early Successes

Cotton cultivation is unique to the South because of geography. The plant thrives in warm, moderate temperatures. It is cultivated in areas below 37 degrees latitude with the right combination of soil, temperature, rainfall, and growing seasons. In order for the cotton plant to mature, a minimum of 200 to 210 frost-free days is required. During the 1849 growing season, the *Albany Patriot* reported a frost in April that killed a large percentage of the young cotton plants. Many plantation owners that year plowed the fields under to start anew. The cotton plant generally needs around twenty-five inches of rain. However, the rain must fall at the right time. Heavy rains early in the season can affect the root system, while rain at picking time can ruin the cotton boll. In 1888 a farmer in the Jones Creek community in South Georgia wrote the *Worth County Local* that he had produced only five bales of cotton from thirteen acres of land due to "too much rain up to last June followed by 40 days without rain."[1]

Cotton was grown in almost every region in Georgia, including the gorges in the North Georgia mountains. It was first grown in the state during the colonial period. Early experiments with a perennial type of West Indian tree cotton failed because the variety was not hardy enough to survive the winter. Sea Island cotton plants from the Bahamas were then introduced to Georgia's St. Simons and Cumberland Islands between 1778 and 1786. Sea Island cotton is often referred to as long-staple cotton since its silky fiber can measure between 1½ inches and 1⅝ inches in length. Its color can range from white to light yellow.[2]

Figure 4.1. This family in Carroll County poses with its sacks and protective hats as it prepares to pick the first cotton bolls of the season, ca. 1900. CAR163, Vanishing Georgia Collection, Georgia Archives.

*Patricia Phillips Marshall*

Sea Island cotton (*Gossypium barbadense*) was well suited to the Georgia coast. It thrived under the hot, humid conditions found on the islands and coastal mainland but did poorly during dry years. Rice and indigo had been the main crops for coastal planters, but a series of severe storms, the American Revolution, and postrevolutionary indigo production in the East Indies combined to turn rice and indigo fields over to Sea Island cotton.[3]

Market demand was another reason Sea Island cotton proved to be an economic boon for the Georgia coast. Considered superior in strength, fineness, and uniformity of fiber, Sea Island cotton was recommended for fine cloth such as muslins, gauze, lace, and cotton-silk blends, as well as for sewing thread. These fabrics were in demand for fashionable clothing between 1790 and 1820. While printed cottons were mainly worn during the day, fine muslin was used for both day and evening dress. Gauze often covered silk on fancy ensembles.[4] What made the cultivation of Sea Island cotton profitable for the Georgia planter was the ease with which the seed cotton could be processed. Sea Island cotton has a smooth black seed that easily separates from the lint or fiber. This separation was accomplished with a roller gin, a simple machine consisting of two upright posts holding one horizontal roller on top of another. The cotton is forced between the two rollers, extracting the fiber and leaving behind the seed.

Soon other Georgia farmers wanted to cultivate this lucrative crop, which by the 1790s was priced at $0.90 to $1.25 per pound of lint. But Sea Island cotton thrived only on the Georgia coast. Farmers who lived in the upcountry, or farther inland, were growing tobacco as a money crop. They were also growing a type of cotton known as green seed or upland cotton (*Gossypium hirsutum*), often described as short-staple cotton because its fiber ranges from ¾ to 1¼ inches in length. Its white fiber was used in the production of ordinary cotton goods ranging from calicoes to sheeting and shirting fabrics.[5]

Upland cotton was never cultivated widely in the Georgia upcountry during the eighteenth century because it was extremely difficult to separate the seed from the lint. Its short fibers clung tenaciously to the green seed, requiring cleaning by hand. Often it was an evening chore done by family members in front of a warm fireplace. Separating one pound of cotton lint often took an entire day. Because it was labor intensive, upland cotton was produced only for home consumption in the making of homespun cloth.[6]

## Invention and Innovation

Because of the increasing demand for cotton, the state had appointed a commission during the early 1790s to promote the invention of a suitable cleaning machine, which would dramatically reduce the labor required to produce upland cotton. It was estimated that two to three million pounds of upland cotton had been grown, but only a small amount had been hand cleaned for sale; the remainder was used on the family farm. An event occurred in 1793 that many consider the prime force behind the dominance of cotton over southern agriculture and economics. On a plantation near Savannah, Eli Whitney was the guest of Mrs. Catherine Greene, widow of General Nathaniel Greene. Here Whitney heard the plantation manager, Phineas Miller, and others talk about the problems of cleaning upland cotton. Whitney tackled the problem, and the result was a machine so simple in its construction it was a wonder that no one had thought of it before. Whitney's gin (some say *gin* is a shortened form of *engine*) consisted of a wooden cylinder embedded with rows of iron spikes (fig. 4.2). When a handle turned the cylinder, the spikes passed through slots cut into a metal plate. On the other side was the seed cotton. As the spikes picked and pulled the cotton lint through the slots, the seeds were left behind. On the opposite side of the cylinder were brushes that removed the cotton lint from the spikes. Whitney's cotton gin was capable of cleaning fifty pounds of cotton lint in one day, an astonishing improvement over one pound per day by hand.[7]

A new generation of the gin soon appeared when another Georgian, inventor and mechanic Hodgen Holmes, replaced the spikes in 1796 with small iron saw blades. This saw gin rapidly spread throughout the state and eventually across the South. The mechanical parts were so simple that a farmer, having observed a gin in operation, could go back to his farm or plantation and easily build his own gin. Whitney and Miller tried to monopolize the young industry by running

thirty gins in eight communities, but they were unsuccessful. In fact, Whitney spent years in court trying to protect his patent.[8]

The cotton gin enabled farmers and planters in the Georgia upcountry to plant upland cotton as a cash crop. In 1806 it was estimated that one upcountry farmer in five owned a cotton gin. This figure increased to one in three by 1820. In the first decade of the nineteenth century, upland cotton sold for around 20¢ a pound. At the same time Sea Island cotton brought 50¢ a pound. Seed cotton (unginned cotton) brought only 2¢ to 3.5¢ per pound. Thus, the value of the cotton ginned by the saw gin dramatically increased.[9]

Some have argued that the invention of the cotton gin was the sole stimulus to the rise in cotton production, and with it the spread of slavery, throughout the South. There were, however, other factors at play. The American Revolution temporarily severed traditional economic ties between the rebellious colonies and Great Britain; this included the importation of consumer goods such as clothing and fancy cloth. Americans were now encouraged to develop a manufacturing base, which included the production of cloth. Many subsistence farm families made homespun (often made from cotton and wool fibers). In Georgia other traditional cash crops such as indigo and rice were on the decline, as already noted: Great Britain found alternative and cheaper sources for indigo, notably in the Caribbean; rice gave way to cotton, which was better suited to coastal weather and less labor intensive. Two other factors increased the demand for cotton in the late eighteenth century. First, a rising commercial class in Great Britain sought to supply that country's spinners and weavers with raw material, that is, cotton. Second, Great Britain's textile industry felt the impact of the Industrial Revolution. Inventions of new machines such as the spinning jenny, power loom, and

Figure 4.2. Whitney cotton gin, patent model. Modern gins still utilize the basic mechanical motion of Whitney's 1793 model. Photo courtesy of the National Museum of American History, Smithsonian Institution.

roller printer capable of producing printed cotton cloth increased the demand for cotton lint. This combination of factors made it possible for cotton to become the king of all crops in Georgia during the nineteenth century. While men in the New England states sought to replicate the English textile mills, southern farmers and planters focused on producing the raw material for those mills. By the 1850s Georgia farmers produced more cotton than they did any other subsistence crops.[10]

Whether one lived on a large plantation or a small yeoman farm, cotton cultivation came to dominate every aspect of life. Cotton was responsible for the rapid development of the middle Georgia piedmont and the southwest portion of the state into large plantation systems dependent upon the labor of slaves. Interspersed between the plantations were small yeoman farms, where most production focused on raising crops for home consumption. Half of all yeoman farms produced only one or two bales of cotton for sale each year because it was so labor intensive. The plantation owners turned to enslaved African Americans to labor in their cotton fields. In 1800 the number of slaves in Georgia was recorded at 59,406. By 1860 this number had increased to 462,198, second only to Virginia. The heaviest concentration of slaves was on the coast, where cotton reigned, and in the piedmont.[11]

Prices for cotton fluctuated throughout the nineteenth century. In the 1820s prices fell to about 12¢ per pound and went as high as 21¢ per pound. By the 1840s cotton sold for 4¢ to 5¢ per pound, a sharp decrease that resulted in an economic depression for the state. However, by the 1850s cotton prices had risen to 11¢ per pound due to market demand: cotton was being used for more than just clothing and quilts. It was woven into cloth for wagon tops and ships' sails, and cotton exports to foreign countries were on the

Figure 4.3. Members of Dan Elder's African American family pose with W. C. Ragsdale, Mrs. Ragsdale and Hunter Ragsdale in Coweta County, ca. 1880. COW 81, Vanishing Georgia Collection, Georgia Archives.

rise. Georgia farmers answered this demand by increasing production. In 1802 the state had produced 20,000 bales of cotton. The number of bales increased to 163,000 in 1833, and by 1859 Georgians were producing over 700,000 bales of cotton per year.[12]

## The Demands of Cotton Cultivation

Cotton cultivation did not require much more investment than labor during the eighteenth and early nineteenth centuries. In the eighteenth century, once the seed was placed in the ground, a broad hoe was used to chop and remove weeds. After 1800 cotton was planted in drilled rows made on ridge tops thrown up by a plow. Cotton rows were about five feet apart, with plants set six inches to one foot apart. The 1850s marked a transition in planting and cultivation methods. The earlier methods of land preparation consisted of careless plowing, which resulted in a loss of topsoil. When the land was played out and no longer produced much cotton, many planters moved on to lands available farther west.[13]

An interest arose during the 1850s in land preservation and a "scientific" approach to farming. Although practiced by only a few at first, these methods became standard during the years following the Civil War and continued throughout the nineteenth century. Cotton production developed a cycle that controlled the lives of farmers both large and small. It began in the late winter with land preparation. A shovel plow was used to plow up the land while turning under any existing vegetation for plant food. The field was then bedded by plowing a series of furrows with a scooter or bull-tongue plow. These furrows were usually set four feet apart and cut deep to accommodate the fertilizer. New fertilizers introduced during the 1850s produced remarkable results. Cottonseed was an inexpensive fertilizer that was supplemented by chemical fertilizers such as guano, which was processed from bird dung. By 1860 guano was widely regarded by agriculturists as the best fertilizer to use. It was applied to the soil with a tin funnel commonly called a guano horn. Later in the nineteenth century, an animal-powered, mechanical fertilizer was employed that resembled the cotton planter in both technique and appearance.[14]

A machine for planting cotton was adopted in Georgia prior to the Civil War and gradually replaced the planting of cotton by hand. A common type of cotton planter was the Dow Law, which had a hopper to hold seed. A front wheel provided motion via crank and shaft to agitate the seed and release it at uniform intervals. A covering board completed the process as it swept the soil across the seed. Planting was done sometime between about April 10 and the end of May. The mechanical cotton planter increased the amount of acreage that could be planted. One man working with a planter and mule could average six to eight acres a day, compared to one acre planted by hand.[15]

At two to four weeks, the cotton was thinned out by "chopping" with a hoe so that the plants were spaced nine inches apart. For the slaves who worked in the cotton fields of coastal Georgia, June was a hard month. They worked in gangs across the fields, often singing in time to the movement of the hoes. Later, plowing with a sweep attachment was used along with hoe chopping to clear the fields of weeds until July, when the crop was considered "laid by."[16] The plant was left to mature until harvest or picking time, usually beginning in September and lasting through the fall. The cotton plant requires several pickings, as cotton bolls open at varying times.

Cotton picking was the most labor-intensive activity of the whole cycle, requiring many hands. The majority of laborers prior to the Civil War were slaves, both men and women. In 1852 Catoe, the driver of Charles Colcock Jones, who owned Montevideo plantation in Liberty County, reported to his master, "We now

Figure 4.4. Dow Law planter. Photo courtesy of the Georgia Agrirama, Tifton (Tift County).

Figure 4.5. Boys and girls were frequently removed from school to help pick cotton. On the Carroll farm Ida Mae Wells Phillips, Bill Wells and Roddie Wells Allgood stand with their sacks full in Gwinnett County, 1908. GWN83, Vanishing Georgia Collection, Georgia Archives.

have all the women picking cotton & from appearance will have no more time to do any thing else it is opening finely & is very white & pretty cotton. I think we will make Thirty Bales unless I am very much deceived." Other planters reported that their slaves could pick anywhere from 60 to 100 pounds of seed cotton a day. George Collier of southwestern Georgia recorded in 1854 that his slaves were picking between 200 and 300 pounds a day, the women picking as much as the men. For example, he noted that Sarah (age seventeen) picked 304 pounds, Mariah (age fifteen) picked 293 pounds, Big Sally (age thirty-two) picked 272 pounds, and Mahaly (age forty) picked 235 pounds. With postbellum freedom, new systems of sharecropping and tenancy replaced slavery to provide the necessary labor force. Many former slaves and landless white farmers became tenants or sharecroppers, exchanging their labor for a home, food, fuel, and the right to hunt and

fish on the owner's property. These systems effectively tied a sharecropper or tenant to the landowner and to the success of the crop.[17]

In the late nineteenth century, both African Americans and whites labored in the cotton fields, with men, women, and children required to do the picking. In 1876 nearly 40 percent of all laborers involved in the production of cotton were whites. In fact, many schools closed during the fall so students could help bring in the cotton crop. In 1896 the editors of the *Douglas Breeze* advocated that the practice be stopped. They wrote, "Some people have an idea that a boy or a girl can learn enough in two or three years to be called educated. They think that a few months in each year, in school when not needed, out of school when there is cotton to pick or sheep to shear or hogs to kill or corn to thin or peas to gather, will suffice to fit them for any duties they will meet after they have grown to

*King Cotton*

Figure 4.6. Cotton picking sacks were often made from old fertilizer and feed sacks. This family in Bartow County is using a sheet instead of a basket to collect cotton from their sacks, ca. 1940s. BRW159, Vanishing Georgia Collection, Georgia Archives.

*Patricia Phillips Marshall*

manhood or womanhood." The editors concluded that this may once have been true, but the "new era" of the 1890s demanded more education for success.[18] It was a cruel reality that for many farm families, the children were needed to help bring in the crops not only for sustenance but to provide the only cash the family might earn through the sale of a bale of cotton. The practice of keeping children from school to work in the fields continued well into the twentieth century.

The quantity of cotton picked depended on the individual, with a child averaging 20 to 30 pounds per day, while an adult could pick between 100 and 200 pounds a day. Sometimes the cotton pickers would hold impromptu matches and challenge each other to a contest. In 1887 in Worth County, J. H. Storey's family held such a match, and the results came in with his son (age fifteen) picking 411 pounds, his thirteen-year-old daughter picking 311 pounds, his ten-year-old daughter picking 186 pounds, his nine-year-old daughter picking 180 pounds, and his two adult field hands picking 306 pounds each. The local newspaper considered this excellent picking with 1,790 pounds of seed cotton by six hands—more than 500 pounds of lint. The paper stated average cotton picking for twelve hands to be a 500-pound bale in a day. The paper also observed the efforts of the children stating, "It demonstrates how serviceable children can prove on a farm."[19]

To pick the cotton, laborers moved through the fields filling long burlap or cotton sacks that hung across their shoulders and dragged along on the ground (fig. 4.6). When full, the sacks were emptied into baskets or wagons at the end of the row. Field scales or steelyards were used to weigh the cotton (fig. 4.7).[20]

Cotton picking was a communal event in most areas, especially in South Georgia. Neighbors could converse with each other while moving down the rows and then share a noon meal prepared by the women. In this way farm families helped one another bring in the crop. J. L. Herring, the editor of the *Tifton Gazette* newspaper in 1918, reminisced about the community cotton pickings in the "old" Wiregrass counties during the nineteenth century: "These 'workings' as they were called relieved the monotony and loneliness of country life; brought people closer together and facili-

tated work, for they gave the task a zip and enthusiasm lacking even with the most industrious when alone. The cotton itself entered more into the home life, for out of each crop was saved the year's supply for knitting thread, or perhaps for the loom."[21]

Once picked, seed cotton was ready for the gin. Prior to the Civil War, most small farmers could not afford a cotton gin. They often took their seed cotton to the gin of a neighboring planter who could gin and sell the cotton for them. Antebellum gins were powered by mules or horses. As seed cotton was fed by hand into the gin, the lint would be dispersed into a side room, where it was gathered by hand and taken to a large baling press. The press had a hand-carved wood screw that would compact the cotton into bales. Be-

Figure 4.7. Laborers in Thomas County weighing in their cotton with a steelyard balance scale, ca. 1895. Original photograph by A. W. Miller of Thomasville, Georgia. THO99, Vanishing Georgia Collection, Georgia Archives.

*King Cotton*

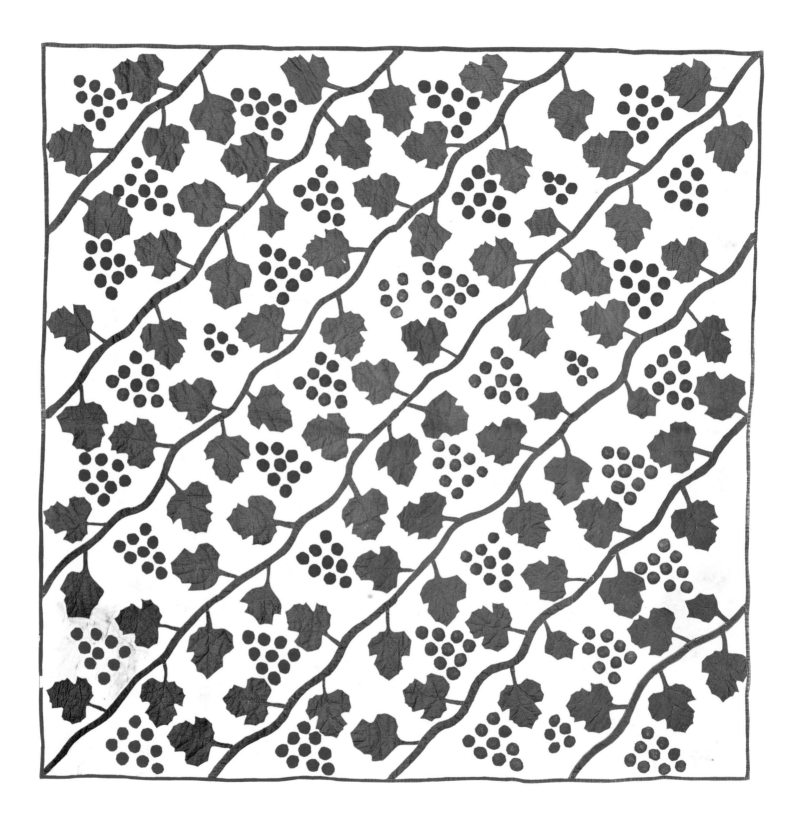

fore the press came into use, ginned cotton was often packed into bags or sacks. Georgia Quilt Project (GQP) volunteers documented a quilt attributed to the estate of Hetty Green in Columbus, Georgia. The ca. 1860 quilt has a lining made from sacks stenciled with the words "Sea Island Cotton" (fig. 4.9). The fabric lining is too coarse to be made from Sea Island cotton, and it is possible the fabric had once been bagging for ginned Sea Island cotton.[22]

By the 1880s there was a proliferation of public gins in small towns and rural communities. In 1900 over 4,700 gins operated in Georgia. The introduction of steam power and improved ginning machinery with mechanical baling presses contributed to the large increase. Contemporary newspapers are full of reports such as "Mr. Joe Norman has built a steam ginnery at his home and will gin cotton for his neighborhood this season. The engine and all the machinery necessary for it was received at Sumner several days ago," and "Mr. J. N. Welch's new 80 saw gin arrived on Monday last and takes the place of the 60 saw gin which did not come up to the requirements of his consumers. The new gin enables him to gin and pack a bale of cotton inside an hour." A review of estate inventories for the 1890s reveals that individual farmers were investing in

gin equipment. In 1891 the estate of James Hancock of Worth County lists a Pratt cotton gin among his farming, blacksmithing, and carpenter's tools. Thomas Warren of Wilcox County owned a sixty-saw gin, a gristmill, an iron cotton press, and an eight-horsepower engine on wheels in 1891. He was obviously grinding corn meal and grits for his neighbors when his cotton gin was not operating.[23]

Like most other rural work sites, the cotton gin served a social function as well (fig. 4.12). Everyone's cotton crop came in at about the same time during the fall months. The cotton gins were a beehive of activity, and farmers with loaded wagons of seed cotton waited patiently for hours for their turn at the gin. Taking the cotton to the gin was an event anticipated by the lucky children permitted to go along. They rode on top of the wagons wrapped in quilts to keep warm during the early morning. While the men talked about crops and politics, the children would marvel at the machinery. The bales produced often represented the only cash the family would have for the coming year.[24]

These cultivation and cleaning processes were the main activities on cotton farms. Both small and large farming operations devoted land and resources to cotton. In 1886 a one-horse farmer in Worth County produced ten 500-pound bales of cotton. An African American farmer, David Moore, in the same county produced eighteen bales of cotton with one horse, which was equal to the output of the Hannon farm that used two horses. Cycloneta, an experimental farm located near present-day Chula (Tift County), used three plows to harvest forty-five bales of cotton. Historically, the majority of Georgia's population lived on farms, and the majority of these farms produced cotton. The 1900 census for Georgia listed 160,865 cotton farms across the state. About 47 percent of all cropland was planted in cotton, and the value of the state's cot-

Figure 4.9. Detail from reverse of Oak Leaf Variation. Family attributes to the estate of Hetty Green (1835–1916), origin unknown, ca. 1860. 90" x 91". Hand-pieced, -appliquéd and -quilted cotton. Collection of Peggy Love. [GQP 2090]

This detail from the reverse of the quilt shows a stenciled "Sea Island Cotton." The lining of this quilt is probably made from bags that once held ginned Sea Island cotton. Photo by Anita Z. Weinraub.

Figure 4.8. Grape Vine. Lavinia Ruth Butts Lewis (1839–1906), ca. 1880. 75" x 76". Hand-appliquéd, -embroidered, and -quilted cotton. Collection of the United Daughters of the Confederacy, Sidney Lanier Chapter. [GQP 1188]

A label on the reverse of this quilt states that Lavinia Lewis made this stunning quilt for her granddaughter, Martha Lavinia Lewis Kadderly. Lewis skillfully used a diagonal set for her pattern of meandering grape vines and leaves to provide a new interpretation of a red, green, and white quilt. She stuffed the individual grapes in each cluster with cotton to achieve a three-dimensional effect. She was no doubt inspired by the native varieties of muscadine and scuppernong grapes gathered each fall by rural women and children.

Figure 4.10. William H. Davis operated a cotton gin on U.S. Highway 29 in Bartow County. Here an unidentified worker tends two gin stands around 1945. Seed cotton is being fed into the gins by a pneumatic feed system that used air suction to remove the seed cotton from wagons. The ginnery was destroyed in the 1950s. BRW26, Vanishing Georgia Collection, Georgia Archives.

Figure 4.11. Laborers work at a baling press in Thomas County, ca. 1895. The ginned cotton was packed into a box that was lined with jute or burlap bagging. Two mules attached to the wood beams turned the giant screw downward and compressed as much cotton as possible into a bale weighing three hundred to five hundred pounds. Although A. W. Miller of Thomasville recorded this photograph during the 1890s, this type of press was also used during the antebellum period. Cotton lint is seen scattered all over the ground. THO138, Vanishing Georgia Collection, Georgia Archives.

*Patricia Phillips Marshall*

ton crop was $57,171,000. All other agricultural products—cereals, fruits, nuts, hay, forage crops, vegetables, and dairy products—were worth $35,876,000.[25] King Cotton was sitting firmly on his throne.

## Homespun

With much of the state's resources devoted to cotton, it stands to reason that the success or failure of the crop directly affected Georgia's quiltmakers. Women accomplished much of a family's textile production at home during the nineteenth century. Prior to the Civil War, cotton garments were made from cotton spun and woven on the farm. On one of his southern journeys, Frederick Law Olmsted, after attending a church service outside Savannah, noted, "In the house were some fifty white people, generally dressed in homespun, and of the class called 'crackers,' though I am told that some of them owned a good many Negroes, and were by no means poor as their appearance indicated." Olmsted had observed the frugality of Georgia's rural population. Even though manufactured cottons imported from northern mills were available in Savannah, the rural "crackers" made their own cloth and saved their money to invest in property. Talula Gilbert Bottoms (1862–1946) of Fayette County remembered, "The women of big families had a hard time when I was a child. They had to spin cotton into thread and weave it into cloth, and then cut garments and make them by hand, for there were no sewing machines in those days."[26]

Estate and inventory records until late in the nineteenth century reveal that most farm families owned spinning wheels and looms. The estate inventory of Timothy Kirkland of Coffee County in 1864 (see pp. 54–55) listed two spinning wheels, one loom, and several bed quilts. The estate of Elizabeth Johnson in

Wilcox County (1891) listed one spinning wheel; the estate of Sarah P. Hancock of Wilcox County (1895) listed a wheel and reel as well as a sewing machine. As the nineteenth century drew to a close, there was a movement to encourage farmers to diversify their crops so as not to be dependent upon cotton and staples purchased from out of state. Southern farmers were urged to grow more corn and raise more hogs to become independent of northern and western markets. This rhetoric was extended in some areas of Georgia to encourage women to return to the production of homespun. In 1889 S. G. Long wrote the *Worth County Local* and reported that farmers in the Jones Creek area were determined to return to the practice of twenty years earlier and produce more at home rather than buy staples from out of state. He cited an example of a widow, A. M. Hill, who along with her daughter, A. T. Hill, ventured to spin and weave again. He reflected, "To hear her spools rattle carried me back to the good old homespun days, when I plowed barefooted and wore my homespun pants."[27]

By returning to the production of homespun, women demonstrated that they could do their part to be more self-sufficient. After all, most rural housekeepers practiced home economy as a way of life. The Civil War left some areas of Georgia totally devastated, especially those in the path of General Sherman's March to the Sea. Talula Gilbert Bottoms wrote: "Salt got so scarce that people dug up dirt from their smokehouses where the meat had dripped, and put the dirt in an old fashioned ash hopper to dry, like lye for soap. They then took the water that ran through the dirt and boiled it down to get salt." However, by the closing decades of the nineteenth century, both homespun and loom weaving were becoming part of the past. In 1889 in Dooley County an eighty-year-old woman was still weaving coverlets. People in the vicinity considered

Figure 4.12. Cotton trading in Norcross (Gwinnett County) on a busy day in 1911. GWN255, Vanishing Georgia Collection, Georgia Archives.

this a curiosity and "came a good long way" to see it. This octogenarian, in addition to weaving, gathered wood, drew water, cooked meals, and washed clothes for a family of five. She also walked four or five miles to visit friends and neighbors.[28] Such was the life of a rural housekeeper.

All of the documentary evidence points to homespun being utilized in Georgia quilts. The term *homespun* refers to cloth produced by hand methods. This includes hand spinning the thread on a spinning wheel and using that thread on a two- to four-harness weaving loom to produce cloth. Although northern textile mills produced a variety of cotton cloth, many rural Georgians chose to make their own cloth to save money. They may have purchased the printed fabric for the quilt top but used their own homespun cloth for the linings. Georgia's Quilt History Days revealed

that many nineteenth-century quilts contained home-spun fabrics.

For example, the quilts made during the mid–nineteenth century by Nancy Lovelace Miller (1810–1858) incorporate a combination of fabrics (fig. 4.14; see also fig. 3.6). The quilt patterns are typical of the time, utilizing red, green, and yellow fabrics that were probably produced in northern mills. However, several of Nancy's documented quilts have linings that were pieced from three narrow lengths of fabric, indicating that they were woven on a domestic weaving loom. In 1910 her quilts escaped destruction when descendant Ola Miller (now Johnson) rescued them. Her aunt, embarrassed because the quilts were old and handmade, had wanted to toss them on a bonfire. Johnson's aunt saw the quilts as representative of a time when life was hard and best forgotten. Today Nancy's descendants see the quilts as heirlooms and still own her spinning wheel,

clock reel, and a wooden box made by her husband, Jacob Miller.[29] For them the quilts and other objects are material evidence of the challenges their ancestors faced in life and ones the current generation wishes to remember.

Life was indeed hard for Georgia families who practiced subsistence agriculture. It was a struggle to raise enough food to feed both family and livestock. The money generated from a bale or two of cotton went to pay taxes and buy additional land and farming necessities, leaving little with which to purchase store-bought items. Many would assume these families lived in economic poverty. However, the prevalence of home-spun cloth in quilts does not indicate that these families were destitute, but rather it reveals how rural farm women economized when necessary.

The women who produced these quilts were frugal and thrifty as well as talented. Spinning thread requires

*Patricia Phillips Marshall*

Figure 4.14. Fig Leaf. Nancy Lovelace Miller (1810–1858), Longcane Community (Troup County), ca. 1850. 74" x 93". Hand-pieced, -appliquéd, and -quilted cotton. Collection of the Columbus Museum of Art, gift of Nancy's great-great-grandson, A. Stephen Johnson. [GQP 2128]

skill, patience, and practice. Cotton is usually spun on a great wheel, also commonly called a walking wheel. This device has a large spoke wheel about three and a half feet in diameter. A heavy cord is wrapped around the wheel rim and the spindle, which is mounted on a post opposite the wheel. Cotton cards are used to comb and card the cotton in preparation for spinning. A card resembles a wooden paddle with a series of spiked "teeth" attached to one side. Cotton lint is combed through the wire spikes by passing one paddle over the other. This combing action straightens the fibers by placing them in one direction. Carding cotton is monotonous work and was often done by the younger children in the family.[30]

Figure 4.15. Cotton cards. Collection of Martha H. Mulinix.

The cotton fiber is then removed from the cards. Called a *rolag*, at this stage it resembles a fluffy roll of cotton. A piece of cornhusk is then wrapped around the spindle, and fibers from the rolag are twisted around the husk. The great wheel turns the spindle, which twists the fibers together as they roll off the spindle tip. This action turns the fibers into thread. As the spindle turns, the spinner, standing, takes two or three steps back, pulling the rolag, which twists into a long thread. She then reverses the turn of the wheel and walks forward again as the thread winds around the cornhusk on the spindle. Eventually a spool of thread is formed.[31] This walking back and forth gave the walking wheel its name.

The next step is to remove the thread from the spindle and measure it. The thread is transferred to a clock reel to be made into a skein. This reel has turned spokes attached to a rimless hub. Instead of a rim, each spoke has a turned peg fastened perpendicular to it. The thread is wound on these pegs, and a mechanism in the reel counts out the number of turns, stopping when a skein is made. The skeins can then be dyed. Indigo (initially produced on the Georgia coast) produced blue; to produce yellow, copperas (ferrous sulfate) was purchased. Walnut hulls and pomegranate were used to make brown and a pale red dye, respectively.[32]

After dyeing, the thread is now ready for the loom. It is transferred to a warping frame, which holds the threads in straight lines so they can be wound on the warp beam of the loom. Each warp (vertical) thread is pulled through a heddle held in place by the harness. Once warped, the loom is operated by pressing foot treadles that lift each harness with its heddles. The warp threads separate and the weaver pushes a shuttle with a weft (horizontal) thread through the open space. The weaver uses the batten or beater bar to press each new weft thread against the previous one, and then repeats the process. The next treadle lifts alternate warp threads for the weft to pass through. Weavers create patterns by using more than two harnesses for lifting specific warp threads.[33]

Once the cloth was made, clothing was cut out and sewn. All construction was by hand until the sewing machine became widely available after the Civil War.[34] In addition to textile production during the antebellum period, rural women also cared for children,

Figure 4.16. Walking wheel. Collection of Sue Kirkland McCranie.

cooked all the meals either over an open hearth or on a wood-burning stove, assisted in food production by tending a garden, preserved fruits and vegetables, and often worked in the fields when it was time to bring in the cotton crop. The old adage that "a woman's work is never done" certainly applied to the women of rural Georgia.

Even after the Civil War and well into the twentieth century, many Georgia women worked in the cotton fields.[35] The GQP documented a number of quilts made of handpicked and carded cotton. Mary L. Beaver of Snellville (Gwinnett County) specifically recalled her youth growing up on a cotton farm when she created her Cotton Boll quilt in 1980 (fig. 4.17). It holds special memories for Mary, who with her eleven brothers and sisters was reared on a farm near Gratis in Walton County during the 1930s and 1940s.

Papa thought nothing of planting 60 to 75 acres of cotton which we gathered by hand, on some days picking as many as four bales. There were no mechanical cotton pickers in those days, and even if there had been, Papa would not have used one. He was a firm believer that if children stayed idle, they grew up lazy and not worth their salt! Even though the work was hard, those were among the happiest days our family ever spent together. The Cotton Boll quilt pattern brought back many fond memories of those by-gone days.

As I began piecing the quilt, I could see Mama making our old sunbonnets, shirts, and pants from feed and fertilizer sacks. She would stiffen our bonnets with homemade starch of flour and water. I wish I had learned to make starch like she did. Each time I tried, I ended up with a pot of flour lumps that the chickens would not even eat! We six girls could always tell whose bonnet was whose, even though they all looked alike. Many a time we crawled under the wagons loaded with

cotton to get out of the rain, not to keep from getting wet ourselves, but to keep our bonnets nice and stiff.

Every time I worked on my cotton boll quilt, I had another precious memory come to mind. I could hear Papa say, "Girls, the cotton bolls are getting freckles. Soon all of you will have to start bending your backs, picking and putting it in the sack." You would think having to wear a pick sack and remembering how sore my back was would be reason enough not to relive the experience, but it was a pleasure making my quilt and remembering those days when cotton was king. I spent many happy hours reveling in the past. Every stitch was a labor of love.

Other documented quilts revealed how the cotton was grown on the farm, picked, and then carded into quilt batts. In 1895 Katherine Malcolm (dates unknown) and Tannie Jones (1862–1950) of Oconee County produced a Mariner's Compass. According to their great-grandson and grandson, the cotton for the quilt was handpicked and dyed and the batts were hand carded. A Turkey Tracks quilt made in 1864 by Mary Rebecca Cearley Thomas (1848–1928) contains cotton grown in Union County (fig. 4.18). It was colored with dyes from native plants. The batts were hand carded before being placed in the quilt.

GQP interviews also revealed the practice of using the "last picking" of cotton for use in the family quilts. Annie Mae Nicholson Ray (1901–1993) of Clarke County remembered, "My father and I picked the last picking of cotton and he took it to the Gin and had it ginned to use in the quilt." The quilt she speaks of was made in 1935 in a Dahlia pattern (fig. 4.19). A quilt made by Mattie Knight Stallings (1882–1964) of Berrien County tells a similar story (fig. 4.20). Apparently Mattie's husband suffered from poor health, and Mattie was responsible for the farming as well as the house-

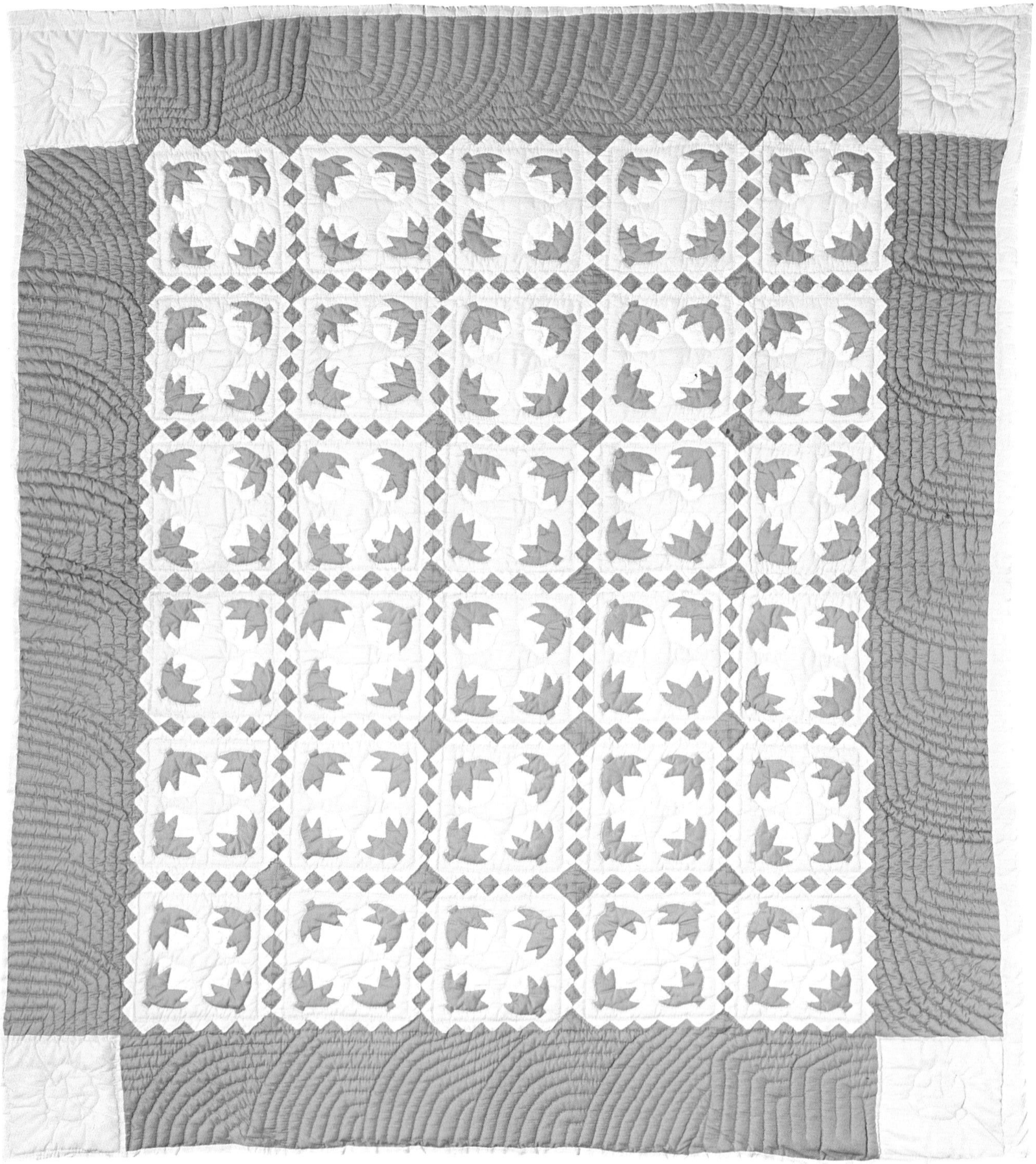

Figure 4.17. Cotton Boll. Mary L. Beaver
(b. 1924), Snellville (Gwinnett County),
1960. 96" x 86". Machine-pieced and
hand-appliquéd cotton blends, polyester batting; hand-quilted. Collection
of Mary L. Beaver. [GQP 3191]

Figure 4.18. Turkey Tracks. Mary Rebecca Cearley Thomas (1848–1928), Blairsville (Union County), 1864. 62" x 87". Hand-pieced and hand-quilted cotton. Collection of Corinne Beaver. [GQP 2631]

Annie Mae Odessa Nicholson Ray, ca. 1916. Photo courtesy of Dottie Whitworth.

Figure 4.19. Dahlia. Annie Mae Odessa Nicholson Ray (1901–1993), Douglas County, 1935. 74" x 88". Hand-pieced and hand-quilted cotton and rayon. Collection of Dottie Whitworth, daughter of the maker. [GQP 2371]

Joe Stallings and Mattie Mariah Knight Stallings in 1899 on their wedding day. Photo courtesy of Jane S. Knight.

Figure 4.20. Star Variation. Mattie Mariah Knight Stallings (1882–1964), Nashville (Berrien County), 1940. 83" x 64". Hand- and machine-pieced cotton, hand-quilted. Collection of Jane S. Knight. [GQP 274]

Annabelle Meadows Bailey, ca. 1920s.
Photo courtesy of Robert W. Bailey.

Figure 4.21. Crazy Quilt. Annabelle Meadows Bailey (1873–1961), Noah (Coffee County), Tennessee, ca. 1886. 64" x 80". Hand- and machine-pieced cotton, silk, and artificial silk (rayon). Collection of Robert W. Bailey, grandson of maker. [GQP 1255]

work and quiltmaking. She would pick any cotton left after the main portion of the crop had been harvested. The local cotton gin would have a "remnant day" when ladies from the community could bring in these last pickings for ginning and then use them in their quilts. Mattie's son remembered as a child carding the cotton to be used in his mother's quilts.

A quilt documented in Andersonville depicts rural life and the material culture associated with it. Although the quilt was made in Noah, Tennessee, by Annabelle Meadows Bailey (1873–1961) and brought to Georgia in 1960 by her grandson, its embroidered decorations are equally representative of country life in Georgia (fig. 4.21). It is a Crazy Quilt made between 1885 and 1895 from both cotton and silk fabrics. Annabelle embroidered the usual flowers typically found on a fancy Crazy Quilt but also added some farm motifs atypical of Crazy Quilts: plow, cultivator, goat cart, farm animals, and insects, even a cockroach. Annabelle's quilt also included an embroidered cook stove with a warming closet for holding food and a pump organ. The inclusion of the stove and in particular the organ probably represented the family's prosperity.[36] Annabelle surveyed her world and embroidered its images onto her quilt. This window into the past gives us a glimpse of farm life. Such was the life of the majority of Georgia's quiltmakers, whose work has been documented through the project.

Wendy Analla, ca. 1990.

Figure 4.22. Queen Alice. Wendy Analla (b. 1951), Ellabell (Chatham County), 1988. 44" x 52". Hand-appliquéd and hand-quilted cotton. Collection of the maker. [GQP 7299]

A self-taught quilter, Wendy has an art and sewing background. She creates traditional quilts but loves to use hand-dyed cotton to illustrate pictures that play with perspective.

## Cotton after 1920

Cotton continued to affect the lives of rural families in Georgia even as its production declined during the twentieth century. Cotton farmers learned the consequences of depending on one crop when the boll weevil infiltrated the state in 1913 and wreaked havoc on the crop well into the 1920s. With its cotton crops devastated, Georgia produced only 600,000 bales in 1923—down from 1.5 to 2 million bales per year in previous years. This, followed by the Great Depression starting in 1929, the New Deal agricultural programs of the 1930s, and World War II, ultimately toppled King Cotton from its long reign as the primary crop for Georgia's farmers. Many turned to other cash crops such as peanuts, tobacco, and livestock. Government price-support policies placed limits on the amount of cotton acreage. Also, the adoption of cotton-picking machinery had an effect as well. In 1963 more than half of the Georgia cotton crop was picked by machine.[37]

What effect did this have on the rural Georgia quiltmaker? Great changes in agricultural methods and machinery occurred in the twentieth century. Farming became modernized with the introduction of government price supports and other policies aimed at helping the average farmer.[38] Although women were freed from the demands of the cotton crop, life on the farm was still one of hard work and sacrifice. Women were constantly finding ways to economize during the lean years of the Great Depression. A quilt made by Lillie Scoggins's mother-in-law near Ashburn (Turner County) was constructed of tobacco sacks emptied by her father-in-law (GQP 313). She would take apart the sacks and then dye the fabric in a solution made by boiling the orange-colored labels from fruit crates. The fabric turned a peach color. Other than the initial purchase of the tobacco, no money was spent on the quilt top. (See chapter 9, "There's Something about Feed Sacks," on the use of feed sacks in quiltmaking.)

The South has never forsaken the cotton crop, though it has had to adjust to increased competition from other regions as well as from foreign imports. Crop production was driven by market demand and the decline of other traditional crops such as tobacco. During the last decades of the twentieth century, the fashion industry created a demand for cotton to use in apparel. Clothing made from all-natural cotton cloth represents a backlash against synthetic fibers, such as polyester, created after World War II. Although cotton as a crop has made a comeback, it will never again exert the broad influence it once had on Georgia's economy and its people. The state's population has shifted from the country into the cities. The generations of Georgians who labored in the cotton fields are quickly passing, and with them the memories and experiences of life on a Georgia cotton farm. Yet cotton fabric and cotton batting are the materials of choice of most modern quiltmakers. Technological improvements have made cotton far easier to obtain than it once was. Admiration is due the quiltmakers who lived and toiled before the evolution of our modern lifestyle. The quilts made by women before the 1920s represent a way of life that is no longer recognizable to the present generation. Perhaps these quilts are the only tangible evidence left to us of a time when cotton was indeed king.

# 5. *Textiles*

## Who Made Them and Who Used Them

**VISTA ANNE MAHAN**

- - - - - - - - - - - - - - - - - - - - - - - - - - - - - - - - - - - -

### *A Story of Child Labor*

Ethel Christopher was in the first grade when she went to work in a cotton mill in 1910. Life in Chattahoochee (now part of Atlanta) was hard, and her family was poor. Her father died when she was three. Her mother took in boarders and did laundry on a rub board. While Ethel was at school, the mill owner came to the house and asked her mother to let the first-grader start to work at Whittier Mill. When her mother said that Ethel would need shoes before she could work at the mill, the mill owner went to the school to fetch Ethel, took her to buy shoes, and put her to work in the mill that very day. By watching the other workers, Ethel learned to spin and could relieve the other spinners at mealtime or when women would take a break to nurse their babies in the mill's early version of day care. When she first started work, Ethel had to stand on a box to reach the machines.

In 1921, at age seventeen, Ethel married Paul Fowler, a spinner and fixer at Whittier Mill. Paul had also gone to work in the mill as a child, starting when he was twelve. Ethel and Paul had five children and lived in the mill village known as Lowerytown. When the little ones were old enough to attend school, Ethel was determined to advance her own education by learning whatever her children were being taught in the early grades. Also wanting to make up for his lack of a formal education, Paul would pick up discarded newspapers and anything else he could find to read. Paul took night courses whenever he got a chance. After their own five children were grown, Ethel and Paul raised a granddaughter, Lynn. Ethel was proud that she was able to read bedtime stories to Lynn, something she had not been able to do for her own five.

Ethel and many other mill women were home quilters. Their batting came from cotton wastes on the floor of the mill, and the mill sold or gave them fabric scraps from time to time. They dyed the mill fabric with pokeberries or clay. Friends and relatives saved their scraps for Ethel, and she would occasionally buy feed bags. The feed bags became aprons, pillowcases, clothes, and underwear, and the scraps left over were used in quilt blocks (see also chapter 8, "Cover"). The quilting frame that Paul made for Ethel in the early 1920s saw many years of service.

By the early 1950s Ethel had given up mill work and was able to quilt more. A relative working at the Atlanta Casket Company could get velvet scraps left over from the casket linings, and Ethel thought the pink and lavender velvet would work out nicely for a quilt for little Lynn. Over the years, its plush feel, pretty colors, and well-worn condition inspired Lynn to name her beloved quilt My Velveteen Rabbit, even though it didn't have a rabbit on it.

The floor under Ethel's quilt frame became Lynn's

Figure 5.1. Ethel Christopher Fowler (1904–1992), ca. 1918 (at about age fourteen). She went to work in a textile mill when she was in the first grade. Photo courtesy of Lynn Patterson.

*Vista Anne Mahan*

126

playground. Ethel and her sister and sometimes a neighbor would quilt at every opportunity, while Lynn played on a folded quilt underneath. As the three women talked, laughed, and dipped snuff, Lynn was cautioned not to overturn their spit cups. Her baby toys were a spool on a cord and a rattle made of a little tin snuff box with a few buttons inside.

When Ethel and Paul moved to the country in 1957, Ethel missed her quilting friends in the mill village. From time to time Ethel's sister came to spend a week or two with her in the country, and they would quilt together for days. At the time of Ethel's death at age eighty-eight, she had made several quilts for each of her children and some for her grandchildren. She had repaired the Velveteen Rabbit quilt so many times that she said if she mended it again, she would have to "patch the patches."[1] Ethel's quilting story is one example of many stories recorded by the Georgia Quilt Project (GQP) that had connections to textile mills. The mills are a significant part of Georgia's history, woven into the lives of its people.

## Setting the Stage for Georgia's First Textile Mills

Georgia's textile mills were patterned after the successful mills built in Massachusetts and Rhode Island in the early 1800s. The history of Georgia's mills follows both the dramatic and the mundane legacy of industrial development. The story features clever inventions, industrial spying, the leadership of business officials, and the lives and labors of a workforce of men, women, teens, and children.

Georgia's early settlement and development were years behind New England's. In 1733, after a two-month crossing and a stay in Charleston, English colonists finally settled the site of Savannah, Georgia.[2] By

Ethel Christopher Fowler, ca. mid-1970s.
Photo courtesy of Lynn Patterson.

Figure 5.2. My Velveteen Rabbit. Ethel Christopher Fowler (1904–1992), Atlanta (Fulton County), early 1950s. 62" x 79". Strippie style, machine-pieced and hand-quilted velvet. Collection of Lynn Patterson, the granddaughter for whom it was made. [GQP 7331]

that time New England settlers had had four generations since the 1620s to clear land, construct buildings, farm, establish shipping and whaling ports, spread inland, and accumulate some wealth. Savannah, by comparison, was still little more than woods and a riverbank, and from a business point of view, the town had poor waterfront facilities, no established merchants, no customs houses, and no credit history.

At the time of the Revolution, Georgia lagged behind the rest of the colonies, and its outlying regions were struggling frontier settlements. In 1783 Georgia's budget included an amount of money to be spent on Indian treaties and defense. Funds weren't available to build and maintain good roads or develop river transportation deep into the heart of the state. It was difficult to get people, goods, and raw materials back and forth. Though Massachusetts had already made land grants of its internal lands by 1750, Georgia was still making land grants in the form of land lotteries to widows, orphans, war veterans, and other Georgia residents until 1832, as Indians were pushed farther west. These land lotteries deeded away nearly three-fourths of the land in Georgia.[3] While New England communities were making progress with local development, much of Georgia was still dealing with Indian hostilities within its borders. Protecting frontier settlements was a Georgia priority.

While Indian problems plagued North Georgia's frontiers in the early 1800s, South Georgia developed an agricultural economy, with cotton and tobacco the favorite crops. Ships loaded with Georgia cotton regularly sailed north to New England mills and across the Atlantic to England. These early textile mills converted raw cotton to cloth. New inventions at the end of the 1700s revolutionized the way cotton and wool were spun and woven into fabric (see chapter 4, "King Cotton").

The old way of spinning and weaving cloth in the home yielded to a mixture of cottage industry at home and work performed at a mill. Raw cotton was cleaned at home, but carding it into strands of fibers and then spinning the strands into thread and yarns took place at a mill. Then the yarn was taken back home to be hand woven on a loom.

After the English invention of water-powered machinery during the Industrial Revolution, the New England mills developed their own machines to spin cotton and wool. Beginning with the 1793 invention of the cotton gin, the whole process of cloth production became easier and more efficient with the ginning, spinning, and weaving machines invented over a twenty-four-year period.[4]

## Lowell, Massachusetts, as the Industry Standard

In the United States in the early 1800s, water power was being harnessed to drive machinery to saw wood, grind flour, and card and spin flax and wool. Francis Cabot Lowell, a Boston merchant with mechanical abilities, wanted to put water power to use to drive the machines necessary for cloth production. While visiting English textile factories in 1811, Lowell figured out the plan of their power looms. Back in Boston, he built his version of the English machinery from memory, and it worked. His mill put the separate processes of textile production under one roof: it carded the cotton fiber, spun and wove it into fabric, then bleached the fabric. The raw material was grown in the South and shipped to New England for processing. In 1821 Lowell built another mill about thirty miles from Boston, on the banks of the Merrimack River. This factory, and later the village that was built around it, was named for Lowell.[5]

Other mills were built in Lowell, and they set the standards that all later textile mills in the United States would strive to copy. Several years later when Georgia's would-be mill owners visited Lowell to inquire about machinery and methodology in running a mill, they saw a state-of-the-art production center and a company-built village to house the workers. Some of the best Georgia mills were patterned after Lowell's model.

These standards weren't confined to the factory. In Lowell, mill officials had built houses, dormitories, and apartments to house the army of workers needed. Most of the early employees in these mills were young, single women from rural New England. Unless the girls had relatives in Lowell, they were required to live in the crowded dormitories run by housemothers who enforced strict rules regarding visitors, curfews, alcohol, and church attendance.[6]

Despite harsh conditions for workers, the cotton mill industry in New England expanded along with the growth of the population. Demand for textile goods was so great that the number of mills in Lowell doubled from twenty mills in 1836 to forty mills in 1850.[7]

Before the Civil War, Lowell was the leading textile producer in the nation. Lowell had the expertise to produce great amounts of cloth and to manage and house a large labor force.[8] Later, when Georgia businessmen looked beyond the bountiful production of the cotton crop itself, they would look to New England, especially Lowell, for the know-how to turn cotton into cloth and for a model mill village.

## Georgia's Antebellum Cotton Mills

As with the early New England mills, the availability of reliable water power determined the location of early Georgia mills. The oldest textile mills recorded in Georgia, built near Augusta and Athens around 1810, were of brief duration. The cost of cloth production was high before efficient water-powered machines were widely available, and England's exported fabric was priced competitively. Though there were some early mill operations in Georgia during the 1820s, most of the fine fabrics used in the South were imported from northern mills or from Europe. Ordinary cloth and coarse fabric were made locally.

By 1828, both Augusta and Athens had made progress in operating textile mills. With sixteen warehouses to store Georgia-grown cotton, Augusta now also had a cotton mill, Belleville Factory, on Butler's Creek. Athens had chartered the Georgia Manufacturing Company, which later became the Athens Manufacturing Company.[9]

As settlers penetrated the frontiers of Georgia, more towns and cities organized themselves, and land was cleared for farming. By 1826 Georgia was the world's leading cotton producer.[10] Though a few mills were built to make cloth from the enormous crop, for many years Georgians concentrated on growing the cotton, not weaving it into cloth.

The town of Columbus, located on the Chattahoochee River, was established in 1827 with just a few stores and one hotel. By 1838, the Columbus Cotton Factory was spinning cotton and carding wool. Two additional cotton mills were built in 1845. Within a few years Columbus was known as the Lowell of the South because of its success as a big cotton center. Sixteen steamboats hauled cotton from there to the Gulf of Mexico.[11]

Though explorers and traders had meandered through, settlers didn't live in northwestern Georgia in sizable numbers until the late 1820s and early 1830s. In 1838 the last twelve thousand Indians were re-

Figure 5.3. In the 1870s the steamboat *Sydney Smith* was one of many steamboats hauling bales of cotton and other goods up and down Georgia's rivers. The *Sydney Smith* is shown at a dock in Rome (Floyd County) on the Coosa River. FLO105, Vanishing Georgia Collection, Georgia Archives.

*Vista Anne Mahan*

moved from their home lands in northern Georgia by the U.S. Army and taken west on what became known as the Trail of Tears, opening more land for development. Land lotteries attracted a growing population to newly opened-up Cherokee land.[12] At the end of the 1830s the Roswell Manufacturing Company was established.

In 1840 Lowell, Massachusetts, had twenty textile mills compared to only nineteen smaller mills in the entire state of Georgia.[13] With Georgia's steady population growth, however, business and industry increased.

From 1845 to 1847, just seven years after the last of the Indians were expelled from northwest Georgia,

a cotton mill was under construction in Trion, a former Indian settlement. Three local businessmen from nearby LaFayette had pooled their money and built a dam, raceway for the river, and mill on the banks of the Chattooga River. This textile mill is still in business today. Trion's early mill employees, like those of most other mills, worked a twelve-hour shift, from 6 a.m. to 6 p.m. In the dark hours of early morning and late evening, light in the building came from candles. After the Civil War, kerosene lamps were used. "Each person brought his own lamp and hung it over his work, then carried it home after work. The way to and from the mill was lighted by pine torches or lighter knots, carried by the person leading the group."[14]

In 1847 Augusta finished a seven-mile canal that linked to the Savannah River. The canal furnished power to Augusta factories and gave better access to the city from the Savannah River. Augusta had ten steamboats to carry bales of cotton to Savannah, headed for northern or European markets.[15]

LaGrange, in Troup County, already had grist mills, saw mills, flour mills, cotton gins, and cottonseed oil mills, and in 1847 it got its first textile mill. The mill cleaned and carded wool. The rest of the process of making wool fabric—the spinning and the weaving—was done at home. A year later, a cotton mill was built.[16]

By the end of the 1840s, Georgia's thirty-two textile mills produced shirtings, bed ticking, linsey-woolsey, jeans, and checks. To transport these textiles, as well as people and other products, railroads were being constructed in Georgia during the 1830s through the 1850s. It took most of three decades to span the state. By the time the Civil War began, Georgia had the best railroads in the Deep South.[17] These rails through Georgia's interior were a boon to cotton planters, merchants, and mill owners.

Many Georgia mills enjoyed success in the 1850s, and by 1860, with its thirty-three cotton mills and another thirty woolen mills, the state led the Southern cotton mill industry and was even called the New England of the South.[18] During these boom years Georgia outgrew its rustic frontier origins. The older coastal areas had benefited for decades from the wealth from business, industry, and agriculture. The newer counties carved out of Native American territory were growing with the expanding roads and railroads upon which farmers and business owners depended.

## Georgia during and after the Civil War

Even with the Civil War underway, some textile mills managed to continue to operate, making cloth for Confederate uniforms, blankets, and tents. No new mills were built, but the old ones ran at full capacity when possible. With men away at war and reduced shipping because of blockades, many mills experienced labor shortages and lacked materials needed in the textile processes. Union forces destroyed machine shops, making it impossible to repair worn-out or broken machinery. The wealth and industry in the state, including many cotton mills, were robbed or destroyed by the enemy. The cotton mills at Columbus, a million-dollar operation, were burned by Union troops. Likewise, mills in the path of General Sherman were destroyed as the Union troops swept through Georgia. The cotton mill at Trion was spared because one of the owners was a Union sympathizer and reportedly gave shelter to General Sherman in 1864; the mill received "protection papers" and Union troops to guard it.[19]

By the end of the war, Georgia had been devastated. Confederate currency was worthless, farm animals had been taken by both the Northern and Southern armies, railroads and many bridges had been destroyed, and communities, businesses, and industries were ruined.

The years of Reconstruction after the war were a struggle for most Georgians. Even if a cotton mill had been spared, few owners had the cash to rebuild mills, repair worn-out machines, or meet a payroll. Despite the odds, some managed to rebuild when three resources were readily available: water power, nearby cotton crops, and cheap labor. In 1866 the West Point Manufacturing Company (forerunner of West Point–Pepperell) was built in LaGrange near the Alabama state line. Ten years later, Bibb Manufacturing in Macon was established and began to bleach, dye, print, and finish fabric. By 1880 Georgia had 49 textile mills, in contrast to the 175 mills operating in Massachusetts.

The relatively few woolen mills in Georgia were generally smaller than cotton operations, and many carded the wool only for the local farmers. From 1875 to the turn of the century, the woolen industry in Georgia declined. (In the twentieth century, Peerless Woolen Mill in Rossville, near the Tennessee state line, was a notable exception: Peerless claimed to be the largest woolen mill in the world.) In the late 1800s farmers wanted to grow cotton, and consequently, operating a cotton mill became the goal of many Georgia businessmen.

Scholars differ on the means of financing the newly organized southern cotton mills. Some sources claim that southern money and the initiative of local merchants built local mills, even though these mills used northern technology and management practices. Other scholars say that the money that helped develop these southern mills came from outside the South and the profits left the South. Even the cloth itself was shipped north for the garment industry.[20] There are case histories to support both versions.

Figure 5.4. Employees at work in the spooler room at Crown Cotton Mills on Chattanooga Avenue in Dalton (Whitfield County), 1920s. WTF256, Vanishing Georgia Collection, Georgia Archives.

In 1881 Atlanta was the site of the International Cotton Exposition, the brainchild of a Boston textile executive. This milestone agricultural world's fair was a showcase for the latest technology and machinery of the cotton industry, and it ignited the imaginations of southern businessmen. For three months people came to see the one thousand exhibits of machinery and methods of farming, ginning, spinning, weaving, dyeing, and printing cotton cloth. Sponsors included textile companies, farming equipment companies, and bankers. Even General Sherman, who had himself directed the destruction of southern resources, sent money to help finance the exposition.[21] As a result of the exposition, Georgians realized that practically every town could and should have a cotton mill.

Merchants and business owners who were able scraped together resources and looked for direction in establishing new cotton mills. They visited southern and northern mill operations for ideas. To start a cotton mill involved more than constructing a building. Money was needed for the machinery in the mill. Roads had to be built, usually from the mill site to a railroad. A dam and raceway were needed, although by now steam was the preferred power in some areas. Housing was needed for workers. Wells and outhouses had to be dug. A school, a church, and a store would be necessary. Teachers and doctors would need to be hired. And finally, recruiters would have to make the rounds to entice workers to hire on for mill work. Many people, often entire families, became wage-earning factory workers, their lives tied to the mills.

After a mill was built, the owners handled its finances but usually weren't involved in daily mill operation. The setup of most southern mills mirrored that of their Lowell counterparts. A superintendent managed production throughout the mill. An overseer looked after each room in the mill and was assisted by a second hand. The overseer and his assistant monitored the productivity of the workers, kept the machinery in working order, provided materials for workers, and had general authority to hire and fire.[22]

The mill itself was usually three to five stories high, with a waterwheel or turbine in the basement to turn the belts, pulleys, and gears that ran the machines. Cotton bales were delivered to the picking room or picking house, where mill hands opened the bales and cleaned the cotton. The first floor of the mill contained the carding room and the drawing room, where cotton was sent through large rollers with fine wire teeth that further cleaned and straightened the fibers. The resulting strands, wound on large spools, went to the spinning room on the second floor, where the cotton was spun, stretched out, and twisted into yarn or threads of varying thicknesses. Doffers, usually boys and girls

*Vista Anne Mahan*

ten to fifteen years old, removed (doffed) bobbins as they filled up. The upper stories housed the looms, where the spools of yarn were wound on a beam and threaded through the loom and harnesses. Then weavers tended the looms, turning yarn into long runs of cloth. In the cloth room workers measured and folded fabric to go through the remaining processes of bleaching, dyeing, printing, and shipping.[23]

Throughout the process, machines did the work, and mill hands tended the machines, spliced yarns together when they broke, and replaced empty bobbins. The male workers were occasionally assigned jobs outside the mill, like digging a grave for a mill employee or painting houses in the mill village.[24]

In each job, the mill employee endured noise, heat, and humidity. To workers accustomed to the heat of farm work, the noise of all the machines was the worst. Breathing the lint was a hazard throughout the mill. Long before government safety regulations came into effect, years of cotton dust in the lungs caused lung disease and even death.

Though it took some adjustment, many workers preferred the life of cotton mill work over the demanding life of the farm. It was not easy to make a living on the farm or in the mill. In both the farm family and the mill family, everybody had to work hard. Farming and crop production were unpredictable, and poor crop prices made it increasingly hard for a family to be self-sufficient on a farm. Cotton mill labor recruiters found that poor farmers, sharecroppers, widows, female heads of households, and single women were ready to give up farming.[25] In 1891 the Trion mill had five hundred employees, three hundred of whom were young girls. Whenever possible, mills hired the whole family, not just girls, as the Lowell mill had. In an increasingly cash economy, family labor made sense to farmers with many daughters who could earn cash

in the mills: the cash from a daughter's mill wage was more useful to the family than a daughter working as a field hand.

Working in a textile mill and living in a mill village was a mixture of benefits and bondage. The mill owners provided a cash wage, homes with cheap rent, churches, schools, and a store where workers could pay for groceries and dry goods on credit. For some families, paying for too many items on credit was their undoing, and as the Tennessee Ernie Ford song warns, they might "owe [their souls] to the company store." The wages were based on a twelve-hour day, and even children eight or nine years old might work sixty-five to seventy hours a week.[26] Mills providing homes, church, store, school, and law enforcement thus had the opportunity to control almost every aspect of mill village life. People weighed the advantages and disad-

Figure 5.5. Warping room in Crown Cotton Mills in Dalton (Whitfield County), 1920s. WTF242, Vanishing Georgia Collection, Georgia Archives.

*Textiles: Who Made Them and Who Used Them*

Figure 5.6. Employees at Beverly Cotton Mill in Elberton (Elbert County), ca. 1905. ELB002–004, Vanishing Georgia Collection, Georgia Archives.

Now mills were being built where they hadn't been practical before. Mills could be built away from rivers if there was transportation to haul coal for steam. Some even installed dynamos to generate electricity. Georgia's cotton mills continued to expand, and owners put money into improving textile machinery.

Occasional labor shortages resulted from mill expansion. To lure more workers, mill owners sought to improve working and living conditions. Around 1900 much of the work force was young—under twenty-five years old—and about equally divided between males and females. Mills provided recreation facilities as a fringe benefit to attract these young workers. Some sponsored semiprofessional baseball teams that competed in textile leagues.[27]

The early 1920s were especially hard on Georgia cotton farmers but not necessarily hard on the cotton mills. The boll weevil had arrived in Georgia in 1913 and had slowly infested the cotton-growing regions, hitting some areas harder than others. The boll weevil decreased southern cotton crops for several years. Still, cotton was available to textile mills from less-affected cotton-growing areas in the South and from states outside the Deep South: Missouri, Arkansas, Oklahoma, Texas, New Mexico, Arizona, and California.[28]

### The Great Depression

The cotton mill business in Georgia hit hard times with the onset of the Great Depression in 1929. The major textile factories survived, but many small ones did not. During the 1930s some Georgia mills showed no profit and just tried to hold on, while some executives found they could profit by making their mills more efficient. Because more modern machinery could be operated by fewer workers, cutting the labor force was a money-saving option for some. This policy was similar to Lowell's techniques of the "stretch out" (work-

vantages of mill work and farm work, and some, when one situation got too tough, would try the other. Mill owners hoped the benefits of cheap housing plus jobs for all family members would attract and retain a steady labor force.

## A New Century

For many cotton mills this package deal of family labor proved successful, and Georgia's textile industry continued to grow. By 1900 Georgia had at least 75 mills, and some experts have estimated there were as many as 120 mills. Some northern textile mills closed and moved south for financial advantages. Southern labor was cheaper, working hours were longer, and the southern textile industries had few labor unions. Because cotton was being grown in the South, southern mills spent less to transport cotton; it was practically at their back door.

*Vista Anne Mahan*

ers operating more machines) and the "speed-up" (machines made to run faster), both of which improved output but required significantly greater worker concentration to run safely. As the Depression wore on, a statewide plan known as Share the Work was instigated to keep as many people employed as possible. Every employee's hours were cut, but the plan allowed more people to have a job. A small paycheck was better than no paycheck.[29]

Jokes about mill life in the Depression reflect the tough times. One worker recalled that his family was "so poor they hardly noticed the Depression." Another joke concerns an unemployed person who saw a mill employee fall out of a third-story window at Crown Mill in Dalton. The unemployed person ran inside the mill to the personnel office, wanting to apply for the dead man's job, but was told, "Sorry, the one who threw him out gets the job."[30]

The old system of textile mill operation was straining under the Depression, the New Deal, and the possible entrance of big labor unions. The National Recovery Administration established codes for hours, wages, and working conditions in industry. Unions tried to organize and strike the textile industry but were largely unsuccessful in Georgia. To avoid the hassles of union organization, some mill owners offered the same benefits unions were fighting for. Other mill owners just fired suspected union sympathizers as a way to intimidate employees. The union at Crown Mills in Dalton was one of the few active unions in Georgia.

A 1934 general strike among southern textile workers gained little for labor and resulted in bitterness for both labor and management. Though some textile factories saw peaceful strikes, the opposition between labor and management turned violent at several locations, and National Guard troops were called in. In Trion two men were killed and nearly twenty were wounded. It was said that mill managers had even installed machine guns on mill roofs to fight off union activities. New laws at the federal and state level were established, and by the end of the 1930s Georgia had child labor laws, free state-supported high schools, and a minimum wage.[31]

## World War II

World War II ended the Depression in the textile mills by providing a brisk business for the war effort. The national defense sent many textile mills into overtime production—twenty-four hours a day, sometimes seven days a week. In contrast to the 1930s, when there were too many workers and not enough jobs, now there were too many jobs and not enough workers to fulfill the demands of wartime America. Though married women had not been a significant part of the cotton mill work force for years, they now filled job vacancies, and some companies set up day care. At the beginning of the war, textile mills had more employees on their payrolls than ever before. Cotton mill workers had been derisively nicknamed "lint-heads," but now they received more respect in their communities because of the mills' defense work.[32]

The mill at Trion had a defense contract from the government to manufacture huge amounts of fabric for uniforms, enough to make uniforms for the whole army. In addition, Trion was to make quantities of gun-cleaning fabric and tent twill treated to repel rain and mildew.[33]

## Prewar Chenille to Postwar Rugs

World War II did not provide a stimulus to the tufting textile industry that had gained momentum in the 1930s and came to dominate the area around Dalton. Defense contracts financed tents, blankets, and uniforms, but there was no call from the army or navy for

Figure 5.7. Endless Chain Variation. Fannie Hammond Knight (1881–1962), Cedartown (Polk County), ca. 1940. 56½" x 80". Hand-pieced and hand-quilted cotton. Collection of Ruth R. Knight, daughter-in-law of maker. [GQP 5235]

Fannie Knight used cotton from the Goodyear Clearwater Mill in Cedartown, where her husband worked, for the batting in her quilt. The fabrics for the top came from dressmaking scraps.

Avice Johnson, 1970s. Avice's husband Percy worked as a sponger, preshrinking fabric at Sewell Manufacturing Co. in Bremen (Haralson County). The company sewed men's dress suits. During her lifetime Avice made more than fifty quilts now with family members scattered throughout Georgia. During the 1930s and 1940s, the Johnsons and others in the community frequently hosted quilting-dinner parties. Photo courtesy of Earline Powers.

Figure 5.8. String Quilt. Avice Matthews Johnson (1907–1997), Danielsville (Carroll County), 1987. 72" x 87½". Hand- and machine-pieced, hand-quilted cotton-polyester blends. Collection of Earline Powers, daughter of the maker. [GQP 3452]

Avice Matthews Johnson carded her own batting for this quilt from cotton grown in Georgia. This exuberant, colorful quilt was made when Avice was eighty years old.

Eva Francis Newsome.

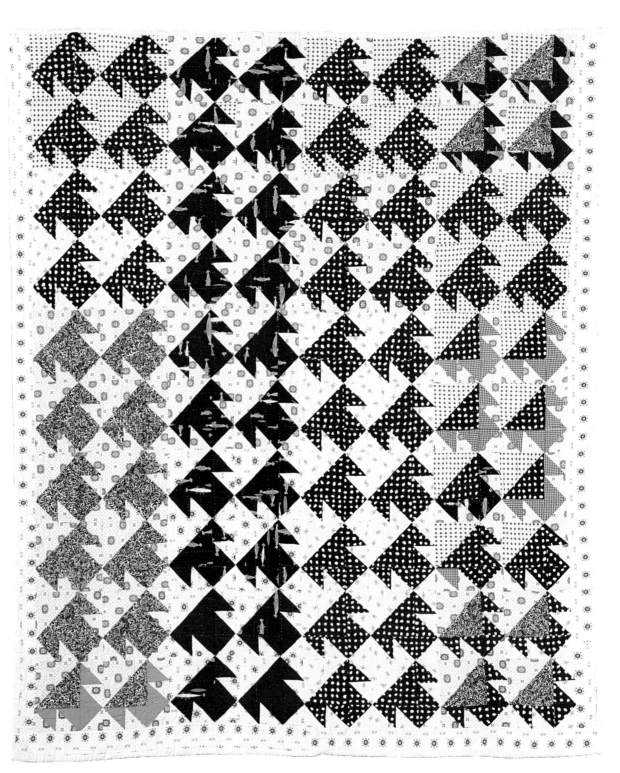

Figure 5.9. T-Quilt. Eva Francis Newsome (1889–1958), Chickamauga (Walker County), ca. 1950. 74" x 82". Hand- and machine-pieced, hand-quilted cotton. Collection of Katie Newsome Ivey, daughter of the maker. [GQP 4535]

Eva Newsome bought yard goods, especially shirting, from the Crystal Springs Bleachery and Cotton Mill in Chickamauga (Walker County) for her quilts.

Figure 5.10. Patriotic Commemorative. Allie Butler Roberts (1886–ca. 1970), Whitfield County, 1944–45. 75½" x 75½". Hand-pieced and hand-quilted cotton. Private collection. [GQP 1477]

Allie Roberts bought cotton scraps at the Lovable Bra Factory in Atlanta to make this quilt during World War II. Allie worked on her quilt to ward off the loneliness and concern she felt for her three sons who were stationed in Europe. Her son Troy reports that her quilt won a twenty-five-dollar prize at the North Georgia Fair in 1946. Allie Roberts was a member of the Busy Bee Homemakers Club, where she and the other members shared patterns.

Figure 5.11. Ethel Partin Stiles uses a wooden block covered with a greasy meat skin to rub a pattern on bedspread fabric. When the tufting stitches are completed, the bedspread is washed and boiled to remove the greasy marks. Ringgold (Catoosa County), 1934. Photographers: Doris Ulmann and John Jacob Niles. CAT007, Vanishing Georgia Collection, Georgia Archives.

Figure 5.12. Mrs. Ralph Haney in her chenille bathrobe with a peacock design. Calhoun (Gordon County), ca. 1934. GOR466, Vanishing Georgia Collection, Georgia Archives.

*Vista Anne Mahan*

Dalton's tufted bedspreads. The bedspread fabric and the yarn were diverted to other war uses, rendering three thousand chenille workers idle.[34]

The modern tufting industry had gotten its start about forty years earlier, when fifteen-year-old Catherine Evans Whitner was taken with a tufted bedspread she saw on her cousin's bed. Whitner decided she could make one for herself and is credited with reviving this variation of candlewicking in 1895. She marked a design with a greasy meat skin on a plain woven spread, then hand sewed yarn along the marked design. After she clipped the yarn between the stitches, she washed and boiled the spread to shrink it. The shrunken spread tightened around the decorative yarn, while the clipped ends of the yarn fluffed out like little pompons. Others admired her bedspread and paid her to make spreads for them. Catherine Whitner enlisted the help of friends and neighbors to fill the orders as they piled up.[35]

A cottage industry blossomed and became widely successful. Many designs for the tufted bedspreads came from traditional quilt patterns. Tufting by hand was replaced by machine tufting in factories, and Dalton became the "bedspread center of the universe." In the 1930s when the bedspreads were made by machine, they were called chenille bedspreads.[36] The chenille industry branched out from its lucrative bedspreads into making bathrobes, rugs, toilet sets, and bath mats. The chenille mills around Dalton shipped their tufted products all over the nation. Tourists who came through Georgia on their way south traveled along a sixty-mile stretch of U.S. Highway 41 known as Peacock Alley. The small factories and home tufters hung their spreads, bathrobes, and rugs on clotheslines to sell to the passing tourists. The popular pattern of tufted peacock bedspreads and other designs made a colorful display.

Sales of chenille rugs were dependable, and the industry embraced innovation to make longer loop rugs, then bigger rugs, and finally wall-to-wall carpet. Each stage challenged designers and machinists to work with fibers, looms, carpet backing, and dyeing to refine the process and make it profitable. In the few years after World War II, the industry changed when the broadloom, nine to twelve feet wide, was invented, and rubber backing began to be used on carpet.[37] As the water-powered loom had changed textile history, the use of Dalton's broadloom changed carpet history and carpet's future.

These new looms used cotton fibers to make cotton floor carpets. Business was so good that mills couldn't keep up with the demand. In 1954 rayon fibers took over the carpet industry, only to be succeeded three years later by nylon. The needs of the carpet mills nurtured side industries such as latex plants, machine parts suppliers, dye plants, and laundries.[38] Just as early

cotton mill owners had gone to Lowell to see how to proceed, carpet manufacturers now came to Dalton to see the latest technology. Dalton became the Carpet Capital of the World, a title it still proudly claims. The desire of a fifteen-year-old girl for a pretty bedspread certainly had far-reaching effects.

## Modern Textile Mills

Without World War II driving Georgia's textile mills, business began a precipitous decline in the postwar period. Between 1946 and 1960, 202 textile mills in the South closed.[39] As the old-line textile giants faced problems, some conquered the obstacles and flourished, but others closed their doors. Cotton mill owners were trying to keep one step ahead of foreign competition. Textile managers installed modern machines, doubling production. Synthetic fabrics challenged the cotton market. Cotton mills now competed with carpet mills for a labor force. Even when the wage was the

Figure 5.13. Part of U.S. Highway 41 in North Georgia was known as Peacock Alley or Bedspread Alley because tufted products, especially bedspreads, were hung on clotheslines and offered for sale to tourists. Bartow County, 1940. BRT126, Vanishing Georgia Collection, Georgia Archives.

same, work in a cotton mill was harsh compared to working conditions in air-conditioned carpet mills.

Housing workers in a mill village, which had served its purpose so well in the early years, was now a burden. Mill owners had previously counted on more than one household member working in the mill. After World War II, however, spouses were employed elsewhere, and new labor laws severely curtailed the use of child labor in industry. Rent was still cheap but wasn't covering the repairs that the old houses regularly needed. Even the lure of cheap housing wasn't enough to ensure a stable work force. Besides, the mill village could not house all the employees, so some workers had the advantage of cheap rent, while the others had to rent at the going rate outside the village. Most mill owners started selling off the mill village houses in the early 1950s. Workers were given the option of buying the house they had been renting, or moving out.

Some northern textile mills had moved south for the advantages of cheaper labor, cheaper coal or electricity, and cotton fields close to the mill. Most of Lowell's mills had closed years ago, in the 1920s.[40] But the South wasn't a panacea, either. The trend of the industry was that fewer workers were needed to operate more and faster machines, and even that increased efficiency might not be enough. Textile leaders had to maintain good management, make technical improvements, work toward tariff protection from foreign goods, and avoid cash flow problems. Textile history is full of stories of those who didn't make it, yet others tell of those who survived.

The twenty-first century has dealt more blows to the textile industry in the United States. With foreign competition and increased costs, more textile mills are closing. Scott Thomas, a manager at Mount Vernon Mills in Trion, explained why this largest denim textile mill in the world continues to be successful in 2005.

The mill is debt free, has state-of-the-art equipment, has few levels of management, and has good relations with customers. It has a stable work force; many of its employees have been there a quarter century. The mill continues a brisk business of selling millions of yards of denim to Wrangler, Levi's, Old Navy, and Gap, as well as to companies who make rental work uniforms. Thomas also discussed the challenges currently facing all American textile mills. Foreign textile mills, especially those in Mexico, China, and Guatemala, have much lower labor costs, no employee benefits, and no safety or environmental concerns, so their costs are lower, which attracts some U.S. companies. Some U.S. textile mills will not survive this tough competition.[41]

### Quilting Fabric at Mill Outlet Stores

Many textile mills offered their mill-end yardage, seconds, and remnants for sale to the public at factory outlet shops. Factory outlets were popular with the mill employees as well as the general public, and the inexpensive fabric at these stores was sewn into clothes and household items. Throughout Georgia, quilters found that the numerous cotton mill outlet stores were excellent sources of fabric for quilts.

Peerless Woolen Mills in Rossville sold quality dress and suit-weight woolens to the public from a store on the mill site. Like many of Georgia's mills, Peerless supported many community efforts. After World War II, the woolen mill donated space at the fabric outlet to establish a public library. The story of June Miller as librarian, quilter, and community leader reveals how the mills and their fabric outlets were a positive influence in the community.

Arriving in Rossville in 1919 as an employee of the local YMCA, June Miller was assigned to work with the young mill women at Peerless to ensure they had wholesome diversions after work. Frequently, they were too tired at the end of the day to support the programs Miller offered, but years later, after World War II, she proposed the idea that Peerless donate space for a public library—an idea supported by Mrs. John L. Hutcheson, the wife of the mill owner. Miller served as the library's director for about thirty years.

In the early 1970s she established a quilting group at the McFarland Methodist Church. The quilters used fabric from several mills in the area. Woolen fabrics for Log Cabin quilts came from Peerless. The mill outlet at Yates Bleachery in Flintstone was a source for large quantities of cotton for the group's quilt blocks and quilt backs. Sometimes thread was obtained from Standard-Coosa-Thatcher Thread Company in Rossville.

These mill outlet stores have been a source of fabric for well-known artists, too. Bets Ramsey, daughter of June Miller, purchased fabric from the same textile mills for her quilts and led quiltmaking workshops in the area. A founder of the American Quilt Study Group, Ramsey is nationally known for her quilts, quilt research, and books. For her outstanding contributions to the quilt world she was inducted into the Quilters Hall of Fame in 2005.

Figure 5.14. Mill Wheel Variation Signature Quilt. Workers at Beaver Duck Mills, Hogansville (Troup County), 1919. 69" x 72". Hand-pieced and hand-quilted cotton. Collection of Anna Carol Culver, great niece of Anna Traber, for whom the quilt was made. [GQP 5294]

The employees at Beaver Duck Mills in Hogansville made this quilt in 1919 as a going-away present for their mill nurse, Anna Traber. The quilt is a variation of the Mill Wheel pattern and has signatures of the mill employees embroidered in the sashing.

Internationally recognized potter Charles Counts (1937–2000) and his wife Rubynelle established the Rising Fawn Quilters in the late 1960s near Lookout Mountain, Georgia. Fabric from the mill outlet at Yates Bleachery went into many of their works. Their one-of-a-kind quilts were exhibited in numerous craft exhibitions around the country, and their quilts are highly prized as art objects.

Fabric donated from cotton mills has been used for many good causes. Frank Pierce, a former owner of Crystal Springs Print Works in Chickamauga, donated cloth to local quilters who made quilts for charitable organizations such as the local Ronald McDonald House, the Chambliss Children's Home, a women's shelter, a group that cared for hospitalized AIDS babies, and others.[42]

## Trion: A Look at Mill Village Life

Trion was built between 1845 and 1847 as a mill town on the site of a former Cherokee village called Island Town. The site in northwestern Georgia was perfect for a mill: the closest competitor was a hundred miles away in Roswell, and the Chattooga River would supply dependable water power year-round.[43]

The mill and its village grew steadily. In 1850, Trion's mill employed 45 people, by 1875 there were 350, and in the 1920s the number rose to 1,500. The factory had its own brickyard at the turn of the century to supply the growing number of mill buildings and to construct new houses and a new school. During this same period an ice plant was built and a sprinkler system installed in the cotton warehouse. At first, the mill produced only yarn, later adding osnaburg—a plain-weave cotton used for sacks.

Four generations of the Bankey family lived in the cotton mill village of Trion and worked at Riegel Tex-

tile Corporation (now Mount Vernon Mills). Born in 1917, Ralph Bankey was able to recall more than seventy-five years of village and factory history, and his father's and grandfather's experiences went back even further. His daughter Jeanne Bille worked at the mill one summer. His sister-in-law, Catherine Hurtt, also worked there, as did her husband, Hester. In fact, at one time just about everyone Ralph knew worked at Riegel Mills.

The mill at Trion was and is a model of success. It was one of the early Georgia cotton mills, and through good management it has survived to today, now making denim for famous jeans makers. Certainly when the first Trion mill was built, it was not in a prime location to capture a big share of the textile business. It had already been in business forty years when the railroad finally came through the county in 1888. Until that time, four to eight covered wagons had hauled the mill's yarn products to market in Rome and returned with supplies, a three-day trip. Ralph remembered how he and other little boys listened to "Old Man Smallwood" tell about leading a wagon train for the mill in the old days.

Ralph and Catherine recalled one story about a day, long before Ralph was born, when eels migrating up the river got caught in the mill wheel. So many dead eels clogged the mill wheel that it stopped turning, and the mill was closed until the mass of eel bodies could be cleaned out. The story ended with three wagon loads of dead eels being hauled away.

The mill closed another time when it was used as a hospital. A typhoid epidemic swept through Trion in 1858, closing the mill and turning it into a temporary hospital. The quarantine was enforced by a guard.

Both Ralph and Catherine talked enthusiastically about their lives in Trion's mill village. Riegel Textiles owned everything in town but had created a pleasant

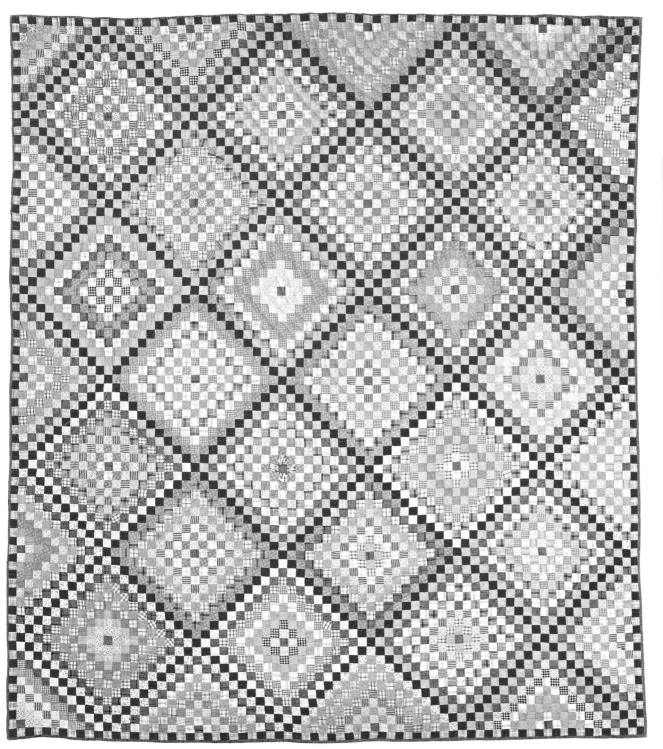

Nora Allen Atwood, ca. 1940s. Nora At-wood worked in the cloth room at Pep-perell Manufacturing Co. in Lindale; she and her family lived in the mill village. Nora bought fabric at the mill store to use in making her quilts. Photo cour-tesy of Emily Collette.

Figure 5.15. Postage Stamp Quilt. Nora Allen Atwood (1893–1950), Lindale (Floyd County), ca. 1912. 90½" x 82¼". Hand-pieced and hand-quilted cotton. Collection of Emily Colette. [GQP 6609]

Nora Allen Atwood made this quilt from hundreds of tiny fabric squares little more than one inch across.

place to live. Both Ralph and Catherine repeatedly said, "We had it made in those days" and "We were lucky people." Their village houses had large rooms with high ceilings and were kept repaired and painted. Single girls lived in dormitories. Families lived in what would be called a duplex or a triplex today. If the house had an indoor toilet, it was shared by all the families. Catherine remembers that during the Depression rent was thirty-five cents per room per week and included electricity. Instead of indoor running water, most houses had an outdoor spigot at the road, and families carried water inside. Most homes had outhouses, but indoor plumbing and toilets were installed after World War II.

The core community was a stable, tight-knit group; however, some "restless" cotton mill people moved from one mill to the next—there were LaFayette Cotton Mills, Crown Mills in Dalton, Crystal Springs in Chickamauga, Peerless Woolen Mills in Rossville, Yates Bleachery in Flintstone, Lindale near Rome, and Summerville Cotton Mill.

Trion's mill village expanded in the early 1930s when the mill complied with the federal labor reform law, and the work schedule changed from two shifts of twelve hours each to three shifts of eight hours. Adding the third shift required the construction of additional housing.

After World War II Riegel's officers began cutting back on some of the company's caretaker-benefactor roles and in 1952 sold off all the mill houses. Ralph bought the house he'd been renting since 1938, staying there until a few years before his death in 2001.

Because few people owned cars, everyone had to walk to the only store in town: Trion's Big Friendly. This store had everything under one roof—grocery store, meat market, cafe, beauty shop, clothing store, hardware store, coal store, drug store, furniture store,

bank, even undertaking and embalming services. Ralph said the coffins, mourning clothes, and material for lining the coffins were always in stock but weren't on display. The bereaved family did not receive visitors in the department store; Ralph explained that the visitation took place at home or a church. Later a funeral home was built.

Though the store was within walking distance of the mill village houses, a shopper couldn't carry many bags of heavy groceries. After items were selected, the store delivered the bags to the home. The Big Friendly also maintained a Rolling Store: a mule-drawn wagon and later a buslike vehicle drove through the streets to provide curbside shopping. The Big Friendly was torn down in the late 1950s to make room for mill expansion, but by then most families had cars to drive to nearby shopping centers.

The Big Friendly also served as a fabric outlet for its mill products, and women came from as far away as Florida, Tennessee, and Alabama to buy cloth. Catherine, who has made so many quilts she has lost count, loved the fabric department. According to Ralph, it seemed that all women in the mill village made quilts, mostly practical quilts to keep warm. Catherine continues to make exquisite quilts today. In 2004, a day after her ninety-fifth birthday, Catherine said she still enjoyed piecing and hand quilting, although she had to give it up in 2005 due to failing health and advancing age. She admitted to having a closet full of fabric!

Ralph bragged unequivocally that Trion had the best dairy products in the world. Dairy products from Riegel's prize-winning dairy were delivered door-to-door. The world's record for butter-fat production was held by the Guernsey cow Green Meadow Melba, right there in Trion.

Another door-to-door service was provided by the laundry truck. Homes had neither washing machines nor indoor plumbing, so either laundry was done by hand or it went on the laundry truck. If clothes required dry cleaning, they went to the Pressing Club, though most folks rarely needed this service. Ice and coal deliveries were door-to-door, too.

If a worker needed money before payday, Riegel issued its own scrip known as kewsters, which came in coupon booklets of one, two, five, and ten dollars' worth. All Trion businesses honored kewsters. The kewsters caused trouble for some workers, much as credit card debt does today.

Ralph and Catherine recalled all the advantages they had living and working in Trion. The people of Trion got a phone system sooner than the surrounding areas. Company physicians would make house calls, and the hospital was impressive for a town the size of Trion. The mill built churches and made donations to them. Mr. Riegel had the reputation of contributing to every worthy cause. Trion had better schools than nearby areas because Mr. Riegel was a benefactor of the schools and paid teachers well. Ralph told about his own high-school football coach going to Mr. Riegel to ask for new uniforms. The immediate answer was reputed to have been, "Get those boys anything they want!" When Ralph was in high school, he took an elective course called cotton mill mathematics that taught gears, pulleys and practical concepts for working in the mill.

Ralph and Jeanne told about Trion's YMCA, which was a big recreation complex. It offered bowling, roller skating, a movie theater, recreation rooms, a gym, an indoor swimming pool (built in 1925), a library, and ten-cent showers. With no showers or tubs in most homes until after World War II, the ten cent showers were popular. This structure, too, was demolished in the 1950s, and a new recreation center and outdoor pool were built.

In 1934 Catherine and Ralph saw the opening of a dormitory or boarding house for 750 girls who sewed in Riegel's glove mill. The glove mill girls came to Trion from nearby towns, as well as nearby states. Ralph remembered that he thought of the girls as "white leghorns" because the white uniforms they wore reminded him of the chicken breed. Unmarried women school teachers lived in this dormitory, too.

For his entire working life—forty-seven and a half years—Ralph worked for Riegel Textiles. His first job was as a shoe clerk at the Big Friendly while he was in high school. He believes that because his father, uncle, and grandfather worked at the mill, he was able to get a "good job" when he went to full-time work: as a loom fixer. He learned to work on every type of loom, most of which were Draper looms from Lowell. Before he retired, he was working on looms Riegel imported from Switzerland. For as long as Ralph and Catherine could remember, the mill bought the latest machinery for every department in order to keep production fast and efficient.

Though both Ralph and Catherine recalled countless advantages they felt they had because they lived and worked in the cotton mill town of Trion, they also remembered some less complimentary aspects of mill life. Certainly compared to today's standards, some conditions were harsh. But hard times were widespread for many Americans from the 1930s into the 1950s. Catherine said that money was scarce, and families made bed sheets by sewing together feed sacks and flour sacks. Accidents in the mill sometimes resulted in serious injury. The streets in the mill village weren't paved.

Until after World War II there were no paid vacations, and Catherine and Ralph only had two holidays, the Fourth of July and Christmas, both of which were unpaid. In the 1940s the mill began to close for

Catherine Mitchell Hurtt, ca. 1990. Photo courtesy of Martha and Galer Wright.

Figure 5.16. Barn Raising at Sunrise. Original design, Catherine Mitchell Hurtt (b. 1909), Menlo (Chattooga County), 1984. 83" x 102". Machine-pieced and hand-quilted cottons and blends. Collection of the maker. [GQP 8157]

the week of July 4, giving everyone a vacation. The mill would service, repair, and replace machinery during that week. During Catherine's and Ralph's early working years the mill had no retirement system. As Ralph put it, "You worked till you died." Work in the mill meant inhaling cotton lint, although monstrous, noisy exhaust fans sucked much lint to the outside. Bushes and surfaces immediately outside the mill windows looked like they were lightly sprinkled with flour or snow. Ralph thought it was in the late 1970s or early 1980s before workers wore masks to protect their lungs. Until 1933, mill workers were still working twelve-hour shifts. In 1934 labor union organizers came to town, and there was a two-week strike. Ralph could hear occasional gunshots from the mill. His next-door neighbor, Mr. Hix, was killed at the mill during the strike. Workers voted the union down.

Both Catherine and Ralph were successful in mill work. Several notable circumstances enhanced the quality of their lives: they were both smart; had intelligent, employed spouses; had good jobs in the mill; and they each had only one child to raise, which made their money go further. Catherine's daughter, Martha, and Ralph's daughter, Jeanne, didn't continue the family tradition of mill work. As Ralph explained, "Kids got smarter and found opportunities elsewhere." Few high-school graduates of the late 1950s and 1960s went to work in the mill. Jeanne worked for Riegel for a few weeks one summer and then went away to college in California on an academic scholarship. Martha went to college in New York. Martha put a gloomier slant on her mill village experiences than her mother did. Martha thinks her parents could have gotten better jobs elsewhere and lived in a better house. It's true that the mill village wasn't one big happy family. Local people rarely got the management jobs, and the top mill officials always came from elsewhere.

❖ ❖ ❖

Mill village life in Trion was a composite of various experiences, some good and some bad, and it was fairly representative of life in textile mill villages across Georgia. If a worker did a good job, maintained self-control about debt at the company store, and didn't have a houseful of children to raise, life in a mill village was tolerable, even good. Wages weren't impressive for the average mill worker, but living expenses were lower in Trion, as in other mill villages, because the mill subsidized the town. Barring accidents, bad debt, bad judgment, or bad luck, a textile worker's life in Trion was as good as anywhere else. Ralph Bankey and Catherine Hurtt saw Riegel Textile Corporation evolve from its role as sole provider of jobs, housing, medical services, churches, store, dairy products, and recreation to a new role as just the largest employer in town. Some might say Trion changed from a mill town where you might "owe [your] soul to the company store" to a town without a company store, whose residents, like most Americans, find a variety of opportunities to spend their money, their energies, and their talents. In that way Trion was characteristic of other large mills, shaping the surrounding community and providing Georgia families an alternative to the subsistence farming life that would most likely have been their lot otherwise.

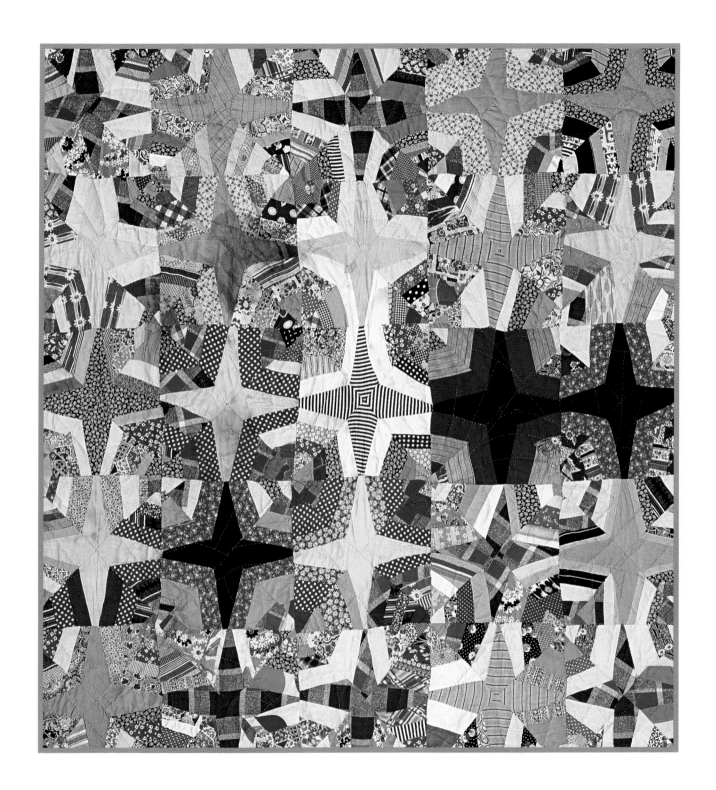

# 6. African American Quiltmaking in Georgia

### ANITA ZALESKI WEINRAUB

One of the great advantages in conducting Georgia's quilt documentation after many other states had initiated theirs was that we were able to benefit from their experiences. In other state quilt documentation projects, relatively few African American quiltmakers participated, resulting in an underrepresentation of quilts known to have been made by African Americans. In planning Georgia's Quilt History Days, the Georgia Quilt Project (GQP) board consulted with several quilt researchers on this matter and made special efforts to encourage black participation. We documented 260 quilts known to have been made by African Americans, representing just over 3 percent of all documented quilts. Given that the state's population is approximately 29 percent African American, this was a disappointing number, since it is believed that there is as rich and abundant a heritage of quiltmaking among our African Americans as among our white population.[1] It was a sufficient sample, however, to gain not only a sense of what Georgia's African American quilts look like, but also insight into the social factors surrounding their making and use.

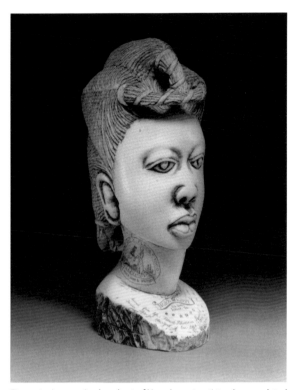

Figure 6.1. Ivory scrimshaw bust of Nora August, artist unknown, dated 1865. This extraordinary piece, although not signed, has several inscriptions carved into the neck: One reads, "Nora August, St. Simons Island, Ga. Carved from life: Retreat Plantation. Presented to the Nurses of Darien, Georgia, the year of our Lord 1865." Another says, "Nora August (slave). Age 23 yrs. Purchased from The Market, St. Augustine, Florida, April 17th, 1860. Now a Free Woman." Also carved into the neck is a medallion depicting a slave in chains kneeling before a woman, perhaps symbolic of Lady Liberty. In the background is a sailing ship and another inscription: "Sold East of Plaza, 1860. Am I not a man and brother."

This medallion, designed by Josiah Wedgwood in 1787, was later adopted as the official seal of the Anti-Slavery Society of London. It has been suggested that the scrimshoner could have been a New England whaler serving in the Union navy or marines and stationed on St. Simons during the Civil War (Union troops invaded St. Simons in March 1862). The Retreat Plantation land is now a golf course at the Sea Island Company resort. The bust of Nora August is on permanent display at the clubhouse near where she lived. Photo by Katherine Wetzel, courtesy of the Museum of the Confederacy, Richmond, Virginia, and the Sea Island Company.

*Anita Zaleski Weinraub*

Aware that a hot debate has ensued in recent years over whether quilts made by African Americans are, as a group, stylistically different from those made by whites, the author compared information on the 260 African American quilts to tallies for all documented quilts (see appendix A). There was more variety in patterns: nearly half of all the quilts documented followed one of ten popular patterns, but only 27% of the African American–made quilts used one of these patterns. Originality was somewhat more common: of all quilts brought in for documentation, 3.1 percent used original designs, but 4.6 percent of African American quilts used original designs. African American–made quilts were more likely to be pieced (73% vs. 65.6% of all quilts documented) and less likely to be appliquéd (9.6% vs. 13.6%) or to incorporate both piecing and appliqué (9.2% vs. 11.2%). There were proportionately fewer crazy, embroidered and cathedral window quilts than among all quilts documented, but twice as many whole-cloth and three times as many yo-yo quilts.

The 260 quilts were also compared to a group of randomly chosen quilts known to have been made by white quilters. Some apparent differences emerged from this examination as well. Because some scholars have suggested that African design elements have been passed down unconsciously among African Americans in the United states, the use of black, red, and red and black—colors common in the arts and crafts from certain regions of Africa—was compared. African American quiltmakers were *more* likely to use black fabrics but no red (10.7% vs. 6.1%), *less* likely to use red fabrics but no black (20.8% vs. 26.9%), and more than twice as likely to use black and red together in quilts (32.7% vs. 13.5%).

In a more subjective analysis, the author found that quilts made by African Americans were somewhat more likely to be asymmetrical, to use polyester or double-knit polyester, and to use bright colors and unusual color juxtaposition. Thirty-five of the African American–made quilts, or 15%, looked different in some way from white-made quilts documented. Slightly more than one half of these "different" quilts were either original designs or of an eclectic or improvisational style. Some of the quilts in the strippie style looked different from white-made quilts. Four quilts had an African theme. The author concluded that some, but not all, of the documented African American quilts have a distinctive look, but the overwhelming majority (85%) were indistinguishable from Anglo American–made quilts.

One quilt that stood out was documented at Old Cassville. The maker, an ancestor of the present owner, was described as coming from "rural folk" (fig. 6.3). The bold, three-color design of this quilt, which forms a sort of cross, is typical of what many people envision when they hear the term "African American quilt." The red and gold stripes, triangles, and diamonds resemble elements of Ghanian kente cloth patterns, supporting the theory of surviving African design influences. This type of quilt was the exception rather than the rule,

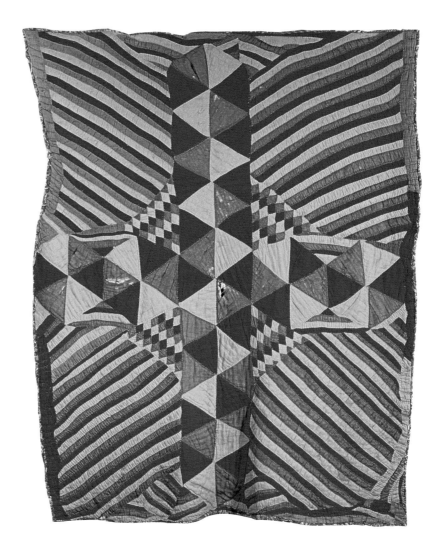

Figure 6.2. African American woman quilting at Louisville High School (now part of Jefferson County High School), March 1991. Until quite recently, the contributions of black quilters have been largely anonymous, as the work of slaves and paid help was absorbed by and taken for granted by the white population. Today we can credit modern quiltmakers for their skill and talent. Photo by the author.

however. In fact, this was the *only* quilt of such a striking design that was brought to a Quilt History Day.

The GQP documented in all segments of the population many quilts that had clearly been well used. However, as a group, the African American quilts seen in Georgia—particularly the older ones—seemed to have been used more and thus were in poorer condition than many of the white-made quilts of similar age. This might be explained by the historically higher poverty rates among African Americans in Georgia than among whites, particularly before about 1970. With fewer resources, including quilts, many families would

Figure 6.3. Original design. Charlotte "Lumpie" Henderson Cotton (ca. 1890–1960s), Cartersville (Bartow County), ca. 1910. 68" x 80". Hand-pieced and hand-quilted cotton. [GQP 1368]

Several years after being documented, the quilt was destroyed in a flood.

Figure 6.4. Chintz Appliqué. Maker unknown, possibly an enslaved African woman, ca. 1800–1830. 104½" x 110". Hand-appliquéd and hand-quilted chintz. Collection of the Sidney Lanier Chapter of the Daughters of the Confederacy, Macon (Bibb County). [GQP 1185]

of the Brown Sugar Stitchers, tended to be smaller and less formal than the predominantly white "guilds" that typically have charters, by-laws, and officers.

Although African American–made quilts were brought to twenty-eight of the seventy-six Quilt History Days, the majority were documented at four Quilt History Days in predominantly black areas. In this chapter we feature the work of several of the African American quiltmakers we met or whose work, if they are no longer living, we documented, and we offer accounts of those four Quilt History Days. The work of other African American quilters may be seen in other chapters.

## Quilts Made by Enslaved Africans

The earliest quilt documented that is believed to be made by an African American dates from the first quarter of the nineteenth century (fig. 6.4). It is an expertly made Broderie Perse chintz appliqué quilt of the type discussed in chapter 2, "Early Quilts." A note, penned on a piece of muslin in a handwriting style of long ago and reflecting the family's oral history, was carefully sewn to the reverse of the quilt: "This quilt was made by an African woman. Bought from a ship in Charleston harbor by John Everingham, this naked savage was trained to be a fine seamstress and waiting maid by his wife Rebecca. She gave the quilt to her great-niece, Rebecca Wadley who gave it to her daughter Tracy Wadley in 1905." Although this description is offensive to modern readers, its sentiments are typical of the early twentieth century. The writer praises the enslaved African for creating such a beautiful piece while crediting the white mistress with teaching the slave. Many Africans would have been familiar with the sewing and weaving techniques of their native lands.[2] This presumed "savage" had talent or experi-

have been unable to put aside quilts "for company," resulting in more wear on the quilts they had.

The African American quilts documented in Georgia were largely made for the same reasons white people make quilts—for their usefulness; for the pleasure of making them; as gifts. Black Georgians also enjoy quilting together (see chapter 10, "Georgia's Quilting Groups"), although contemporary black quilting groups encountered by the GQP, with the exception

*Anita Zaleski Weinraub*

------------------------------

ence that enabled her to adapt and quickly learn the new Anglo-European needlework techniques taught to her by her mistress. The quilt is physical evidence that she was an accomplished needlewoman and anything but a "savage."

A few white quilt owners stated that their quilts were made with the help of slaves on the ancestral plantation. No diaries were found among these owners to support the assertion, though it should be possible to confirm that the ancestors of the current owner did indeed own a plantation and/or slaves. Other sources record that skilled African American seamstresses were valuable and sought after in the antebellum period.[3] Certainly some slave seamstresses would have been responsible for quiltmaking as well as dressmaking. We cannot dismiss the possibility that many antebellum quilts attributed to a white ancestor were in fact made in part or in whole with slave labor.

That slaves made quilts for their own use is well documented. The Federal Writers' Project conducted interviews with more than two hundred former Georgia slaves from 1936 to 1939. Informants were asked a series of questions about their lives as slaves, including queries regarding living conditions and daily life. The passage of more than seventy years since the end of the Civil War and the advanced age of the people interviewed must be taken into account when considering the accuracy of the statements. But when the same information is reported again and again by unrelated subjects and by different interviewers, it can be reliably believed to be in large part accurate. Of the 120 interviews reviewed for this chapter, about half contained mentions of quilts. Most references were in passing, merely noting, for example, that there were always plenty of quilts to keep warm, or that their bed consisted of a mattress stuffed with wheat straw and quilts made from old clothes. Some former slaves stated that

Figure 6.5. A little boy poses in his cabin in Greene County, 1941. The GQP documented several quilts similar to the one seen on the bed (left foreground). GRN22, Vanishing Georgia Collection, Georgia Archives.

female slaves too old to work in the fields cared for the small children of others, and made quilts while doing so. Several described group quilting activities, or quilting bees. Georgia Baker, who grew up on the Stephens plantation in Taliaferro County, stated in 1938: "There warn't no special cornshuckings and cotton pickings on Marse Alec's place, but, of course, they did quilt in the winter because there had to be lots of quilting done for all them slaves to have plenty of warm covers, and you knows womans can quilt better if they gets a parcel of them together."[4]

Callie Elder, from the Billy Neal plantation in Floyd County near Rome, stated: "Old Aunt Martha what nursed the chillun while their Mammies work in the field was the quilting manager. It warn't nothing for womans to quilt three quilts in one night. Them quilts

Figure 6.6. Wall hanging or small quilt. Possibly Leota Whitham, African American, LaGrange (Troup County), ca. 1880. 30" x 34". Hand-appliquéd cotton with homespun border. Collection of Robert Reeves. [GQP 8167]

Although not a quilt, this (now) framed piece of hand appliqué is interesting for the images it contains. Note the man and boy in stovepipe hats, the soldiers in blue and gray, the heart in hand, the bales of cotton, the elephant, a lighted cabin, and the man drinking whiskey atop a mule. Also the fox with the red eye. Either of the last two images could be interpreted as representing the devil (temptation). The elephant brings to mind those in the quilts of Harriett Powers (fig. 7.2).

had to be finished before they stopped to eat a bit of the quilting feast. Marse Billy divided them quilts out amongst the Niggers what needed them most."[5]

One former slave, Nancy Boudry, was proud of her quilt-making ability and sent her granddaughter to find her quilt: "'Git 'um, Vanna, let de ladies see 'um,' she said; and when Vanna brought the gay pieces made up in a 'Double-Burst' (Sunburst) pattern, Nancy fingered the squares with loving fingers. 'Hit's pooty, ain't it?' she asked wistfully, 'I made one for a white lady two years ago, but dey hurts my fingers now—makes 'em stiff.'"[6]

Charlie Hudson, who grew up with his mother on the Bell plantation in Elbert County (his father was on another plantation), stated: "They went from one plantation to another to quiltings. After the womans got through quilting and ate a big dinner, then they asked the mens to come in and dance with them."[7] The similarity to descriptions of "white" quiltings is obvious.

Although African Americans in Georgia were freed from slavery more than a hundred years ago, the memory and oral history of slavery persists among much of Georgia's black population. A quilt brought to the Quilt History Day at the Noble Hill School in Old Cassville had the following note attached to it, the owner confirming the information during the interview: "This quilt was made by my great aunt, Karan Moore, who was eight days old when Freedom was declared" (fig. 6.8). Born in slavery, Karan Moore grew up to become a domestic; she and her husband King raised one son, spending their lives in Bartow County. Moore's quilt is typical of many made during the 1930s—in the strip style and using the colors popular during the period, it was made of scraps left over from cutting out fabric to sew clothing. Its colors remain strong, and the piece is in good condition for its age.

Figure 6.7. Although it appears that this woman is "ironing" a quilt, it is likely the quilt was used as padding to cover a rough board so the woman could iron clothing. A large wash kettle is in the yard, and it seems to be wash day. Although the photo was taken in Thomas County ca. 1900, washing would have been done in much the same way in rural Georgia during slavery. The quilt is in the Princess Feather pattern. Note the unusual circles appliquéd onto the feathers. The GQP documented a quilt very similar to this one, which was made by an African American woman in Ohio in the late nineteenth century. THO176, Vanishing Georgia Collection, Georgia Archives.

Other than the already-mentioned quilts brought in by white owners who claimed they were made by slaves, no quilts documented were known to have been made by slaves. However, several quilts dating from the beginning of the twentieth century made by descendants of Georgia slaves were seen.

## Quilt History Day at Noble Hill School

Through an introduction by Martha Mulinix, the author of chapter 8, "Cover," GQP met an exceptional African American woman with whom Martha worked for many years. This led to an opportunity to document quilts in a small community just north of Cartersville (Bartow County). Dr. Susie Wheeler is a retired educator. Having earned a doctoral degree in education, and following a successful career as an administrator in the Bartow County Schools, she has received many professional honors. One of her many accomplishments is the effort she spearheaded during the mid-1980s in her own community of Old Cassville to restore a part of Georgia's African American heritage.

Figure 6.9. Noble Hill School, 2005. Photo by Anita Z. Weinraub.

Figure 6.8. Star. Karan Moore (1865–1945), Bartow County, ca. 1939. 64" x 72". Hand-pieced and hand-quilted cotton. This quilt was sold out of the family several years after being documented. [GQP 1388]

There was no public education available to African Americans in rural Georgia during the 1920s. Julius Rosenwald was a Jewish philanthropist from Chicago and CEO of Sears, Roebuck and Company who, during the early part of the twentieth century, gave millions of dollars to the cause of educating black children.[8] Local communities would contribute half the cost of building a school; Rosenwald's foundation would match it. More than 5,300 Rosenwald schools were built, mostly in the southern states. One such school was built on Noble Hill in Old Cassville—Wheeler's father, along with several others in the community, put up the money and land to build it. Noble Hill School opened for the 1922–23 school year and for many years served the community, which also paid the salary of the teachers. When the county took over education of all children during the 1950s, the school closed and eventually fell into disrepair.

During the mid-1980s, Wheeler saw the potential of the school to illustrate for today's schoolchildren and others the extraordinary efforts earlier African Americans had to make in order to obtain an education. She initiated a movement to reacquire the land and to restore the school she had attended as a child. In 1985 the school reopened as a state historic site, and today it plays a role in educating schoolchildren about African American history. Wheeler serves on the board of directors.

The Noble Hill School sits upon a rural hilltop well back from busy U.S. Highway 41. Inside, its two classrooms are light and airy due to the large windows along each side of the building. The school was the setting of a Quilt History Day in June 1990, coordinated by Dr. Wheeler and with the assistance of the curatorial staff. Local residents brought in family quilts to be documented. A picnic-style lunch was served on the peaceful grounds of the school.

More than fifty African American quilts were documented at the Noble Hill School. According to the owners, they were primarily utility quilts, made by women from necessity. They were all twentieth-century quilts, many dating from the 1930s and 1940s.

## Quilt Day in Louisville

A second fruitful venue for documenting African American quilts was Louisville (Jefferson County). The population of the county is approximately 75 percent African American, and the racial mix of the schools reflects this percentage. Through a referral by Dr. John Burrison of Georgia State University, English teacher Jane Donahue at Louisville High School (now part of Jefferson County High) contacted the GQP and proposed that we conduct a Quilt History Day at the school, using students from English classes as our volunteers. Delighted with the suggestion yet somewhat apprehensive of the potential chaos of changing our volunteer force every fifty minutes, the board went forward with the plans. The school gym was to be the project's home for a day, with plenty of space to spread out all phases of the documenta-

tion and with bleacher seating for quilt owners. Jane laid the groundwork with her volunteer students and planned everything in great detail, including a tour of the town for the visiting volunteers the day before the event. The local senior center brought its quilting group to the gym to demonstrate quilting in the frame. The Quilt History Day was open to the public, and the students were encouraged to bring in quilts from their homes and to ask family members about them. The willingness and enthusiasm of the students more

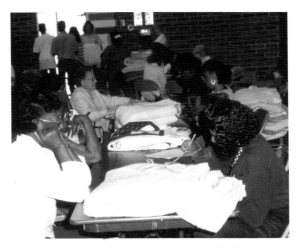

Figure 6.10. (*top*) High-school students at Louisville High School (Jefferson County) hang a quilt for photography, March 1991.
Figure 6.11. (*bottom*) Students at Louisville High School help interview quilt owners and record information about their quilts and their makers. March 1991. Photos by the author.

than made up for the minor confusion of exchanging workers every time a class period ended, and a lot was accomplished that day. Not only were more than sixty quilts brought in for documentation, but there was an opportunity for contact between two groups of people whose lives would otherwise not have intersected.

The Louisville quilts, for the most part, dated from the 1960s and later, with many from the 1970s and 1980s. Several included polyester and polyester double-knit fabric. They were mostly traditional patterns such as Pinwheel, Star, and Fan. Some were asymmetrical, with blocks that did not come together evenly.

## Quilt History Days in Atlanta

Atlanta Life Financial Group, formerly the Atlanta Life Insurance Company, is the world's largest insurance company with African American stockholders in the majority. Its headquarters is located on Auburn Avenue—a street of great significance to African American history—along which are also found the Ebenezer Baptist Church, the King Center (formerly the Martin Luther King Jr. Center for Nonviolent Social Change), and King's birthplace, now a national historic site. Founded in 1905 by Alonzo Herndon, a former slave, Atlanta Life developed from a long tradition of mutual-aid societies among African Americans. Herndon's is a great success story. His entrepreneurial abilities and his shrewd business acumen enabled him to prosper despite the great number of obstacles, legal and otherwise, facing African Americans in the business world.[9]

Sponsored by the fledgling APEX (African American Panoramic Experience) Museum directly across the street from Atlanta Life's headquarters, a Quilt History Day was held in Atlanta Life's spacious main floor auditorium. Unfortunately, the combination of a commercial location, traffic, and limited parking facilities resulted in sparse attendance; only eighteen quilts were documented that day. However, some valuable contacts were made with the local community, which subsequently led to further participation by African Americans at other Quilt History Days held in the Atlanta area.

Not far from Auburn Avenue the GQP found another site for a Quilt History Day in Atlanta. This was Emmaus House, a community outreach center created by Father Austin Ford, a white Episcopal priest. Ford left his comfortable, suburban congregation in the 1960s when he felt called to help those with greater need. Purchasing a home in what is now the stadium area near downtown Atlanta, Ford ministered to the local residents, creating a church and neighborhood community center offering after-school child care and a meal program. The center has become a focal point of positive change for the area, and a variety of classes and services are offered there. Emmaus House opened its doors to the GQP for two days in 1991. Some local residents participated as volunteers, and many quilts from the neighborhood were brought for documentation.

## Mattie Elder

During the Emmaus House Quilt History Days, the GQP was reacquainted with Mattie Elder. Elder first encountered the GQP when, as a volunteer with the Washington Park Sunshine Club, she displayed some of her quilts at the 1989 Dogwood Festival in Atlanta's Piedmont Park, where two GQP volunteers participated in the same "Grandma's Backyard" vignette. At Emmaus House, it took little encouragement to convince Ms. Elder to bring in some of her family's quilts, since she is eager to share her love of quilts with oth-

Mattie Elder poses with her sampler quilt, 1995.

Figure 6.12. Sampler. Mattie Woods Elder (b. 1915), Atlanta (Fulton County), 1992. 90" x 105¼". Hand- and machine-pieced, hand-quilted cottons and blends. Collection of the maker. [GQP 7143]

Elder pieced the blocks of this cheerful sampler over a period of twelve years and spent another six months quilting it.

Harriet Jones Swann, ca. 1935. Photo courtesy of Mattie Woods Elder.

Figure 6.13. Spider Web. Hand pieced by Hattie Jones Swann (1876–ca. 1947), ca. 1930; finishing borders added and hand quilted by her granddaughter, Mattie Woods Elder (b. 1915), Atlanta (Fulton County), 1989. 70" x 82½". Cottons with some feed sacks. Collection of Mattie Woods Elder. [GQP 8170]

ers. She brought yet more of her family's quilts to be documented to a Marietta Quilt History Day in Cobb County in 1992, thus affording the GQP the unique opportunity to document the work of five African American quiltmakers in the same family spanning five generations. Mattie Elder, who was born in 1915 on her great-grandfather's farm in Rockdale County southeast of Atlanta, learned to quilt by watching her mother, grandmother, and aunt. During her working years she quilted very little, instead completing high school and then beautician's school at night after working during the day in a beauty parlor. Eventually

Figure 6.14. Streak of Lightning. Top hand pieced by Cleo Swann Woods (1896–1940), Conyers (Rockdale County), ca. 1919; hand quilted by daughter Mattie Woods Elder (b. 1915), Atlanta (Fulton County), 1980s. 67" x 88". Cotton, tobacco sacks. Collection of Mattie Woods Elder. [GQP 6724]

Half of the tobacco sacks in this quilt were dyed with tea leaves.

Elder operated her own beauty shop from her home, a comfortable brick bungalow in the West End neighborhood of Atlanta. The home was built by her uncle during the Great Depression, when his wage was fifteen cents per hour.

Elder closed her shop and retired in 1980 due to pain in her legs, probably from the long hours on her feet her trade required, and severe pain in her hands, possibly due to the hot oil treatments she administered. She began quilting again at that time, setting up a frame in her dining room. She quilted several family tops she inherited and created many beautiful quilts of her own. Poor eyesight and failing health now prevent her from creating quilts.

Mattie Elder owns several quilt tops pieced by her grandmother, Harriet ("Hattie") Jones Swann, who was born in 1876 in DeKalb County. She has quilted some of them and carefully recorded information about them on the backs (see also fig. 9.11). She has also quilted a top pieced by her mother, Cleo Swann Woods (1896–1940), from tobacco sacks (fig. 6.14). As a wedding gift in 1942, Mattie Elder was given a quilt top by her mother-in-law, Callie Elder. Mattie added borders to the top to make it larger and then quilted it in an all-over diamond design. This quilt, named Basket, is one large, exuberant basket pieced by hand from many small triangles, with three whimsical flowers peeping out from the top (fig. 6.15).

Elder has a son, who does not quilt, and no daughters. But her family's quilting tradition continues. She made a quilt in 1985 with her granddaughter, Tiffany, when Tiffany was ten years old. The placement of the fabrics (scraps given to Elder by a friend who worked in a blouse factory) in this simple one-patch design they call Candy Sticks creates a pleasing effect (fig. 6.16). Ms. Elder and Tiffany pieced the top together by machine, and Elder hand quilted the large piece.

Cleo Swann Woods, ca. 1940. Photo courtesy of Mattie Woods Elder.

*African American Quiltmaking in Georgia*

Figure 6.15. Basket. Top hand pieced by Callie Elder (1890–1971), Union City (Fulton County), ca. 1942; finishing borders added and hand quilted by Mattie Woods Elder (b. 1915), Atlanta (Fulton County), 1980s. 75" x 87". Cotton, some feed sacks. Collection of Mattie Woods Elder. [GQP 7140]

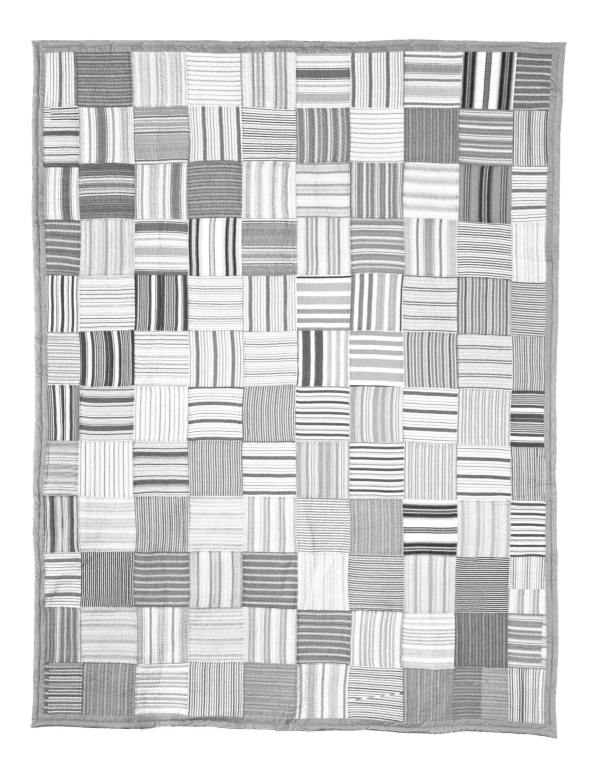

Tiffany Joy Elder at age ten in 1985, the year she made the Candy Sticks quilt with her grandmother. Photo courtesy of Mattie Woods Elder.

Figure 6.16. Candy Sticks. Top machine pieced by Tiffany Joy Elder (b. 1975) and her grandmother Mattie Woods Elder (b. 1915), Atlanta (Fulton County), 1983; hand quilted by Mattie Woods Elder, 1983. 75" x 96". Cotton and blends. Collection of Tiffany Joy Elder. [GQP 6727]

Annie Howard, ca. 1995. Photo by the author.

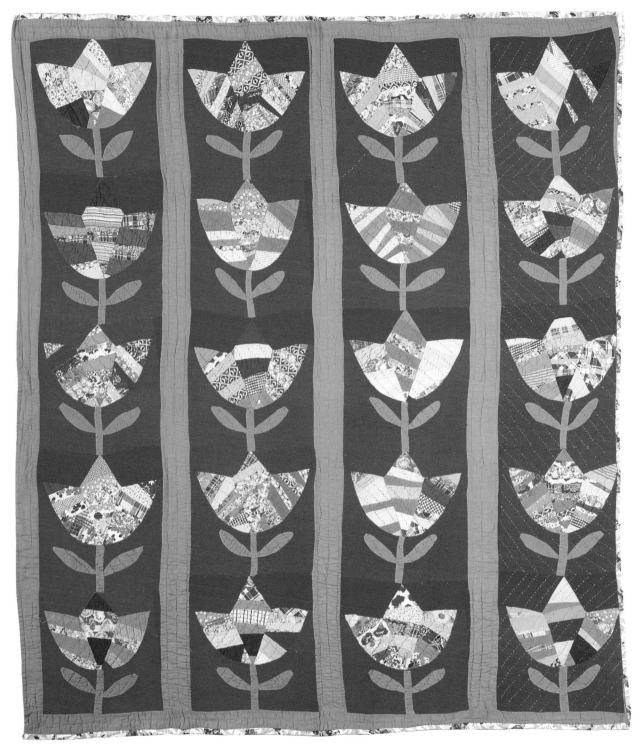

Figure 6.17. Tulip Quilt. Blocks pieced by Mary Lizzie Parham (1883–1955), Putnam County, undated; top constructed by Annie Parham Howard (1913–1999), Morgan County, ca. 1960; hand quilted by Julia Ford, Morgan County, ca. 1960. 75" x 87". Cotton with flannel backing. This quilt was lost, along with other personal items, during Annie Howard's move to Ohio in 1997. [GQP 8160]

## Annie Howard

The GQP first met Ms. Annie Howard at a documentation of Morgan County quilts sponsored by the Madison-Morgan Cultural Center in 1989. Then in her seventies, she was a petite woman with eyes that twinkled and skin as smooth as that of a much younger woman. Annie Howard began quilting in her midthirties after her marriage. She learned by watching other women in her neighborhood quilt—"folks visited and helped each other in those days." Howard was born in Putnam County near Eatonton, where her grandparents were almost certainly slaves; the 1860 census reveals that there were almost no free African Americans in this county at the time.[10] Her grandfather farmed and raised horses, and her grandmother was a midwife. Annie Howard was taken out of school when she was seven and put to work in the same white household in which her mother worked. It was not until after her marriage in 1945 and her move to Morgan County that Howard began putting blocks together, and she put her first quilt in the frame after the cotton was planted. Her husband purchased narrow strips of lumber from the sawmill for the frame, which he suspended from the ceiling in their home. Howard's mother also made quilts, until age and infirmity brought her quilting days to an end.

Among the possessions most dear to Howard were some quilt blocks in a Tulip pattern that her mother, Mary Lizzie Parham (1883–1955), pieced before her death. Howard cared for her mother in her later years since she was the only one of the six siblings able to do so at the time. After her mother's death, Howard created a quilt made from the string-pieced tulips her mother had made (fig. 6.17). She chose a green fabric for the stems and leaves and red for the background and sashing. Not knowing how her mother had in-

Figure 6.18. Fan Quilt. Annie Parham Howard (1913–1999), Madison (Morgan County), ca. 1993. 68" x 77". Hand-pieced and hand-quilted cotton-polyester with lace. Collection of Annie Lucy Brown, granddaughter of maker. [GQP 8161]

Ms. Howard purchased the purple fabric used on this quilt's border during a day trip to a fabric store in Statesboro. Although she originally set out to make a traditional fan quilt, the blocks looked too empty to her, so she added the eight-pointed stars. This quilt was quilted by many at the Morgan County Senior Center.

tended to set the blocks together, she did so in the only way that made sense to her: assembling the flowers in strips so that they would all be going the same way. A friend, Julia Ford, quilted the top. Although she sold some of her quilts over the years, Howard, who had one child, a daughter, said that she would never sell the tulip quilt because it was a link to her mother.

Howard quilted at the Morgan County Senior Center for many years. Having always regretted the fact that she had to leave school at age seven, in her later years Howard sought tutoring and learned to read—at the age of seventy-seven. Numbness in her right arm eventually prevented her from quilting, so she found enjoyment in looking after her garden and watering her flowers, a colorful profusion of marigolds, zinnias, and petunias. She continued to visit the center regularly until 1997, when ill health required that she move in with her daughter in Ohio. She passed away in 1999.

## Quilts that Represent a Connection to a Loved One

Vernard Jordan of Athens in Clarke County owns a special memento from his past: a quilt his mother made for him commemorating his birth in 1909. When she completed it nine months later, she inscribed it to him joyfully in large, embroidered letters (fig. 6.19). Jordan, a native of Oconee County (as were his parents), was the first son born to Laura Savannah Stroud Jordan (1875–1952) after two daughters, and she was thrilled with her little boy. He remembers her always admonishing her children to do right (although he adds that they did not always obey). Although his mother made many other quilts, no others have survived, having been "used up." This one, named Diamond Ring, was kept as an heirloom. Mr. Jordan still has his mother's quilting frame.

Becky Chambers is a white, recently retired middle-school teacher in Harris County and the first female mayor of Hamilton. As a child in the 1950s she often visited her Wisenbaker grandparents' large farm in Lowndes County near Lake City in South Georgia, and she lived there for part of her childhood. Tobacco, some cotton, and a small amount of sugar cane were grown there. Shorty and Rosa Chislom were an African American couple who worked on the farm and lived in a small house owned by Becky's grandparents near their home. To the best of Becky's recollection, Shorty was a farm hand, having come to work on the farm before his marriage to Rosa. Rosa became the Wisenbakers' housekeeper. Shorty taught Becky how to ride a horse and even showed her a drunken pig (the pig had gotten into some moonshine). He once spanked her when she wandered too near some quicksand in an area off limits to her. Becky describes the Chisloms as concerned with preserving what they could of their past life. Becky remembers the couple with great affection; she does not remember their being treated as servants or employees, but rather as family members who participated in many activities, including fish fries by the lake.

Apparently, the affection between the Chisloms and Becky was mutual, because during a brief illness that proved fatal, Rosa asked her husband to give Becky a quilt that she liked and that Becky remembers always being on a bed in their small home. Rosa had told Becky that the quilt had been made by Rosa's own mother, Les Zanders (fig. 6.20). It has a bold, unusual design whose inspiration is unknown. Becky treasures the quilt because of the memories of Rosa and of her own childhood that it evokes. She laments that, being only fourteen when Rosa died in the late 1950s, she was not yet interested in learning about the histories behind family treasures. She vaguely remembers Rosa working on patches and that she would help with quiltmaking in her grandmother's home, but she is sure that there was no frame set up in the small house Rosa lived in. She does remember other quilts in the Chislom home, specifically in the Wedding Ring and Shadow Box patterns, as well as a small Crazy Quilt that adorned a table. She said that Rosa also sewed useful items such as curtains.

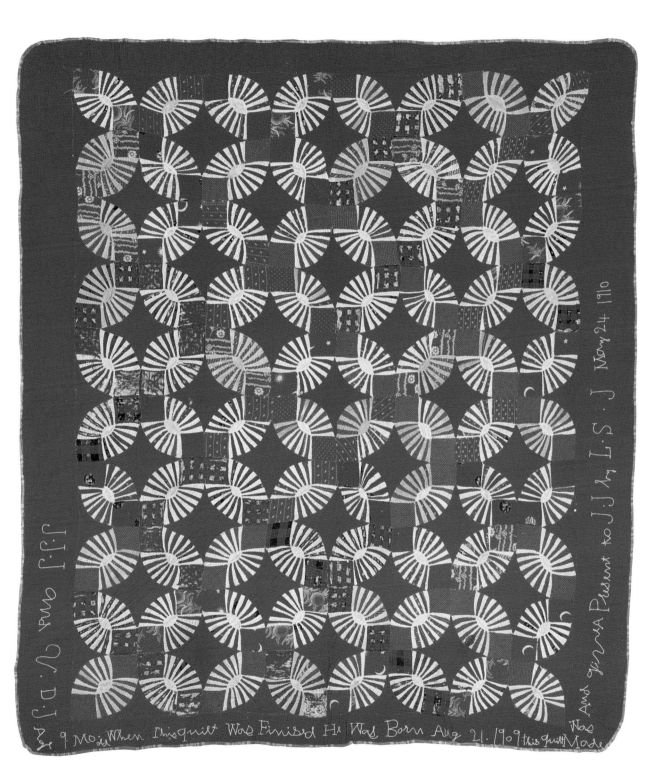

Laura Savannah Stroud Jordan, ca. 1930.
Photo courtesy of the Jordan family.

Figure 6.19. Diamond Ring. Laura Sa-
vannah Stroud Jordan (1876–1952),
Jackson County, 1909–10. 72" x 80".
Hand-pieced and hand-quilted cotton.
Collection of Vernard Debue Jordan.
[GQP 2464]

Around three of the borders is embroidered "J.J.J. and V.D.J. Age 9 months
old when this quilt was finished. He
was born August 21, 1909. This quilt
was made and given a present to J.J.
by L.S.J. May 24, 1910." Vernard Jordan
confirms that the quilt was a joint gift
to John Jackson Jordan and Vernard
Debue Jordan, Laura's husband and
son, respectively. John Jackson Jordan
was born enslaved in 1862 in Jackson
County and was freed when he was
three years old.

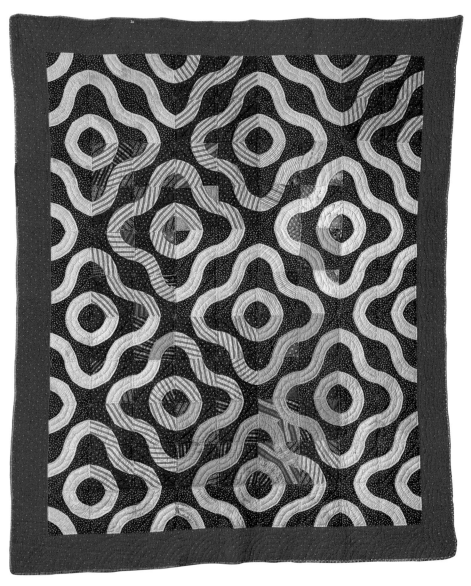

Figure 6.20. Original design. Les Zanders (dates unknown), near Lake City (Lowndes County), early twentieth century. 68" x 80¼". Hand-pieced and hand-quilted cotton. Collection of Becky Chambers. [GQP 8657]

A similar account of affection between employer and employee, white and African American, is told by Evelyn Riden Sheffield, who grew up in Morgan County a few miles from the community of Bostwick. Lissie Thomas King was employed by Evelyn Sheffield's parents as a housekeeper for forty years. One of Ms. Sheffield's earliest memories is of crying with her mother at the living room window while Lissie was taken to the hospital, seriously ill. Lissie recovered and continued to live in a small house on the property with her husband, one child, and two nephews she raised. Lissie's parents were sharecroppers, and her husband was a farmer and sawmill worker.

When Evelyn married in 1948, Lissie presented her with a magnificent quilt in the Lone Star pattern (fig. 6.21). It was used for many years on the Sheffields' bed and then put away when it began to show signs of wear. Evelyn estimates that Lissie was in her fifties when she made the quilt; she also made several others, including one for Evelyn's brother and another for a Riden cousin.

Figure 6.21. Lone Star. Lissie Thomas King (dates unknown), near Bostwick (Morgan County), 1948. Hand-pieced and hand-quilted cotton. Collection of Evelyn Riden Sheffield. Photo courtesy of the Madison-Morgan Cultural Center. [GQP MAD-37]

## Contemporary Quiltmakers

Gwen Procter-Johnson, an enthusiastic quiltmaker and volunteer, helped coordinate the Quilt History Days held at Emmaus House in Atlanta and volunteered at several others. Now in her seventies, Gwen has been quilting for more than forty-five years. She is a prolific quiltmaker and just "can't get enough of it," a sentiment we heard again and again all over Georgia among enthusiasts, black and white alike. A member of three local quilting guilds, Procter-Johnson enjoys making the traditional patterns, such as Grandmother's Flower Garden, Ohio Star, and Churn Dash. She is particularly proud of the sampler quilt she completed during the 1980s (fig. 6.22). Piecing by machine and then quilting by hand, Gwen makes more than seven quilts per year. She has never sold any of her work, nor does she take commission work. It's merely an absorbing hobby. She has taught both her daughters to quilt, and she has made many quilts for them as well as for her grandchildren. Several years ago she organized a group of women at her church and taught them quiltmaking basics. The group donated many of the quilts it has made to homeless shelters and to a local children's hospital. Gwen's daughter now coordinates the group. Procter-Johnson has formed another group, the Union City–Campbell County Quilters. All of the members are at least seventy years old, and Gwen is now teaching the newcomers how to quilt. During her convalescence after a heart attack in 2003, Gwen hand quilted a white-on-white quilt that she considers her masterpiece.

O. V. Brantley of Atlanta is lucky enough to be able to surround herself with the quilts she loves. Anyone having occasion to visit the Fulton County Attorney's Office will immediately be drawn to the artwork—the walls are full of Brantley's quilts! Quilting is a form

Detail of Atlanta Album (This Ain't Baltimore!), GQP 8654.

of therapy and relaxation for her, and a needed stress-reliever, given her high-profile position as the Fulton County Attorney. Brantley is amazed at the amount of attention her quilts generate from visitors—it seems everyone wants to talk quilts when they see hers displayed. She began quilting in 1999 after purchasing a how-to-quilt book at a local fabric store. Since then, quilting has developed into a consuming passion. Brantley gets her ideas and inspiration by reading a lot of magazines and books, as well as from her fellow guild members (she is a founding member of the Brown Sugar Stitchers—see more about them in chapter 10, "Georgia's Quilting Groups"—and says that she "owes it all" to Maxine and Roz). She likes to put her personal twist on patterns and just goes with what moves her when making a quilt. This is seen readily in her interpretation of the classic Baltimore Album quilt, which Brantley named Atlanta Album (This Ain't Baltimore!) (fig. 6.23). She acquired many of the

Gwen Procter-Johnson, ca. 1980.

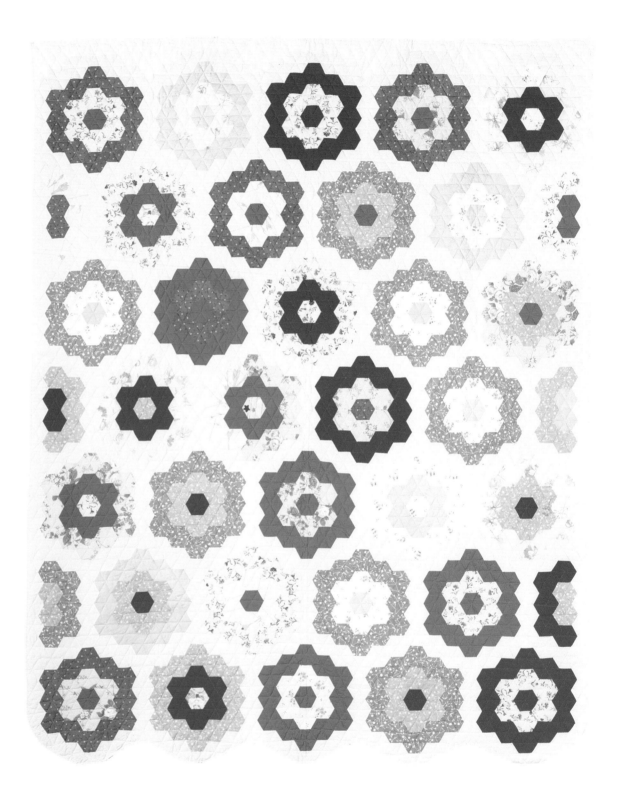

Figure 6.22. Grandmother's Flower Garden. Gwen Procter-Johnson (b. 1934), Seattle (King County), Washington, 1989. 80" x 98". Hand-pieced and hand-quilted cotton and cotton blends. The Old Campbell County Quilters in Fairburn (Fulton County) helped with the quilting. Collection of the maker. [GQP 8171]

O. V. Brantley, 2005. Photo by France Dorman.

Figure 6.23. Atlanta Album (This Ain't Baltimore!). O. V. Brantley (b. 1954), Atlanta (Fulton County), 2004. 74" x 94". Machine-pieced and -appliquéd cotton; machine quilted by Sylvia Davis. Collection of the maker. [GQP 8654]. Photo by France Dorman.

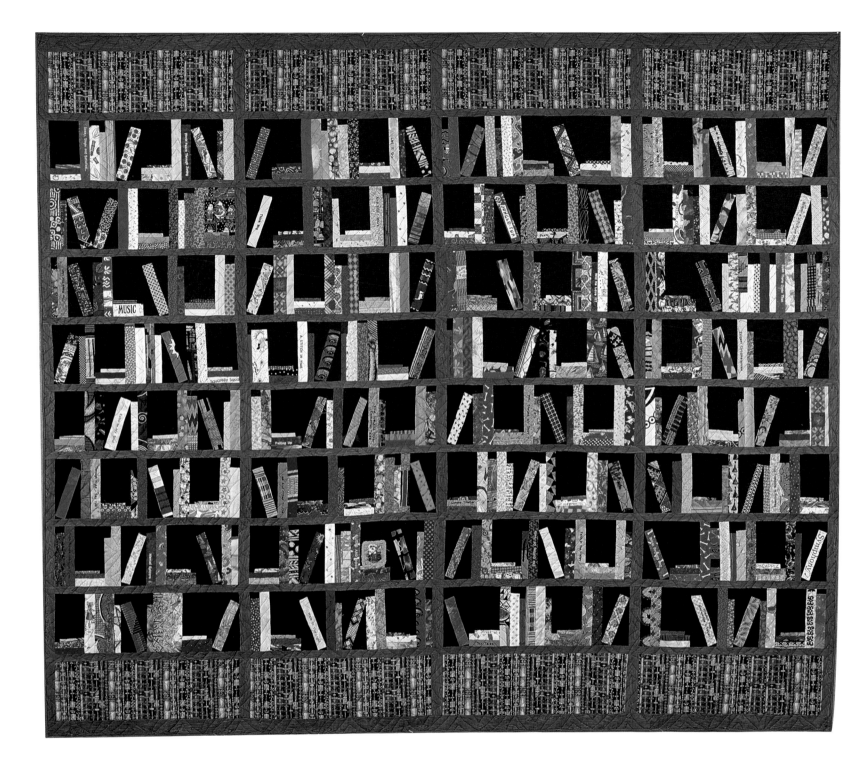

African fabrics in the quilt when fellow guild members conducted a fabric exchange in order to make African Coin quilts. She started with a pattern from a magazine and then did it "her" way, carefully choosing the variegated threads for the machine appliqué. The walls in Brantley's office and in the reception area and conference rooms of the Fulton County Attorney's Office are her personal gallery. She also makes an original design quilt each year to honor her staff, always including her daughter, India, in those quilts. The 2003 quilt was a "library" style quilt: each staff member chose the title of a book he or she would like to write. A friend machine embroidered the titles on the spines of the books in the quilt (fig. 6.24). Some of the titles, such as *World Peace through Zoning, Lies and Other Truths, And Still I Work*, and *Mental Epicure*, reflect a bit of tongue-in-cheek humor.

O. V. views quilts as a metaphor for life: "I love the notion of putting together pieces that may be ugly standing alone, but become gloriously beautiful when made a part of the whole." Quilting also helps her in her work as it reaffirms that one must have a great deal of patience and take the long view of things. Mother to India, born in 1992, Brantley turns into a super-mom after working hours and always has some hand-work with her to fill the time while waiting in the carpool line, during sports practices, and so on. A prolific quiltmaker, she loves to give quilts as gifts because she knows the recipient will appreciate the work that went into the making of it. A native of Arkansas, Brantley is fortunate enough to have eight quilts made by her grandmother in the mid–twentieth century. They are

Detail of Fulton County Attorney Law Library Quilt, GQP 8653. O.V.'s daughter is represented in this quilt by the *Aliens and Dogs* book, complete with a photo in cloth of her beloved shih tzu.

Figure 6.24. Fulton County Attorney Law Library Quilt. O. V. Brantley (b. 1954), Atlanta (Fulton County), 2003. 86" x 102". Machine-pieced cotton; machine embroidery by Brenda Wade; machine quilted by Sylvia Davis. Collection of the maker. [GQP 8653]. Photo by France Dorman.

displayed on an Internet site, and O. V. has created a foundation in her grandmother's honor dedicated to the preservation of antique African American quilts.[11]

✤  ✤  ✤

The 260 African American–made quilts documented by the GQP were of many kinds, of many skill levels, ages, colors, and styles, made by an equally diverse population of women. Each quiltmaker had her own creative vision and incorporated into her quilts her own personal preferences regarding pattern and color and fabric selection and style, just as white women do. As a group, these 260 quilts paint a picture of a talented, creative, and varied group of women (and two men—see one of them in fig. 8.10) who made and make quilts for cover, as gifts, as vehicles of creative expression, and from a desire to create something lasting to leave behind. Can quiltmakers of any race be described any differently? African Americans are a significant part of the Georgia quilt story—the quilts studied in this chapter are only a tiny sampling of the many African American quilts around the state. That some, but not most, African American–made quilts are distinctive is indisputable. After all, let us remember the creative artistry of Harriett Powers, an illiterate African American woman from Athens, Georgia, who is featured in the next chapter.

# 7. The Darling Offspring of Her Brain

## The Quilts of Harriett Powers

### CATHERINE L. HOLMES

- - - - - - - - - - - - - - - - - - - - - - - - - - - - - - - - - -

Jennie Smith stopped when she came upon the quilt hanging in the colored section of the 1886 county fair in Athens, Georgia. Amid the stalls of agricultural implements, prizewinning bales of cotton, celebrated jams and jellies, and careful needlework, the quilt's bright colors, with its watermelon-pink blocks, green sashing, and purple and yellow spotted animals, caught her eye. On closer examination, she saw that each of the quilt's eleven appliquéd squares depicted a scene from the Bible. The unique artistry captivated the twenty-four-year-old Smith. After searching out the quilt's maker with some difficulty, since fair entries were anonymous, she found her to be a "negro woman, who lived in the country on a little farm whereon she and her husband make a respectable living." Smith offered to buy the quilt on the spot. Its maker, a former slave named Harriett Angeline Powers, declared "it was not for sale at any price."[1]

The quilt Smith noticed that day and later purchased would one day belong to the Smithsonian Institution's National Museum of American History. A second, similar quilt that Powers made in the late 1890s would be held by the Boston Museum of Fine Arts. Both quilts illustrate scenes from the Bible and life in Georgia during the eighteenth and nineteenth centuries on blocks of varying sizes: a host of animals from Noah's ark cavort on one block, and stars from a spectacular 1833 meteor shower shoot across another. In 1974, author Alice Walker would describe the Bible quilt held at the Smithsonian as

> a quilt unlike any other in the world. In fanciful, inspired, and yet simple and identifiable figures, it portrays the story of the Crucifixion. It is considered rare, beyond price. Though it follows no known pattern of quilt-making, and though it is made of bits and pieces of worthless rags, it is obviously the work of a person of powerful imagination and deep spiritual feeling.[2]

In 1990, art historian Mara R. Witzling would argue that in its "powerful visualization of a cosmology and innovative use of materials," the Powers Bible Quilt could be compared to Michelangelo's Sistine Chapel ceiling. Prominent twentieth-century artists like Faith Ringgold would pay homage to Powers's quilt through their own art.[3]

As compelling as her quilts, Harriett Powers's life story traverses the tragedy of slavery, the hope of Reconstruction, and the difficulty of life in Jim Crow Georgia. Born October 29, 1837, she grew up on a 262-acre farm on Beaverdam Creek in Madison County, Georgia, just northeast of Athens. The piedmont did not support many of the enormous cotton plantations that so captured the imagination of visitors who traveled in the antebellum South or, later, the millions of readers and viewers who read or watched *Gone with*

Figure 7.1. Harriett Powers, ca. 1897. This is the only known photo of Powers. A sun and cross similar to those found on her quilts can be seen on her apron. Courtesy, Museum of Fine Arts, Boston. Photography copyright 2006 Museum of Fine Arts, Boston.

*the Wind*. John and Nancy Lester, who had moved with their respective families from Virginia to frontier Georgia at the end of the eighteenth century, lived with Powers and her mother on a farm large enough to support their family with its eight children as well as half a dozen slaves.[4]

John Lester had inherited property and several slaves when his father died in 1806. A decade later, when

Nancy Lester's father died in 1816, he bequeathed her and her children even more slaves. Although the couple successfully amassed both slaves and property during the early years of their marriage, as he grew older John Lester's ability to manage his farm and family faltered, then failed altogether. In 1836 the local court found John Lester guilty of "wasting and mismanaging" the estate and appointed his wife guardian of their children. John left the family in disgrace and Nancy Lester became the head of the household, running the farm with the help of her youngest son, John, youngest daughter, Sallie, and six slaves. Harriett Powers, born the following year to the only female slave on the Lester plantation, was perhaps named for Harriet Lester, the third of the Lester daughters, who had married and moved to Walton County in February 1836.[5]

Almost a hundred years later, Powers's son, Alonzo, described his childhood on the Lester farm, which probably differed little from his mother's childhood. If so, as a young girl, Powers gathered mussel shells from the banks of Beaverdam Creek for the slaves to use as spoons. She fetched water or herbs when her mistress requested and brushed flies away from food while the white family dined. Old Mistress, as the slaves called Nancy Lester, would not allow anyone, black or white, to whip the slave children, although her daughter, Sallie, was a different story: "Sometimes . . . Miss Sallie would get mad with us for a trifle and start to whip us. You ought to have heard us yell, 'Old Mistress, Old Mistress!' Out she would come. Her curse word was, 'Drat your infernal soul.' 'You jus want to beat my little niggers to death,' she would say. Then Miss Sallie would leave a-running." There were occasional small kindnesses. Sometimes Nancy Lester made taffy for the slave children or, when they were sick, medicine from chinaberry roots or sassafras tea.[6]

As she grew older, Powers's workload increased so that by the time she was twelve she spent long days weeding, hoeing, and picking crops of wheat, corn, potatoes, and cotton. Although male and female slaves alike worked in the fields, female slaves also cooked, sewed, and tended to their own housework. Powers's mother cooked for the Lester household, and both women made fabric. After harvesting cotton, Alonzo Powers remembered, the slave children "would pick out the seed with our hands. My mother [Harriett] would card it; my grandmother would spin it. She put it on brooshes and made a bank. Every time it filled it would click. Then she started another one. Young mistress [Sallie Lester] was the weaver and she made all our clothes."[7]

Harriett, her mother, and another young slave girl, possibly Harriett's sister, and five male slaves lived in two slave houses on the Lester property until the Civil War ended. As chattel property, slaves could not legally marry, but when she grew older, Harriett, like many other slaves, "jumped the broom" nonetheless. She married Armsted Powers, several years her senior and the sole slave belonging to James Nunn, who owned a smaller neighboring farm roughly ten miles away from the Lester property. "Away marriages," as they were called, were common among slaves, and were preferred by many who did not want to be put in the situation of watching helplessly as their spouses were, as historian John Blassingame notes, "beaten, insulted, raped, overworked or starved." All slaves were required to carry passes if they left their owner's property, so to spend time with Harriett, Armsted had to get a pass from Master Jimmy. "He got to come to see my mother twice a week," Alonzo Powers recalled decades later. "If he slipped out without the pass the 'patterollers' got after him and if he out-run them and got back to his Marster he was safe, but if he didn't, he got a whipping. Twenty-five licks was what he would get."

Even as a very old man, long after his father and slavery had passed away, Alonzo Powers remembered how many lashes his father received if caught at night without a pass.[8]

Harriett and Armsted's marriage carried the full support of the Lesters, as well it should have: their fortune increased each time Harriett had a child. Slave babies who survived infancy became valuable property to use for labor or to sell for profit. By the time the Civil War broke out, Harriett had at least one daughter, Amanda, and a son, Alonzo.[9]

Except for infrequent dances and annual corn shuckings with slaves from neighboring farms, Powers spent most of her slave life in unrelenting labor. She rarely left the Lester property except when she and the other slaves received permission to attend church. Although they had to walk several miles to get there, once inside, sitting among the other slaves on one side of the church while whites sat on the other, Powers listened to readings and sermons on the Bible.

Like Nancy Lester, Harriett Powers could not read or write. For both women, Bible stories made up a rich oral tradition of epic tales and songs. Many slaves memorized Bible passages and catechisms because, as one missionary to slaves said, "to those who are ignorant of letters, their memory is their book." Powers's experience of slavery further fashioned her understanding of what she heard. Many slaves found special significance in Christianity's attention to suffering, redemption, and hope of rebirth that free people could not understand, and they translated the message of the Bible in terms of their own experience.[10]

Though no Civil War battles were fought in Madison County, the war nonetheless devastated the area. Most able-bodied white Southern men—including the young John Lester, who went in place of his older brother, Franklin—fought in the Confeder-

ate army. Everyone who remained at home—slaves, women, children, and the elderly—faced hunger, as scarce food and even scarcer money made for unbridled inflation. Powers experienced Yankee occupation firsthand when Union soldiers passed through Beaverdam Creek and forced her to cook "fifteen bushels of peas and three middlins of meat," her son recalled. "They didn't wait for them to get done. The peas just got hot and swelled. They taken them and left with all the good horses they could catch of ours and all the money they could find." That money had been discovered when soldiers cut open the bosom of Nancy Lester's dress and "gold and silver went everywhere." Lester's son Franklin fared even worse. The soldiers first hung him up by his toes and then bored into his head with an auger until he finally divulged the hiding place of his money.[11]

In May 1865 the Confederacy surrendered, and all African Americans became citizens of the United States. Harriett Powers remained on Nancy Lester's farm, living with her husband for the first time. Free, the couple prospered amid the very circumstances under which they had previously hungered. Armsted, able to profit from his own labor for the first time, raised "a bunch of hogs and put them in the cellar and sell them at a very high price," sold "wheat at sixty dollars a bushel," and made at least one pair of shoes from rawhide and dried maple pegs, which he sold for an astonishing one hundred dollars. After Nancy Lester died in 1871, Harriett and Armsted rented land in nearby Sandy Creek, where they grew cotton, potatoes, and corn and raised cows, pigs, and goats. By 1874 the couple had assets worth more than $350, and by 1880 they owned a four-acre farm in Sandy Creek. One year later they bought the Singer sewing machine that Harriett would use to make her quilts.[12] By the standards of all blacks and many whites at the time, Armsted and Harriett Powers were enormously successful, their accomplishments all the more notable given the South's economic decline.

Powers made the first of her two quilts known to exist after the purchase of a Singer sewing machine (fig. 7.2). Depicting eleven scenes from the Bible, Powers later called it her sermon in patchwork, according to journalist Lucine Finch, and said she intended to show "where sin originated, outen de beginnin' uv things." Indeed, reading her quilt from top to bottom and left to right, she begins her sermon with temptation, "Adam and Eve in the Garden of Eden, naming the animals and listening to the subtle whisper of the 'serpent which is beguiling Eve,'" and concludes with redemption, "the Holy Family: Joseph, the Virgin and the infant Jesus with the star of Bethlehem over his head. Them is the crosses which he had to bear through his undergoing." She made the people largely symbolic, the animals more expressive and colorful, and scattered the sun, moon, and stars throughout. In the first block, the serpent's eyes glow, his feet protrude, and he is curled around temptation, which Powers represented by an ambiguous form. In another block, Judas Iscariot is suspended over the "star that appeared in 1886 for the first time in three hundred years," amid thirty pieces of silver paid to him for his treachery and counted out for Powers by a Missy Coomby. This blending of contemporary symbols and Old and New Testament stories reveals Powers's understanding of the Bible and the world around her.[13]

Although Christian influences are obvious, African design traditions shaped Powers's quilt as well. The blocks of irregular shape and size and the deliberate lack of symmetry echo intentionally random elements many African artisans incorporated in textiles to avoid evil spirits, which were believed to travel in straight lines. More, scholars have noted striking similarities between the figures on her Bible quilts and tapestries made by the Fon people of Benin and the Ewe, Fanti, and Ashanti of Ghana. Powers's quilts do not echo a single African tradition. Instead they resonate with the various textile practices of many tribes and demonstrate a unique aspect of American slave culture, in which different African cultural traditions blended as they never would have on the other side of the Atlantic. Powers was born in Georgia, as were her parents, but African influences clearly survived in her work.[14]

For whom or what purpose Powers made her first quilt remains unknown, but in November 1886 she exhibited it at the Northeast Georgia fair held in Athens. The regional drew crowds of people eager to take in horse races and exhibits of everything from paintings to poultry. The Athens *Banner-Watchman* described Wednesday at the fair thus:

> Yesterday the clouds broke and the sun burst in all beauty and brightness upon the fair. It made everybody happy and the grounds were crowded all day. It looked like a carnival. The schools emptied themselves into the halls and the grand stand was crowded long before the hour of the races to view the entries in the cattle ring, which were shown in front of the judges stand. The streets were crowded from an early hour, and the string of people and vehicles to and from the grounds made almost a continuous procession all day long.[15]

Jennie Smith was among the most significant exhibitors. A young white artist, teacher, and collector, Smith had studied art extensively in New York and Europe before settling at the Lucy Cobb Institute, where she taught art to privileged white girls. For the fair in 1886, Smith assembled a sizable exhibition featuring the work of her Lucy Cobb pupils as well as her own work. The local paper reported that though the "fair regulations require all exhibits to be nameless . . . if

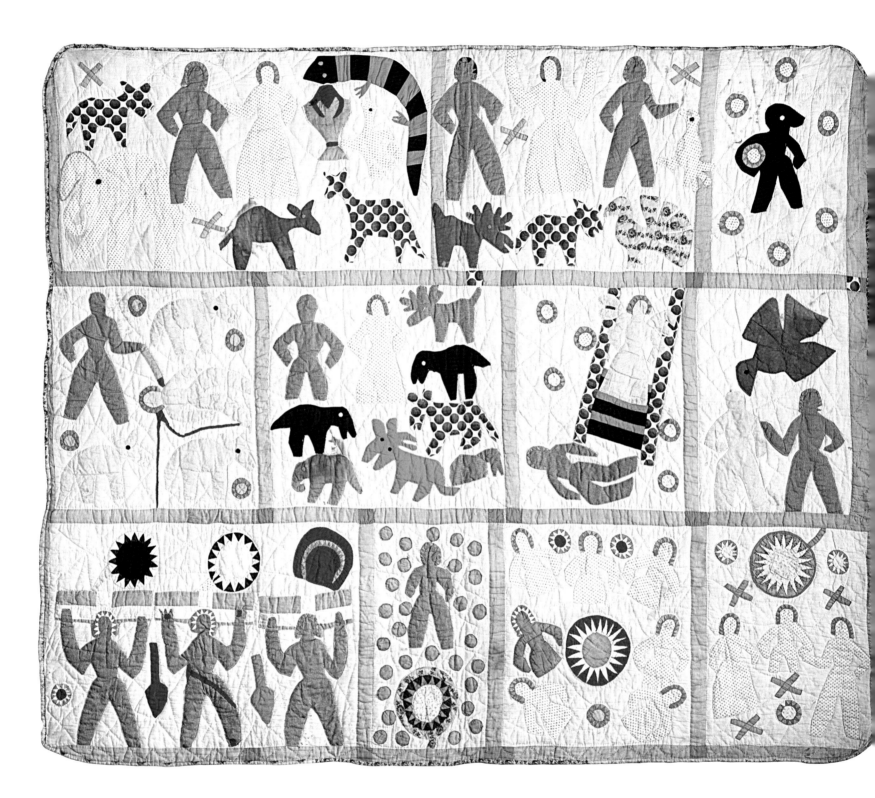

Although according to Jennie Smith, "all word painting would look pale and faded compared with the original [Bible quilt]," she knew it was important to record what Powers told her each block meant. The following are excerpts from Smith's Bible quilt "Key."

**Description of squares, left to right and top to bottom:**

Square 1: Adam and Eve in the Garden of Eden, naming the animals and listening to the subtle whisper of the "serpent which is degiling Eve."

Square 2: Eve has "conceived and bared a son."

Square 3: "Satan amidst the seven stars."

Square 4: Cain "is killing his brother Abrel and the stream of blood, which flow over the earth" is plainly discernable.

Square 5: Cain here goes into the land of Nod to get him a wife. There are bears, leopards, elks, and a "kangaroo hog."

Square 6: Jacob's dream "when he lied on the ground" with the angel ascending or descending the ladder.

Square 7: The baptism of Christ, [with] "the Holy Sperret extending in the likeness of a dove."

Square 8: "Has reference to the Crucifixion."

Square 9: Judas Ascariot and the thirty pieces of silver! . . . The large disc at his feet is "the star that appeared in 1886 for the first time in three hundred years."

Square 10: The Last Supper.

Square 11: "The next history is the Holy Family: Joseph, the Vargint and the infant Jesus with the stare of Bethlehem over his head. Them is the crosses which he had to bear through his undergoing. Anything for wisement. We can't go back no further than the Bible."

the looker on could have been told the artist of many beautiful conceptions admired during the week, he or she would have been amazed at the fertility of Miss Smith's genius and the rapidity [with which] she executed her work." Thus, Smith brought a considerably experienced and sophisticated frame of reference to

her impression of Powers's Bible quilt in 1886. Though Powers had not used quilting techniques typically prized at the time—hers was sewn mostly by machine, her quilting stitches were not particularly fine, and she did not design her quilt according to a known pattern—Smith was nonetheless captivated by the quilt and asked to buy it. Powers turned down the offer, but Smith asked to be notified if Powers ever changed her mind.[16]

For the remainder of the decade, Harriett and Armsted continued to prosper and their family grew. They had at least two more daughters, Nancy and Lizzie, as well as another son, Marshall, and they continued to accrue livestock, tools, and household goods. However, the racial and economic climate in the South became increasingly difficult for black people. Lynchings were regular front-page newspaper fare, and formerly unwritten practices of segregation were increasingly codified into law. Furthermore, the South's economy, crippled by the abolition of slavery, continued to spiral downward. While whites struggled, African Americans toiled at the bottom of the economic heap.

By 1891 Harriett and Armsted Powers had fallen on hard times. They were forced to sell two acres of their farm, and Harriett contacted Jennie Smith about selling her quilt.[17] As Smith later wrote, "She arrived one afternoon in front of my door in an ox-cart with the precious burden in her lap encased in a clean flour sack, which was still enveloped in a crocus sack. She offered to sell it for ten dollars but I told her I only had five to give. After going out consulting with her husband she returned and said 'Owin to de hardness of the times, my old man lows I'd better tech hit.' Not being a new woman, she obeyed."[18]

Powers gave Smith a "full description of each scene with great earnestness," and Harriett returned several times to visit "the darling offspring of her brain." As many have observed, had this pathetic sale not taken place, and Smith not recorded Powers's explanations of each block, there is little chance that the quilt would have been documented or preserved.

A troubled decade followed this difficult transaction. Unable to support his family with their markedly reduced acreage, Armsted probably hired himself out as a laborer. Harriett would have remained on their farm while Armsted worked for other farmers and labored in town. In the midst of this, in 1895, Jennie Smith arranged to have Powers's Bible quilt displayed at the Atlanta Cotton States and International Exposition (see fig. 1.9). More than one million people visited this exposition, which boasted a unique attraction: the Negro Building, devoted solely to the industry and cultural evolution of African Americans. Entirely constructed by and filled with works by African Americans, the Negro Building took center stage despite the fact that it was tucked into the far southeastern corner of the exposition grounds, behind the Mechanical Building and near the carnival-like Midway. A reporter for the *Southwestern Christian Advocate* wrote: "The exhibits are a study. Art, industry, literature, science, philosophy are all here and grandly proclaim the capacity of the Negro to do something worthy of the admiration of all men."[19]

The Bible quilt hung in an area of the Negro Building reserved for the works of former slaves. This area honored former slaves and their handiwork while at the same time  presuming their earlier position along the timeline of African American cultural evolution. Because the exhibits within the Negro Building demonstrated how far black Americans had come in the thirty-five years since the end of slavery, the slave section marked the beginning of the American trajectory, preceded by the "lowest savage life of darkest Africa."[20]

Exhibits in the slave section included a sizable display of one woman's canned goods, an intricate table "constructed of thirty-five kinds of wood from Georgia and containing, in all, 736 pieces," and a white bedspread woven from packaging twine, of which "not a piece was bought." Descriptions of two quilts in the slave section survive, recorded on the pages of an 1895 African American newspaper: one, a silk quilt made of "at least 1000 pieces"; the other, the Bible quilt, described as "made by a poor, ignorant slave who could neither read nor write and whose knowledge of the Bible came from stories told her by others. Each square represents one of these stories and it is not only curious but amusing to see the impressions these stories made upon the mind of one who could not understand them."[21]

Among the visitors who attended Atlanta's Cotton States and International Exposition were faculty wives from Atlanta University, one of the leading African American universities in the country. The women commissioned Powers to make another quilt as a gift to Charles Cuthbert Hall, chairman of the Atlanta University board of trustees and president of Union Theological Seminary in New York.[22]

This second quilt, larger and more complex than the first, included both scenes from the Bible and more contemporary scenes of natural wonder (fig. 7.3). Some events portrayed in the quilt had occurred during her lifetime. Powers was nine years old when the memorable "red light night of 1846," probably a meteor shower, occurred. The "Cold Thursday of February 10, 1895," when icicles formed from a mule's breath and bluebirds and people froze, is substantiated by climatological data indicating subzero temperatures in Athens at the time. However, Powers depicted two other events that had occurred before she was born. One was the dark day of 1780 when smoke from enormous forest fires in Canada or New England covered the sun so that even at nine o'clock in the morning, "candles were lighted in many houses; the birds were silent and disappeared, and the fowls retired to roost. . . . A very general opinion prevailed, that the day of judgment was at hand." The other was the spectacular Leonid meteor storm of 1833, which one witness described as "the grandest and most beautiful scene my eyes have ever beheld. It did appear as if every star had left its moorings, and was drifting rapidly in a westerly direction, leaving behind a track of light which remained visible for several seconds." Many were awestruck or afraid. Powers learned of these long-past events just as she had learned the Bible, through oral stories passed from generation to generation. During the nineteenth century, many evangelical Christians believed these events heralded the second coming of Christ.[23]

Although it is unknown who recorded Powers's explanations of the second quilt, her voice nonetheless rings true. As with the first quilt, she portrayed Bible stories in her own, strikingly personal way. In the first square, Job's crosses flank his coffin with stars at each of its four corners, as it hovers above Job praying for his enemies. In the sixth square, two sea turtles escort the whale as it swims up to swallow Jonah. God's all-seeing eye and merciful hand are found in several squares, while angels of wrath and everlasting punishment appear in others.

No one knows whether Powers made other quilts. She spent her last years, as she had her entire life, working on the farm where she lived. She had many opportunities to hear her son Alonzo preach, as he was a Baptist pastor for more than twenty churches, some as far away as Atlanta. Her other two remaining children also married, and Powers had at least fourteen grandchildren.[24] Perhaps she continued to visit her quilt at

Jennie Smith's. Armsted died the day after Harriett's seventy-second birthday, on October 30, 1909. Harriett died two months later, on January 1, 1910. The *Athens Banner* noted her death on January 4, 1910, with a tiny notice under the headline "Aged Colored Woman Dies in Athens" on page 8: "Harriet Powers, an aged Negro woman who held the esteem of many Athens people, died from pneumonia Jan. 1st. Her remains were carried to her old home near this city for interment Sunday." She was buried in the Gospel Pilgrim Cemetery in Athens, where she and Armsted share a simple, hand-carved granite tombstone erected by their son Marshall Powers.

In 1914 Lucine Finch, a musician and writer who had interviewed Powers before she died, published an article entitled "Sermon in Patchwork" in *Outlook* magazine. She wrote: "There is a certain wistfulness about the old quilt that touches something fine in us. It is the unbidden pathos of any simple expression that comes from the deep heart, where sincerity bides her time in infinite patience."[25] There is pathos in the stories of both Powers and her quilts, but there is more. Powers's quilts describe a nineteenth-century African American woman's world for which precious few sources now remain. Her stories tell us much about her worldview, a combination of the sacred and the secular, mythical, and personal. Indeed, through Powers's depictions of mankind's most profound suffering and despicable behavior, as well as mercy, redemption, and the wonders of God's world, we see how one woman understood the world around her, one that included slavery and freedom, unceasing work, and angel dreams.

Figure 7.3. Bible Quilt, ca. 1898. Harriett Powers (1837–1910), Athens (Clarke County). 69" x 105". Machine-pieced, hand- and machine-appliquéd, and hand-quilted cotton. Courtesy, Museum of Fine Arts, Boston. Bequest of Maxim Karolik. Photography copyright 2006 Museum of Fine Arts, Boston.

Powers applied most of her appliqué for this and her earlier 1886 quilt with a Singer sewing machine. However, she applied the flowers, suns, and stars on her quilts using a much more complex method. She hand-pieced each out of as many as forty miniscule triangles of fabric, cut out circles in the quilt top, and then inset each flower, sun, or star into the resulting holes. Powers made ten such stars for the block depicting the meteor shower of 1833 in the center of this quilt.

The author of the second Bible quilt's "key" is unknown.

**Description of squares, left to right and top to bottom:**

Square 1: Job praying for his enemies. Job's crosses. Job's coffins.

Square 2: The dark day of May 19, 1780. The seven stars were seen at 12 N. in the day. The cattle all went to bed, chickens to roost and the trumpet was blown. The sun went off to a small spot and then to darkness.

Square 3: The serpent lifted up by Moeses and women bringing their children to be healed.

Square 4: Adam and Eve in the Garden. Eve tempted by the serpent. Adam's rib with which Eve was made. The sun and moon. God's all-seeing eye and God's merciful hand.

Square 5: John baptizing Christ, and the sprit of God descending and rested upon his shoulder like a dove.

Square 6: Jonah cast overboard of the ship and swallowed by a whale. Turtles.

Square 7: God created two of every kind. Male and Female.

Square 8: The falling of the stars on November 13, 1833. The people were fright[ened] and thought that the end of time had come. God's hand staid the stars. The varmints rushed out of their beds.

Square 9: Two of every kind of animals continued. Camels, elephants, gheraffs, lions, etc.

Square 10: The angels of wrath and the seven vials. The blood of fornications. Seven headed beasts and ten horns, which arose out of the water.

Square 11: Cold Thursday, 10 of Feb. 1895. A woman frozen while at prayer. A woman frozen at a gateway. A mule with a sack of meal frozen. Icicles formed from the breath of a mule. All blue birds killed. A man frozen at his jug of liquor.

Square 12: The red light night of 1846. A man tolling a bell to notify the people of the wonder. Women, children, and fowls frightened but God's merciful hand caused no harm to them.

Square 13: Rich people who were taught nothing of God. Bob and Kate Bell of VA. They told their parents to stop the clock at one and tomorrow it would strike one and so it did. This was the signal that they entered everlasting punishment. The independent hog that ran 500 miles from GA to VA. Her name was Betts.

Square 14: The creations of animals continues.

Square 15: The crucifixion of Christ between the two thieves. The sun went into darkness. Mary and Martha weeping at his feet. The blood and water ran from his right side.

Figure 7.4. The grave of Harriett and Armsted Powers, Gospel Pilgrim Cemetery, Athens (Clarke County). Photo by the author.

# 8. *Cover*

## Everyday Quilts

### MARTHA H. MULINIX

---

Some quilts were made not for sale or to show but for use by the family. Their designs might have been determined more by the materials at hand than by any style or trend; their construction techniques might have been adapted to suit not only the talents of their makers but the time it was possible for the maker to devote to quilting. Such quilts have been referred to as utility or utilitarian quilts, although it is doubtful that their makers used such a designation. Known most often as everyday quilts or bed quilts, in some areas such quilts are simply referred to as cover or "kiver." The latter term reflects the Anglo-Saxon speech patterns inherited from English ancestors and retained in the Southern Highlands until well into the twentieth century.

S. W. Puryear (1867–1939) retained vestiges of these peculiarities of speech throughout his life, and his family provides examples of the handed-on tradition of quilting and other folk arts. S. W. and his wife, Viley Ann Tate Puryear (1869–1945), owned acreage in Walker County, some valley land, but also some mountain land. The family farmed in an area designated since the 1930s as John's Mountain Wildlife Management Area of the Chattahoochee National Forest. They also operated the general store and U.S. post office at Zone, Ga., and raised eleven children (one died in infancy). Cattle and a variety of fowl provided food. A flock of sheep supplied the wool that was spun into thread to be woven into blankets or knitted into socks, caps, and mittens.

In this family, quilting was a true salvage art. Clothing was made at home, and scraps were carefully saved for quilt tops. Viley Ann was making quilts before she was married (1886) and continued throughout her active life. Viley Ann sorted scraps by color and size, laying aside larger pieces for borders or stripping. She cut smaller bits of fabric into squares or other geometric shapes for use in four- or six-inch patterns or two- or three-inch designs, depending on the size of the scrap.

The traditional Nine Patch was a popular design of the period for using fabric scraps. Another favorite, 'Round the Mountain, is constructed by adding squares around a center square until a full-size quilt is achieved. Viley Ann's version of Odd Fellow was an overall design of octagons, each of a different fabric. A style established later, in which no fabric is used more than once, became known as a Charm Quilt.

Viley Ann almost certainly shared patterns and possibly scraps with other women in the community. Her daughters later reminisced about "spend-the-nights" with friends. All the girls arrived at the designated

Figure 8.1. S. W. (1867–1939) and Viley Ann Tate Puryear (1869–1945), ca. 1938. As her girls married, Viley Ann gave each one "cover for one bed," usually three quilts, but when Florence married and moved to northern Kentucky, where the winters were longer and colder, she sent her away with five quilts.

house with their scrap bags and spent the evening cutting and exchanging patches for their own Odd Fellow quilts.

Even the smallest bits of cloth could be salvaged for quilt use. Some quilters used one-inch squares to make the Postage Stamp design. For frugal quilters such as Viley Ann, a string-pieced quilt was the ultimate design for utilizing the smallest snips of fabric. One of her surviving string quilts has several pieces that can be completely covered with a thumb.

String piecing was done on a base, usually paper

from outdated Sears catalogs, magazines, or newspapers. A paper pattern was cut in the desired shape, and small, irregular strips, or "strings," of material were stitched onto the paper to cover the pattern. A loose basting tack usually held the outside pieces in place until the whole could be trimmed to the shape of the paper. These paper-backed units were then pieced into blocks or an overall design to make the quilt. The papers were usually torn away before the quilting was done.

Lula Puryear Hefner (1889–1982), daughter of S. W. and Viley Ann, told of one family in the community who did not take the paper out before quilting. Lula disliked spending the night at that house because the paper in the quilts always rattled when anyone turned over in bed. However, the paper added welcomed warmth in the unheated bedrooms, which were often the children's lot.

Since the primary purpose of quilts was warmth for sleeping, the inner layer was most important. In Georgia, wool was not commonly used as a filling unless it was a threadbare blanket whose life was extended by being quilted between a top and lining. Well-worn and much-washed, quilts sometimes served as fillings, too.

Cotton, grown in Georgia since colonial days, was the most common quilt filling or batting. (Earlier chapters explain more fully the process of cleaning cotton and the changes the cotton gin and other inventions made in cotton production.) Before the advent of the cotton gin, removing the seeds from the "cotton wool" was a laborious, time-consuming task shared by even the children in the family. This was a sit-around-the-fire activity that occupied the hours between sundown and bedtime, a time for read-aloud sessions from the Bible, the classics, and the few periodicals that were available. Sometimes popcorn, peanuts, or chestnuts roasted on the open fire provided an element of fun that made the tedious task more bearable. In preginning days, the prepared cotton was hand carded into batts to be used as the "wadding," as S. W. called it, in the "kiver." When the cotton gin became commonplace in farming communities, the last picking of cotton, or "scrap," was reserved for quilts. Ten pounds of ginned cotton made batts for two to five quilts, depending on the thickness preferred by the quilter.

The bottom layer, or lining, of the quilt was often made from salvaged material, such as old bedsheets. Bags and sacks produced for the packaging of feed and seeds or flour, meal, sugar, and tobacco were also carefully washed and utilized for linings. Viley Ann took great pride in her ability to "get the letters out of the sacks." Often Viley Ann dyed this material at home, using natural pigment sources such as walnuts, indigo, or red clay to obtain specific colors. Yard goods were available from the family store, and she sometimes used gingham, or "checks," for backings.

Quilting, the stitching that holds the three layers of the fabric sandwich together, was strictly utilitarian on these quilts. Often the design of the patchwork was ignored, and the quilting itself formed an overall pattern—fan, parallel lines, or crosshatch—to stabilize the batts within the quilt. Although quiltmakers tried to make their stitches neat and even, the stitches were not the fine quilting or intricate patterns executed on the Sunday best or company quilts of the same time period. Thread used was common ball thread, #8 sewing thread, or sometimes sack ravelings.

A bed-sized quilt provided a challenge when it came time for the quilting. Most quilters used some kind of frame to hold the three layers in place. It could be as simple as four narrow boards or even "slivers," the throw-away strips salvaged at the sawmill. These four narrow boards might have holes bored through them

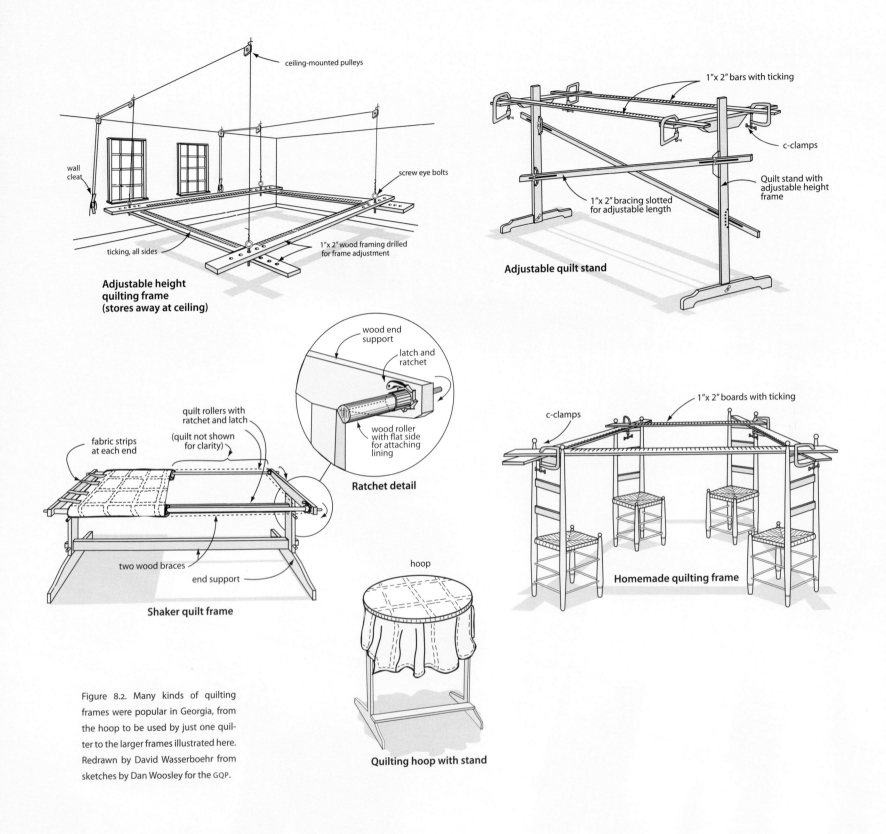

ceiling-mounted pulleys

wall cleat

screw eye bolts

ticking, all sides

1"x 2" wood framing drilled for frame adjustment

**Adjustable height quilting frame (stores away at ceiling)**

1"x 2" bars with ticking

c-clamps

1"x 2" bracing slotted for adjustable length

Quilt stand with adjustable height frame

**Adjustable quilt stand**

wood end support

latch and ratchet

wood roller with flat side for attaching lining

**Ratchet detail**

fabric strips at each end

quilt rollers with ratchet and latch

(quilt not shown for clarity)

two wood braces

end support

**Shaker quilt frame**

hoop

**Quilting hoop with stand**

c-clamps

1"x 2" boards with ticking

**Homemade quilting frame**

Figure 8.2. Many kinds of quilting frames were popular in Georgia, from the hoop to be used by just one quilter to the larger frames illustrated here. Redrawn by David Wasserboehr from sketches by Dan Woosley for the GQP.

for a long nail to connect them at each corner to hold them in a square. Some quilters used four C-clamps for this purpose. The quilt's lining could be fastened to the boards by sewing through a series of holes along the length of the boards, held in place by rows of headless tacks nailed into the boards, or pinned to a heavy piece of fabric permanently tacked to the wood. These four-square frames needed to be held at a convenient height for the quilter. In some areas, it was customary to stand while quilting, though most often quilters sat as they worked.

Many quilting frames were attached by rope or sturdy cord to four ceiling hooks that allowed the frame to be raised out of the way for storage. Thoughtful quilters were careful not to rock the frame and cause a fellow quilter to mis-stitch or prick her finger, resulting in blood on the quilt. Other quilters supported the frames in various ways: sawhorses, chairs, or stands built specifically for this purpose. Regardless of the type of frame, with large frames the quilting process always started on the outer edges and the quilted area was rolled inward as the quilters worked toward the center.

More sophisticated freestanding quilting frames were the work of furniture makers or woodworkers. Various designs were used to roll the quilt and to support the carefully crafted frame. The number of rollers varied, and the techniques for stabilizing the quilt after each roll took various forms. With such freestanding frames, a quilt was fitted onto the frame and rolled up for the quilting to begin in the center, working out to the edges. In general, this type of frame was only thirty or so inches wide, so it didn't require that an entire room be devoted to quilting.

A 1920s freestanding frame made by Ben F. Mulinix (1878–1964) for his wife Iva (1892–1936) is on display at the Bartow History Center in Cartersville. A

Figure 8.3. People quilting standing up, using surplus commodity cotton. Greensboro (Greene County), 1941. Though not as common as seated quilters, quilting while standing up is the practice among some Georgians. Photo courtesy of the Library of Congress, Photo Duplication Service.

Figure 8.4. Woman quilting in her cabin, Augusta, ca. 1885. Quilting frames were frequently suspended from the ceiling on large hooks. They could be raised out of the way by pulleys when not in use. Photo from Williams Photographic Collection, courtesy of the Hargrett Rare Book and Manuscript Library, University of Georgia.

freestanding frame of this design is also on display in the Women's Quarters at the Shaker Village in Pleasant Hill, Kentucky. R. E. Mulinix (b. 1920), son of Ben F., makes a modification of this frame for present-day quilters.[1] One of his frames is displayed in Shaping Traditions: Folk Arts in a Changing South, a perma-

*Cover: Everyday Quilts*

- - - - - - - - - - - - -

Figure 8.5. Lone Star. Hand pieced and appliquéd by Aurie Hefner Holsomback (1873–1942), Armuchee (Floyd County), 1930s; hand quilted by her niece Martha H. Mulinix (b. 1921) in the 1980s. 81½" x 82½". Cotton. Collection of the Atlanta History Center, gift of Martha H. Mulinix. [GQP 1409]

As the South developed industrially and many people found employment in the local textile mills or garment factories, another source of materials became available to the thrifty homemaker-quilter: scraps salvaged from the workplace. One such quilt is now a part of the permanent textile collection at the Atlanta History Center (fig. 8.5). As a young woman in the 1930s, Ivena Holsomback (1905–1999) worked at the Spread House in Sugar Valley and brought home scraps to her mother, Aurie Hefner Holsomback (1873–1942), who pieced a Lone Star top from the fabrics. The folk art flowers in the corners of the quilt are irregularly placed, strategically machine appliquéd to cover holes and grease spots already in the cloth. Evidently Aurie did not consider this top worth quilting, but years later a niece spent many hours turning it into an award-winning example of the creative quilting of the 1980s and 1990s.

The same women who in their youth quilted from necessity, to keep their families warm, found much pleasure in continuing to quilt in later years. They could exercise the thrifty habits of their youth and middle years; the craft was a diversion to pass the time; they created handmade articles to pass on to their descendants.

Many quilts brought for documentation to Quilt History Days were not quilts made to showcase fine fabrics or expert techniques. Instead, utilitarian quilts are pieces of family heritage valued by present owners. For example, at Summerville, Asa Mulinix (b. 1971) took great pride in presenting a quilt made by his great-grandmother, Lula Puryear Hefner (1889–1982), when she was over eighty years old.[2] Now a keepsake, the string quilt had been pieced on paper and contains a variety of fabrics (fig. 8.6). Seldom are these creations used for cover nowadays, but they are ceded places of honor in modern homes or incorporated into the home's decor.

nent exhibit curated by John A. Burrison at the Atlanta History Center.

R. E. says that although as a child he was sometimes present around the quilting frame, he never quilted. Later in life, however, audience participation demonstrations of the Mulinix Frame found him stitching away at quilt exhibits, craft shows, and other public events. R. E. attended classes, lectures, and workshops and became knowledgeable and appreciative of quilts and quiltmaking.

*Martha H. Mulinix*

Asa Mulinix (b. 1971) and great-grand-mother Lula Puryear Hefner (1889–1982), 1977. Asa was excited to see his great-grandmother working on his quilt. During the Summerville Quilt History Days in 1990 he proudly brought this quilt to be documented, and when he purchased his first home in 1994 it was installed in a place of honor on his bedroom wall.

Figure 8.6. String Quilt. Lula Puryear Hefner (1889–1982), Bartow County, 1976–77. 55" x 92". Machine-pieced and hand-quilted cotton and blends. Collection of Asa M. Mulinix, the great-grandson for whom it was made. [GQP 474]

Figure 8.7. Family in Jackson County with some of its quilt tops, 1908. Forming a backdrop to the photo, the quilt tops are clearly of the "cover" variety and typical of those found in any rural Georgia home of the period. JAC015, Vanishing Georgia Collection, Georgia Archives.

Scrap bag quilts were prevalent at most documentation sites throughout Georgia. The workmanship usually indicated that the quilts had been produced by the most practical, timesaving methods possible with service in mind. This was evident in the amount of quilting done and in finishing techniques used on the quilt edges. A self-finish back over front or front over back was popular. An otherwise all hand-stitched quilt often had a machine-finished edge. Presumably, this produced a sturdier, more wear-resistant end result.

Although Quilt History Days were not conducted in each of Georgia's 159 counties, quilts from throughout Georgia were brought in. A survey of the collected data revealed many examples to illustrate the characteristics for cover quilts. A few follow here.

*Martha H. Mulinix*

From Bartow County, a scrap bag Step Around the Mountain illustrates the oft-repeated story of a thrifty woman providing cover for her family. Lemma Harris (1888–1970), affectionately known as Ma Harris, was widowed in her twenties. With four children to support, she worked in the textile mills during the 1940s. By saving every scrap she could, Lemma hand pieced tops and stored them in an old trunk until she had time to finish them for members of her family. She gave hand-stitched quilts as wedding gifts to her grandchildren. Her grandson, Joe Frank Harris (b. 1936), received the Step Around the Mountain when he married (fig. 8.8).

Joe Frank served as governor of Georgia from 1983 to 1991. His wife, Elizabeth Carlock Harris (b. 1940), accepted the Honorary Chairwomanship of the GQP, a position she still holds. In remarks made at the project's kickoff ceremony on February 22, 1990, Mrs. Harris stated the reasons she believes Ma Harris made quilts: "Number one, she wanted to provide for her family. Quilting was a way. Secondly, she was also thrifty. She took scrap pieces and put them together. Lastly, quilting was solace for the soul. It was an expression of herself, and it was the therapy she needed." These three points could well be included in the definition of cover that begins this chapter.

Lemma Harris (1888–1970) and grandson Joe Frank Harris (b. 1936), ca. 1939. Joe Frank Harris was governor of Georgia from 1983 to 1991. His wife, Elizabeth Carlock Harris, is honorary chairwoman of the GQP. Photo courtesy of Elizabeth C. Harris.

Figure 8.8. Step Around the Mountain. Alice Eulemma Hice Harris (1888–1970), Cartersville (Bartow County), ca. 1960. 69" x 78" Hand- and machine-pieced, hand-quilted cotton and blends. Collection of Mr. and Mrs. Joe Frank Harris. [GQP 2698]

The colorful scrap bag quilt with seersucker backing is typical of Lemma's usual utilitarian gift for such an occasion. Grandson Joe Frank still values the quilt that was a wedding gift from his "Big Ma" (Lemma).

Figure 8.9. Star. Bessie ("Beck") Caudell Kirby (b. 1916), Martin (Franklin County), 1931. Hand-pieced and hand-quilted cotton and feed sacks. Collection of owner. [GQP 7329]

Beck's, a shop that began business in the 1940s doing custom sewing and alterations in Toccoa in Stephens County, was operated by Bessie ("Beck") Caudell Kirby (b. 1916). As of 2005 Beck continued to do alterations but worked out of her home. After her mother died (and was buried on Beck's fourteenth birthday), Beck found herself taking over many of the household chores, including sewing for the family as her mother had done. Her first quilt was string pieced on paper with family sewing scraps of cottons including feed and/or flour sack materials (fig. 8.9). The quilting is fan (also called Baptist fan or shell in some parts of Georgia), a design usually marked by starting at the corner of the frame, placing an elbow on the edge of the quilt and marking the arc with chalk. Beck eyeballed subsequent arcs at one- or two-inch intervals to complete the fan. Rows of fans cover the quilt. If fans were begun from both sides of the quilt, a backbone formed where the two sides met. Beck worked in a pants factory and a thread mill for a few years before she opened her shop.

She expresses amazement that so many of today's women do not sew. She says, "I do believe the Good Lord put me here to sew."

James McClarty (d. ca. 1922), the father of Jimmie Mc-Clarty Tinch (b. 1919) of Cartersville in Bartow County, made a handmade patchwork quilt, a variation of Basket (fig. 8.10). Mr. McClarty died when Jimmie was very young, and her mother earlier in the same year. Sisters Henrietta and C. Ferrell had died as infants, and brother Joe lived only to be eight or nine. The only "mama" she remembers was her mother's sister, Ella Boyd, who reared Jimmie, an older sister Jennie Vee, and a brother Pless Columbus (P.C.). P.C. was nine years older and supplied most of the information that Jimmie has about her family. Both mother and father were born in Georgia. James McClarty came from a rural background in which quilting was a necessity; he learned to quilt when he was a child. Later he worked for the railroad and at the time of Jimmie's birth was living in Pennsylvania. Ill with measles, the whole family was further weakened by exposure to the cold while trying to put out a fire in their home. All suffered a major setback and were never well again. James McClarty managed to bring his family back to Georgia, where his wife Julia died; he did not live long after her death. Jimmie remembers playing in the scraps while Mama Ella pieced quilts, and later she made quilts for her own family. However, the Basket quilt provides a tangible link to the parents she never knew.

Figure 8.10. Basket. James McClarty (d. 1922), Veronia, Pennsylvania, ca. 1912. 68" x 82". Hand-pieced and hand-quilted cotton and flour sacks. Collection of Jimmie Tinch, daughter of the maker. [GQP 1357]

The McClarty family, early 1900s. James McClarty (d. 1922) is on the right side of the back row.

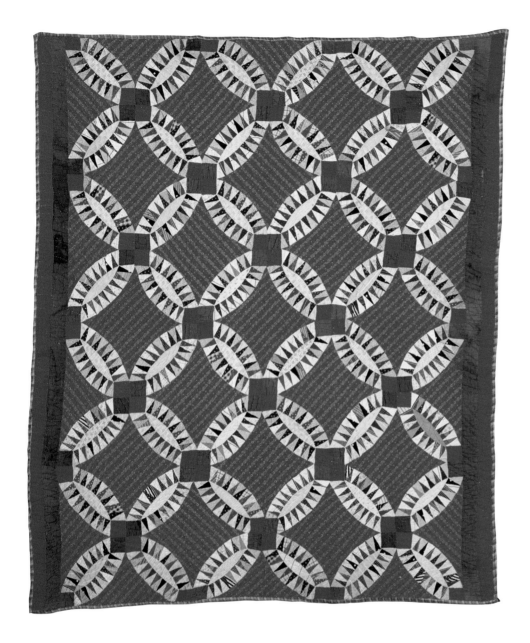

A Pickle Dish quilt from White County made by Sarah Crumly Jarrard (1853–1925) exemplifies the tradition of using even the smallest scraps to produce an outstanding quilt (fig. 8.11). The wide variety of colors and fabrics in the cover, composed mostly of small triangles, indicates a scrap bag quilt made after the larger pieces of fabrics had been utilized for other patchwork. The quilting is a modified fan design with two closely placed rows alternating with a wider space. Back-to-front finishing by machine produced a sturdy quilt expected to see much use. Sarah's family farmed and also operated a country store. Since such businesses usually handled some dry goods, and often the woman was allowed to choose that part of the stock, it is likely that Sarah chose yardage especially to complete her quilt. It is possible that much of the hand piecing of this intricate pattern was done between customers while minding the store.

Figure 8.11. Pickle Dish. Sarah Crumly Jarrard (1853–1925), White County, ca. 1890–1910. 82" x 83". Hand-pieced and hand-quilted cotton. Collection of Vista Anne Mahan, great-granddaughter of the maker. [GQP 568]

James and Sarah Crumly Jarrard, ca. 1910. Photo courtesy of Claire Stringer Schenk.

*Martha H. Mulinix*

In 1934 in Treutlen County, Florrie Hutcheson McCrimmon (1889–1981) pieced a quilt as a wedding gift for her son, Lyman, and his wife, Bertha Warnock McCrimmon. A group of local ladies gathered for a quilting party and completed it (fig. 8.12). The prints were sewing scraps from dresses, shirts, skirts, and aprons made by Mrs. McCrimmon. At present, Carolyn McCrimmon Tarpley, granddaughter of the maker, owns the quilt. Carolyn's son, David Tarpley, and her daughter, Pamela Tarpley Lewis, have enjoyed the quilt, too. Now there are five great-great-grandchildren to learn from the treasured family heirloom. When she brought the quilt in to the Soperton Quilt History Day, Mrs. Bertha Warnock McCrimmon O'Brien, for whom the quilt was made, noted that it has covered many through the cold nights before the time of push-button heat.

Figure 8.13. Oak Leaf and Reel. Sophronia Lansford Beaver (1859–1936), Rossville (Catoosa County), ca. 1900. 68" x 83". Machine-appliquéd and hand-quilted cotton. Collection of Elizabeth Hess, granddaughter of the maker. [GQP 4492]

Figure 8.12. Crow's Foot. Florrie Hutcheson McCrimmon (1889–1981), Treutlen County, 1934–35. 70" x 75½". Hand- and machine-pieced, hand-quilted cotton and feed sacks. [GQP 2715]

For family use, Sophronia Lansford Beaver (1859–1936) of rural Walker County used machine appliqué to shorten the task of making her Oak Leaf and Reel (fig. 8.13). A quilt of this pattern was often the result of long hours of fine handwork, but access to a machine made it possible to produce the quilt in much less time. This maker's neat, even hand-quilting stitches stand out; however, the quilt is finished front to back by machine.

Margaret Sophronia Lansford (1859–1936) and James Harvey Beaver (1854–1932) were married April 30, 1879. This photograph was taken at their fiftieth anniversary in 1929. Photo courtesy of Elizabeth Hess.

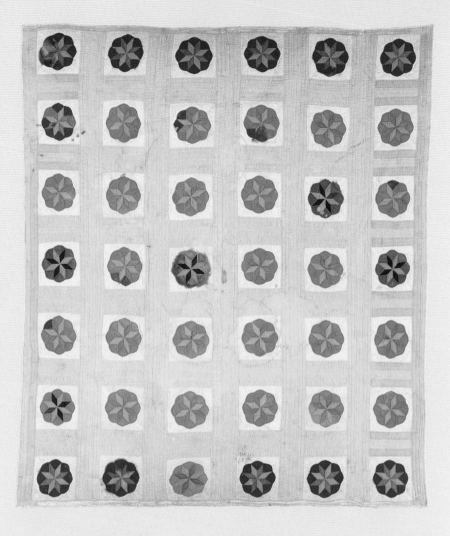

Figure 8.14. Eight-Point Star Varia-tion. Mrs. John Oscar Harrell (dates unknown), Grady County, ca. 1890–1910. 70" x 79". Hand-pieced and hand-quilted, home-dyed cotton. Collection of Pauline Hewlett, grand-daughter of maker. [GQP 4972]

Pauline Hewlett of Clayton County brought in an Eight-Point Star Variation, believed to have been made around 1900 (fig. 8.14). Her grandmother, Mrs. John Oscar Harrell (dates unknown), in rural Grady County, made this quilt. All solids, the green, red, and yellow appear to be home dyed. A back to front finish by machine is evident on this otherwise all-handmade quilt. This well-loved cover is worn, faded, and damaged, supporting the assumption that this quilt was made to be used and has been used by three generations.

The GQP's attention to all types of quilts has encouraged people to take pride in the fact that simple cover quilts had been made and used in their own families. Quilt History Days throughout the state awakened an interest in family and local community culture as cherished keepsakes were documented.

Worn-out quilts have made convenient packing material for America on the move as well as welcome additions to camping and/or picnicking gear for several generations of nature lovers. Many of them have been cut up and recycled as placemats, pillows, toys, wall hangings, and other items. Some have been turned into high-fashion expensive clothing.

Other quilts serve their main purpose—cover for beds—and are then casually discarded. One such quilt was picked up in the woods near a remote mountain cave in North Georgia. This specimen provides a diligent researcher the challenge to determine by careful examination the history of a quilt without the benefit of firsthand information from the maker or user.

The found piece (fig. 8.15) shows a quilt within a quilt, illustrating the common practice of renewing a worn quilt by re-covering it. The outer quilt measures 71" × 78". The first or inner top was string pieced in seven-inch squares randomly interspersed with whole squares. Both hand- and machine-piecing techniques were used. The backing appears to be made from flour sacks. "Snow White" and "flour" are reversed because the sack was turned so the lettering would face the inside. The batting is cotton, possibly hand carded. The diagonal quilting with a #8 white thread appears to follow the seams of the blocks in lines about two inches apart, with approximately five stitches to the inch. The solid border was finished back over front by machine. Clearly identifiable as a cover quilt, the choice of materials seems to indicate this is from the Depression era of the 1930s.

Two patchwork tops were used for re-covering. Both have a wide range of fabrics, indicating their source as the scrap bag.

The upper top is the Churn Dash pattern with 12½-inch squares set five wide and six long with 1½-inch strips and corner posts. All the strips are solid orange and light tan. Throughout the quilt, blues, pinks, greens, tans, and lavenders are seen in stripes, florals, checks, plaids, and limited amounts of plains. Only hand stitches are evident in this top.

The quilt backing is made entirely of two-inch squares. The color arrangement suggests the backing is made of two joined pieces. Long lines in one direction are done by machine, but there are many hand seams. It is difficult to decide whether the machine work was in the original construction or if this stitching was reinforcement after the piece was used. The backing fabrics are more varied than those in the Churn Dash side. Dimities and voiles are interspersed with the more common cottons. Colors range from bold black-and-white checks to faded solids.

The refurbished quilt is neatly tacked with a tight-twist white thread that follows the patchwork design. The quilt was finished by hand with the back over the front method of binding.

If such a quilt could tell its own story, perhaps it would reminisce about the industrious housewife who spent many hours providing cover for her family. It would tell of years of service—first as a new quilt covering the company bed and later as a much-worn old quilt making a pallet for a visiting grandchild. Certainly it would relate with pride the fact that memories of this and other quilts have become a part of the cultural heritage of the maker's family, still handed down from generation to generation.

Figure 8.15. The two sides of a quilt within a quilt. Maker unknown, place unknown, ca. 1930s. 71" x 78". Hand- and machine-pieced, hand-quilted and -tacked cottons and feed sacks, with some dimities and voiles. Collection of the author. [GQP 8166]

*Cover: Everyday Quilts*

203

# *9. There's Something about Feed Sacks…*

**ANITA ZALESKI WEINRAUB**

- - - - - - - - - - - - - - - - - - - - - - - - - - - - - - - - - -

*The quilts that's made from the old sacks, the old feed sacks, they are the warmest, sweetest—they feel different from any other quilt that you can use.*

—Hazel Fulton, Cartersville

Hazel's observation sums up Georgians' feelings about feed sacks: Georgians have a soft spot in their hearts for feed sacks. Whether they evoke an earlier time when we imagine life to have been simpler, whether they bring back memories of making do and living through the Great Depression on a farm, or whether they remind us of mothers and grandmothers who wore feed-sack aprons and made curtains from feed sacks, they always elicit a warm response. Most native Georgians over the age of sixty remember feed sacks.

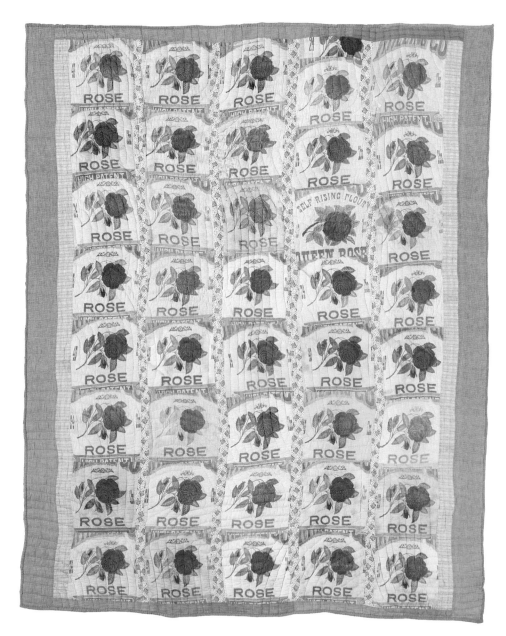

Figure 9.1. Rose Pattern. Maker unknown, place made unknown. Purchased. Made before 1950. 62" x 75". Machine-pieced and hand-quilted cotton feed sacks from Rose Flour Milling Co. Collection of the Litton family. [GQP 1588]

*Anita Zaleski Weinraub*

- - - - - - - - - - - - - -

206

Manufacturers packaged and sold feed, seed, and household staples in factory-made cloth sacks beginning in the mid-1800s; sacks used to transport or store goods prior to that time were home sewn.[1] During that period, cotton bag manufacturers provided the farmwife or homemaker with free fabric for home sewing. This continued until the 1950s, when paper packaging and bulk delivery became more cost effective, ultimately leading to the decline of the cotton bag industry in the 1960s.

According to Georgia Quilt Project (GQP) findings, feed sacks began to be used in Georgia quilts during the second half of the nineteenth century. At that time, sacks were usually used as a backing for a quilt, not typically as a fabric used on the front except sometimes as the sashing fabric between blocks. Manufactured sacks were printed with the name of the company whose product was packaged inside the sack, the company's location, the contents and weight of the sack, and the name of the sack manufacturing company. They often incorporated an illustration or the company's logo—Jim Dandy, Pillsbury, Rose Flour (fig. 9.1). These sacks were white or off-white, and quilters carefully bleached the lettering from the fabric before sewing with it (though they weren't always successful). They also sometimes dyed the cloth to match or coordinate with the squares of the quilt or the quilt top.[2]

The earliest documented quilt containing sacks dates from around 1860. It was found in a hope chest in 1906 somewhere in South Georgia. The inked legend on the back of the quilt, made in the Blazing Star pattern, is still visible: "Jackson Mills, 49 lbs. 'Diadem' Flour, Buchanan & Brother, Americus, Georgia, Esquire Manufacturers."[3] A fancy border surrounds the lettering. Several examples of quilts with feed-sack backings appear elsewhere in this book.

Depending on the product they held, the texture of the sacks varied; the larger granules of fertilizer, seed, and chicken and hog feed could be packaged in coarser cloth, whereas the finer flour, salt, and sugar required a more tightly woven fabric. Sacks varied in size as well, from a small tobacco sack, to one that held ten pounds of sugar, to the large fifty- and hundred-pound sacks of chicken and hog feed. The sheer variety of textures and sizes of sacks increased their potential uses. In general, larger sacks are the ones Georgians referred to when interviewed for this chapter. When the top and side stitching was unraveled and one of these sacks was opened up, it yielded just over a yard of fabric. Georgians repeatedly observed that four sacks were required to back a quilt.

Home economy was practiced in almost all Georgia households both from tradition and from necessity. Few goods were purchased. Anything that came into the household was reused; brown paper that purchases had been wrapped in was smoothed and folded for future use, and the string that tied the wrapped purchases was wound into a ball for reuse. Even scraps of soap were saved and pressed together to make a "new" bar.

As we have already seen in chapter 1, "Background for Quilting in Georgia," the South—Georgia included—was in an economic depression well before the 1929 stock market collapse. Among the textile collection of the Georgia Agrirama in Tifton is a post–Civil War quilt made of dyed feed sacks that the donor family called the Hard Times Quilt. Thrift and conserving cash were indeed a way of life on Georgia's farms.

The GQP documented more than four hundred quilts containing feed sacks. Of these, twenty-eight were attributed to the nineteenth century (seventeen with an estimated date of 1899 or earlier, and eleven

Figure 9.2. Detail of Anchors Aweigh. C. M. Newman (dates unknown), Hixon (Hamilton County), Tennessee, top ca. 1919, hand quilted in 1990. Hand-appliquéd and hand-quilted bleached feed sacks. Purchased from the estate of C. M. Newman. Collection of Mary Hendricks. [GQP 4474]

with an estimated date of 1900). Only twenty of the quilts bear dates (five of which are 1974 or more recent). The earliest dated feed-sack quilt, Anchors Aweigh, was made in 1919 (fig. 9.2). The top has a solid white feed-sack background with appliquéd red and blue anchors. Its name suggests that the quiltmaker had some connection to the navy—perhaps a family member was serving in the navy during World War I or she saw the pattern somewhere and reproduced it in a burst of patriotism in the colors of the U.S. flag.

Although many products were packaged in cotton bags, the majority of quilt owners indicated they knew their quilts to be made from chicken feed sacks. Such sacks would have been readily available to many farmwives as a direct result of the development of Georgia's poultry industry.

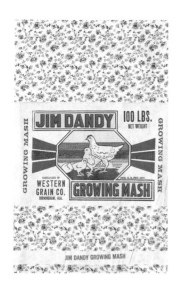

Figure 9.3. The labels could be removed by soaking them in water, yielding just over a yard of fabric in the hundred-pound size. Collection of the author.

*Anita Zaleski Weinraub*

Jesse Dixon Jewell of Gainesville (Hall County) was a prominent figure in the poultry industry's transformation from a home enterprise to a large-scale modernized industry. Most Georgia farmers during the 1920s and 1930s were so cash poor they did not have the means to buy chicks to raise. Jesse Jewell, owner of a feed store, supplemented his income by buying chickens from farmers and transporting them to Atlanta to sell. He convinced a bank to make him a loan and persuaded feed manufacturers to extend him credit. He then contracted with farmers for them to raise chicks and provided them with both the chicks and the feed. When the birds went to market, Jewell made a cash settlement with the farmers, which resulted in a profitable situation for all concerned—the entrepreneur, the farmer, and the consumer, who could now purchase chickens at a lower price.

Eventually, Jewell expanded his business both horizontally and vertically, enlisting the services of ever-increasing numbers of farmers and building a hatchery and a chicken processing plant, thus fully integrating his enterprise. Several factors—the economic depressions and then the food shortages during World War II, along with the absence of price controls that the government imposed on other agricultural products—contributed to the poultry industry's taking a foothold and then thriving in Georgia, beginning in the 1920s. Between 1947 and 1960, broiler production in the Southeast increased by 365 percent.[4] Throughout Georgia, especially throughout North Georgia, many quilt owners stated that the family had raised chickens to sell. The farmwife, then, would have had an ample supply of feed sacks with which to embellish her surroundings.

The feed sacks that Georgians recall most vividly are those made from bright floral prints. Beginning in the mid-1920s, the white feed-sack fabric with let-tering stamped on it was gradually replaced by floral, striped, plaid, and other patterned fabric. Instead of the ink stamping found on white sacks to identify the feed, printed sacks had a paper label, spot, or band that could quickly be removed by soaking in water (fig. 9.3). This was a great timesaver and boon to the farmwife, who now had ready-made colored, patterned fabric to use. This innovation resulted in an explosion of feed-sack popularity by the late 1930s. Women sent their men to the local feed and seed store with instructions to bring back three or four sacks, all of the same design (this was enough for a woman's dress). No longer was one bag of feed just like the next one, and Georgians have told of shopkeepers who grumbled when asked to get a bag of feed from the bottom of a pile just because the sack would match another or because one pattern was preferred over another. As these new sacks caught on, bag manufacturers would sometimes print a design with, for example, a border pattern, for use as a pillowcase or curtains. They even prestamped sacks with children's dress patterns and doll patterns.[5] Georgia's feed-sack era stretched from the Great Depression beginning in the 1920s, through World War II, and into the postwar prosperity of the 1950s and even the 1960s.

This period is well within the memory of many living Georgians, which made for lively recollections during the Quilt History Days. A woman in Mableton told us she had discovered three hundred whole sacks with labels removed, washed, ironed, folded, and stored in the attic by her mother. One quilt we documented was a beautifully made, colorful quilt in the Double Wedding Ring pattern, made by Electa Archer Harris of Deepstep in Washington County (fig. 9.4). Harris's quilt had taken second place in a 1958 quilting contest at the Georgia State Fair—all quilts submitted had to be made *entirely* from feed sacks.

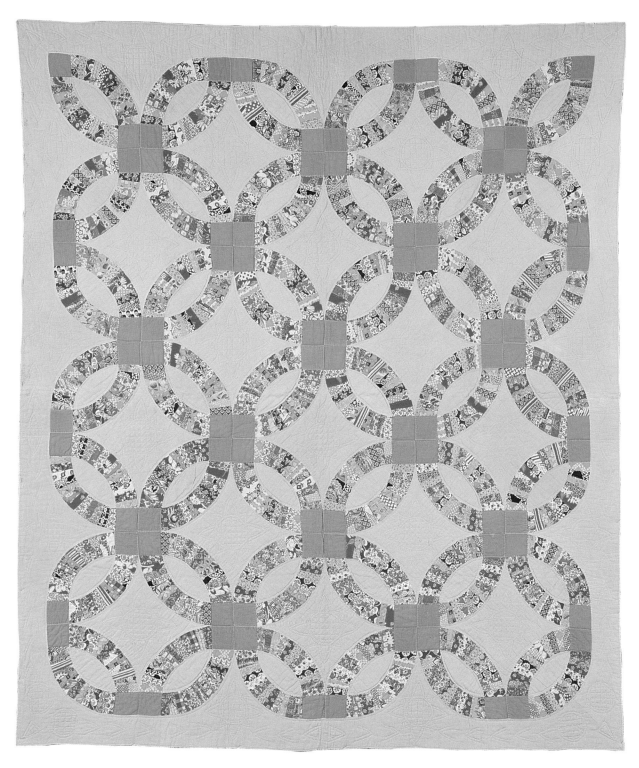

Electa Archer Harris, early 1980s. Photo courtesy of Kyla Andrews.

Figure 9.4. Double Wedding Ring. Electa Archer Harris (1923–2002), Deep-step (Washington County), 1958. 71" x 82". Hand-pieced and -quilted cotton feed sacks, some home dyed. Collection of Kyla Andrews, daughter of maker. [GQP 5655]. Photo by France Dorman.

Figure 9.5. (*left*) Nelle Bannister Dooley in her high-school graduation dress made of feed sacks. Dawsonville (Dawson County), 1943. Photo courtesy of Nelle Bannister Dooley. (*right*) Ellie Lou Merritt Whitmire was also a member of the Dawsonville High School class of 1943; sixty years later, her granddaughter Lisa Francingues modeled Ellie's graduation dress made from feed sacks. Photo by the author.

After her marriage in 1942, Lucy Nell Flowers of Norcross kept twelve or fourteen chickens. She used the fabric from the chicken feed sacks to make housedresses. Flowers recalls, "Cotton cloth was hard to find during the war—you couldn't just go over to Rich's [an Atlanta department store] and get it." She also made her children pajamas from feed sacks and still has some ironed and folded sacks stored at home.

The thirteen girls of the Dawsonville High School class of 1943 demonstrated their patriotism at the graduation exercises in a unique way—instead of caps and gowns that they would only wear once, the girls wore floor-length dresses they made from feed sacks.[6] Beloved homeroom teacher Mrs. Sirmons is credited with the idea. Dawson County was one of the North Georgia areas where the poultry industry burgeoned during World War II, and even people who lived in town had backyard chicken houses, frequently made from inexpensive wood slabs obtained from the local sawmill. Feed sacks were found in nearly every home, guaranteeing an ample supply of cloth for the dresses. Each girl chose her own pattern and then sewed her dress either by herself or with the help of a family member who sewed (fig. 9.5). Songs from all the branches of the armed forces were sung at the graduation ceremony. Several of the graduates recall that during those times, everyone banded together to support the war effort.

One of Hazel Fulton's (b. 1919) earliest memories is of holding the lamp for her mother so she could quilt in the evening after a long day at work in the fields. She was five years old at the time. Her mother did all of her sewing by hand since she didn't own a machine. Hazel also remembers wearing striped feed-sack underwear she thinks was made from sugar sacks. She resented having to wear homemade underwear; her younger sister's were store-bought.

Hazel married at sixteen; in 1942 she and her three small children moved to Cartersville to live with relatives. Hazel worked for Goodyear Tire and Rubber for thirty-five years, most of those as a spooler in the twister room, later as a licensed practical nurse there. She wore work dresses and work aprons made from floral feed sacks (aprons were a work necessity to protect her clothing from the oil and grease in the twister room).[7]

Hazel didn't begin to quilt until she retired. She has made several quilts from feed sacks and has collected enough sacks to make many more (fig. 9.6). She is one of many Georgians who continue the tradition of making quilts from available goods.

*Anita Zaleski Weinraub*

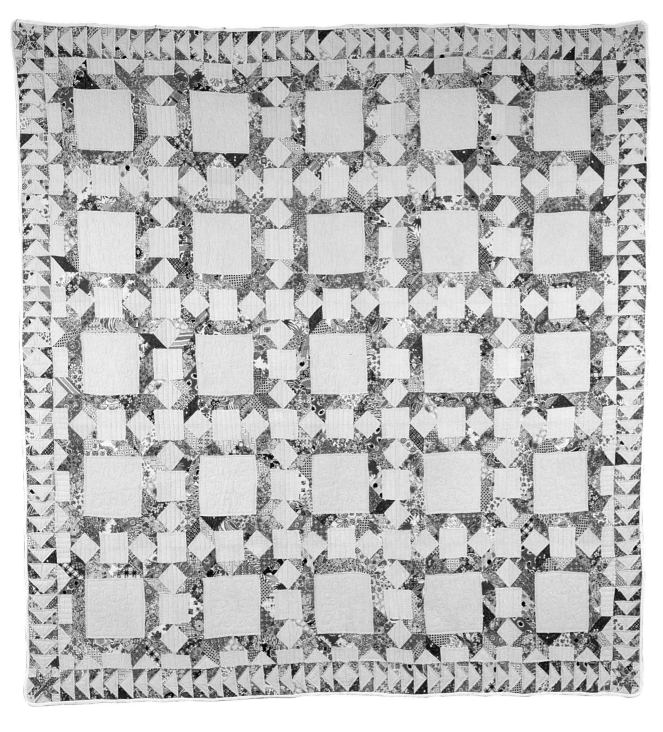

Detail of embroidered inscription on the back of Chicken Feed Sacks quilt, GQP 8652.

Figure 9.6. Chicken Feed Sacks quilt. Hazel Fulton (b. 1919), Cartersville (Bartow County), 1999. 86½" x 88½". Machine-pieced and hand-quilted cotton feed sacks. Collection of the maker. [GQP 8652]. Photo by France Dorman.

In 1986 granddaughters-in-law Judie and Jane Glaze (who are sisters-in-law) and great-granddaughter Marianne Glaze Burrows (Judie's daughter) hand quilted a quilt top made by Violet Ramsden Glaze (1891–1986) of Stone Mountain (DeKalb County) around 1927. This top was one of five quilts rescued from a discard pile during the cleanup of Violet's household after her death. The sashing fabric in the simple Nine Patch design is of white feed sacks dyed a beige-pink (fig. 9.7). Violet had turned the lettered side of the sack fabric to the inside, but on the front of the quilt, backward lettering still faintly shows through: *growing mash* (feed), *laying mash*, *Atlanta*, *Georgia*, and *Macon*.

Violet Glaze kept chickens and a cow at her home in Stone Mountain on Hairston Road, often referred to as Buttermilk Row. She sold eggs, sweet milk, buttermilk, and butter from her home. She also had a peddler's wagon, from which she sold eggs on the square in Decatur. Glaze made aprons, quilts, and quilt tops from feed sacks and used fertilizer sacks to make bedsheets and pillowcases. Her daughter-in-law, Lillie Kate Hughes Glaze (1907–2001), also used plain feed sacks for bedsheets and pillowcases. Lillie saved the thick thread used to seam the sacks, the "sack ravelings," for basting quilts into her wooden floor frame, which was supported by chairs (see fig. 8.2). She made underwear for her husband from plain sacks and used printed sacks for her six children's dresses and shirts, for aprons, and for her own housedresses. For each of her children's firstborn children, she made a simple quilt by machine from two feed sacks with batting between.

Lillie Kate's daughter-in-law, Judie Glaze, wore maternity tops made from feed sacks soon after her marriage in 1957. Judie later made a nightgown from feed sacks for her daughter Marianne, who in turn dressed her own children, twins Eric and Emily Burrows (born

Judie Glaze, Jane Glaze, and Marianne Glaze Burrows, May 2006. Photo by the author.

in 1989), in matching feed-sack outfits made for them by a quilter friend. Marianne has also made a quilt using the old sacks. Feed sacks have been used by five generations of the Glaze family.

Judie, Jane, and Marianne are enthusiastic quilters who pooled their talents by quilting Violet Glaze's top to create a lasting family heirloom. After finishing the quilt, the women drew straws to determine who would have the honor of owning it—Judie was the lucky winner.

Blanche Vandiver, who made many quilts, allowed her daughter and future daughters-in-law to each choose five quilts from her cupboard when they married. Lynn Vandiver chose a colorful fan quilt (fig. 9.8) upon her marriage to Blanche's son Arnold in 1962.

Mamie Belle Wiley grew up in the small South Georgia town of Hahira (Lowndes County). Her father was a telegraph operator for the railroad, and her mother was a homemaker who made quilts, often using feed sacks. Mamie Belle did not remember wearing clothing made from feed sacks. After graduating from Valdosta State University, Mamie Belle taught elementary school in Laurens County for two years before moving to Social Circle in Walton County in 1949 to continue her teaching career. Several years ago,

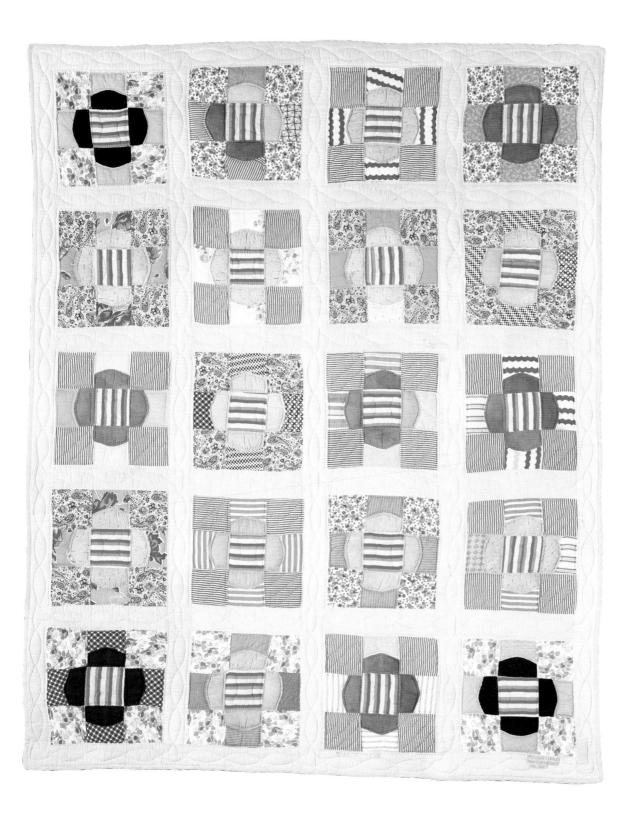

Violet Ramsden Glaze feeding the chickens in her yard, ca. 1936. Photo courtesy of Judie Glaze.

Figure 9.7. Nine Patch. Hand pieced by Violet Ramsden Glaze (1891–1986), Stone Mountain (DeKalb County), ca. 1927; hand quilted by Judie Glaze (b. 1940), Jane Glaze (b. 1936), and Marianne Glaze Burrows (b. 1960) in 1986. 64½" x 80". Cottons, including feed sacks. Collection of Judie Glaze. [GQP 0056]

Blanche Vandiver working in her garden, 1970s. Photo courtesy of Arnold and Lynn Vandiver.

Figure 9.8. Fan Quilt. Blanche Marie Brawley Vandiver (b. 1911), Dial Community (Fannin County), ca. 1950–60. 63½" x 82". Hand-pieced and -quilted cottons, mostly feed sacks. Collection of Arnold and Lynn Vandiver. [GQP 5077]. Photo by France Dorman.

Detail of figure 9.9. Bethlehem Star, GQP 3051.

a friend in Laurens County came upon some quilt tops that her mother, Mattie Perry Green (1882–1961), had made during the 1930s. Knowing that Mamie Belle had taken up quilting after her retirement, the friend gave her one of the tops, made of scraps of feed sacks, in the Bethlehem Star pattern (fig. 9.9). In 1988, Mamie Belle hand quilted the multicolored top.

Another brightly colored quilt of feed sacks, this one in the Monkey Wrench pattern, was purchased at an estate sale in Ellenwood (fig. 9.10). The quiltmaker, Rosie Bell Morgan Jones (1891–1989), was a rural Henry County homemaker. Her husband raised chickens, and Rosie Bell made clothes for her three children from feed sacks, using the scraps in quilts. Although from humble fabrics, the quilt reveals the maker's flair for design and color—small green and white nine-patch cornerstones are at the intersections of the sashing between the blocks. The bright yellow sashing is made of dyed feed sacks. The family believes that Ms. Jones made the quilt during the 1920s.

African American women used feed sacks in the same ways and for the same reasons white women did in Georgia. Not putting usable fabric from feed sacks to further use was considered wasteful. Several Quilt History Day participants told of using sacks to make children's clothing, aprons, curtains, and other household items.

Mattie Elder was born on her great-grandfather's farm in Rockdale County in 1915. When she was four—around the time the boll weevil was beginning to take hold in Georgia—her family moved to the small town of Lithonia in neighboring DeKalb County, where her father took a job as a stone cutter in the local quarry. The family kept chickens, hogs, and a cow. Elder recalls that her family was very poor; she remembers not having bread to eat with the plentiful hog meat because they didn't have money to purchase flour. Her mother and grandmother would patch everything made of cloth: from tablecloths to pillowcases to clothing. After Elder moved to Atlanta in the early 1930s to attend beauty school, she had a regular supplier of feed sacks: her uncle worked in the Atlas feed mill in Atlanta and would bring damaged sacks home. Elder taught herself to sew with feed sacks; the first dress she ever sewed for herself (around 1944) was made from them.

Detail of figure 9.10. Monkey Wrench, GQP 8174.

Mamie Belle Wiley, 2004. Mamie Belle contributed to many annual quilt shows held at the United Methodist Church in Social Circle. Photo courtesy of Molly Kimler.

Figure 9.9. Bethlehem Star. Hand pieced by Mattie Perry Green (1882–1961), Laurens County, 1930s; hand quilted by Mamie Belle Wiley (1926–2005), Social Circle (Walton County), 1988. 75" x 91". Cotton with feed sacks and blends. Collection of the Wiley family. [GQP 3051]

Figure 9.10. Monkey Wrench. Rosie Bell Morgan Jones (1891–1989), Henry County, ca. 1920s. 64½" x 82". Hand-pieced and -quilted cotton feed sacks, some home dyed. Collection of Julia Anderson Bush. [GQP 8174]

Figure 9.11. Tiger's Paw. Top hand pieced by Harriet Jones Swann (1876–ca. 1947), Ellenwood (DeKalb County), ca. 1920; hand quilted by her granddaughter Mattie Woods Elder (b. 1915), Atlanta (Fulton County), 1989. 79½" x 90". Cotton feed sacks. Collection of Mattie Woods Elder. [GQP 6726]

Figure 9.12. In this array of feed sacks are several novelty prints. Collection of the author.

Figure 9.13. A rare feed sack but one that is a favorite among Georgia collectors is this one featuring a *Gone with the Wind* motif. Collection of the author, photo by the author.

Elder inherited and quilted several of her grandmother Hattie Jones Swann's (1876–ca. 1947) quilt tops. Some of them incorporate feed sacks (fig. 9.11). More of Ms. Elder's family quilts are pictured in chapter 6, "African American Quiltmaking in Georgia."

Feed sacks were a free resource for frugal housewives in Georgia and elsewhere. When times were hard, the colorful feed sack buoyed the home economy and brightened, both literally and figuratively, many modest homes. The feed-sack era is remembered with great nostalgia by most Georgians.

In recent years quilters have rediscovered feed sacks, scouring flea markets, antique shops, and Internet auction sites for them—prices for a single sack can be as high as a hundred dollars, though they currently average between fifteen and forty dollars. Especially desirable are sacks featuring novelty prints—fabrics depicting anything from tubes of lipstick to Mexican sombreros (fig. 9.12) to French poodles near the Eiffel Tower to *Gone with the Wind* motifs (fig. 9.13). Responding to this demand, several fabric manufacturers now have lines of reproduction feed-sack fabrics and fabrics evocative of the lively prints. Georgia's love affair with feed sacks is not over yet.

Fig. 9.14. Stephanie Weinraub (b. 1990) enjoys a favorite book while wearing a feed-sack dress made for her by her mother, the author. A feed-sack quilt forms the backdrop of this 1994 photo.

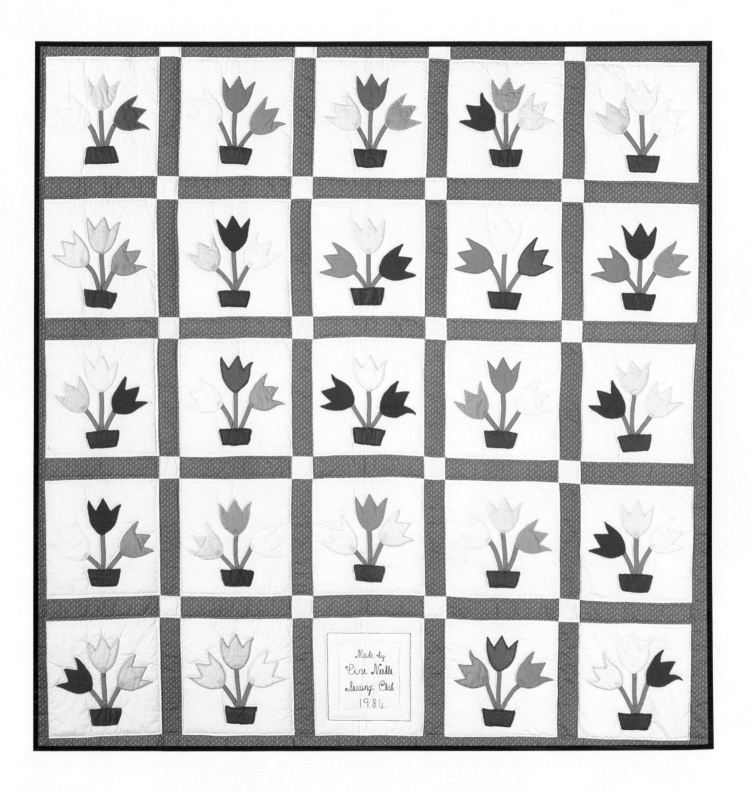

Made by
Pine Needle
Sewing Club
1984

# 10. Georgia's Quilting Groups

## Shared in the Making, Shared in the Giving

**JANICE MORRILL**

- - - - - - - - - - - - - - - - - - - - - - - - - - - - - - - -

In Georgia, as elsewhere, quilts have often been created as part of a group activity, and folklorists and other researchers have explored the dynamics and purposes of quilting groups in a substantial body of literature. In addition to documenting individual quilts, the GQP conducted a survey of contemporary quilting guilds throughout the state. Researchers from the project also interviewed some of the sewing clubs that have been in existence in Georgia—some for over fifty years—to explore the role that collaborative quiltmaking has played in these women's lives.[1] This chapter places some of the findings about Georgia's quilting groups within the historic contexts of group quilting, especially in the Southeast.

Today, as in the past, an obvious, practical reason for sharing the labor of quilting is the many hours needed to complete a single quilt top and sew the many minute stitches that hold together the layers of the quilt. Although many women have made quilts on their own, many hands working together can finish a quilt in a fraction of the time it would take one person. Gift quilts that commemorate a particular event, such as a marriage, birth, or a scheduled fund-raiser, inevitably face a race against the calendar.

In many instances, a woman pieces her quilt top alone and then draws together a group to assist with the quilting. Many Georgians recall neighbors and family being called on to quilt the completed top. Mamie Hannah Dugan, born in 1911 in Paulding County, Georgia, describes her mother's quilting parties:

> The quilting groups in North Georgia in the earlier decades of this century that I remember were informal but planned gatherings of family and neighbors. The piecer of the quilt prepared it for quilting, notified those nearby, and adjusted the daily routine to accommodate a day at the quilting frame. . . .
>
> Then oral invitations were sent out to those living nearby for a day of quilting. . . .
>
> There would be a light lunch for those who could stay the day, and thus the social functions of food, fellowship, newssharing, and artistic creation were all fulfilled in a day.[2]

Impromptu and informal quilting groups composed of neighbors and friends have been typical within black as well as white rural communities in Georgia. African American Jewel Edwards, who grew up in the farming community of Register (Bulloch County) during the 1940s, recalls neighbors assisting her mother in preparing much-needed quilts for the family. An-nie Howard, an African American from rural Putnam County, had similar recollections from the 1920s.[3]

Some contemporary quilting groups operate similarly but somewhat more formally. Beginning in the late 1970s, a group of about twelve quilters in Ephesus (Heard County) began gathering each week during the winter at a member's home to quilt the hostess's prepared top. After completing one woman's quilt, they would turn the following week to working on the quilt of the next hostess. Since 1983 this group has held quiltings in the same building (the old city hall, now used as a community center); continuing their tradition from the days they quilted in each other's homes, the member whose top is being quilted provides refreshments. The membership of the group has changed over the years, but its longevity bears witness to the observation of one member, Mrs. Lonnie Rogers, that "quilting is alive and well in Ephesus, Ga."[4]

Still, reasons for joining a quilting group go beyond the efficient accomplishment of a task. As Rogers notes, "We would all work together and have a wonderful time together and get a lot of work done at the same time." Many women who quilt in groups cite the pleasure of company as an important aspect. Wilma Cornelius was a member of the Pine Needle Sewing Club of New Lois (Berrien County) for more than sixty years. As she put it, "You can sew and you can visit—that's the greatest thing."[5] For the Pine Needle sewers (organized in 1932), the social aspect of the group is clearly important: group membership is by invitation only, with preference given to families of members. Club minutes from past years note that the group instituted a fine of five or ten cents as a way to discourage members from attending but not participating in the sewing—inflation has driven the fine up to twenty-five cents. During the 1970s, the county weekly ran several articles describing the meetings in various members' homes.

> The Pine Needle Sewing Club met Thursday, June 17, at the lovely country home of Gladys Knight on the Cecil Road with Myrtie Lou Griffin assisting as co-hostess.
>
> Everyone stopped on the way in to admire the beautiful garden of petunias, calladium bulbs, marigolds, altheas, coleus and hydrangeas....
>
> Little sewing was done as the social hour was spent with much talk about gardens, canning, freezing, and pickling, with some exchange of recipes and chatting with visitors. Carrie brought the finished quilt that the club helped her quilt at the last meeting.
>
> Delicious party refreshments of sandwiches, cookies, dainty sweets with cherry punch were served from the dining table which was overlaid with a beautiful white cloth. In the center was a lovely arrangement of blue, pink and rose hydrangeas.[6]

More recently, the Pine Needle sewers helped Berrien County celebrate its sesquicentennial in 2006. Gathered around a quilting frame, the members rode a float in the Nashville parade.

For the Pine Needle Sewing Club, quilting and other sewing have certainly been part of the fun, but the sharing of special refreshments, showing of one's home, and just being neighborly are additional sources of pleasure to the members.

That quilting gatherings provide an opportunity to socialize is often cited as a rationale for nineteenth-century rural quilting parties and bees. In the rural South, quiltings were only one example of the reciprocal work exchanges between neighbors. John A. Burrison cites several written descriptions of nineteenth-century daylong get-togethers in which work—shucking corn, log rolling, or completing a quilt—was followed with festive foods and dancing. According to Burrison, such gatherings accomplished major tasks and simultaneously helped break the isolation experienced by members of farming families.[7]

Contrary to popular conceptions, however, quilting was not primarily a rural phenomenon during the nineteenth century, nor were all quilts strictly utilitarian. Quiltmaking came to the United States as a popular trend of the wealthy, and women of leisure devoted many hours to decorative sewing and to producing impressive quilts for display. Many sewing groups of the nineteenth century involved urban women of leisure who sewed more for the symbolic value of sewing than out of necessity. According to Pat Ferrero, a "cult of domesticity" was created in response to industrialization as a way of encouraging women with increasing amounts of time on their hands to remain within the home. For these women, the products and processes of quiltmaking expressed social ideals of femininity: quilts symbolized "the frugal and industrious use of scraps both of fabric and time, and the creation of a practical and beautiful product that embodied women's role of nurturing and serving others."[8]

Quiltmaking, it seems, has long served to provide more than warm bedcoverings and an opportunity to get together. By Ferrero's interpretation, beginning in the nineteenth century, quilting served as a way of building identity for many women, and as a way of expressing values. So what does a quilt symbolize? Quilts—whether constructed by urban or rural women, by an individual or by a group—are aesthetic and technical achievements. They serve as tangible, lasting markers of a woman's skill and hard work. By virtue of these characteristics, and because quilts are often shared—in the making and in the giving—quilts communicate something about their makers. Their

Figure 10.1. Tulips in Pots. Pine Needle Sewing Club, New Lois Community (Berrien County), 1984. 82" x 100". Hand-appliquéd and -quilted cotton. Collection of Jane S. Knight. [GQP 4721]

This quilt was one of seven made as fund-raisers. The proceeds from each quilt were designated for a different charity. The lucky winner of this quilt was Gladys D. Knight, a member of the club who worked on it. It now belongs to her daughter-in-law.

weighty symbolic value is how several researchers explain the modern-day quilting revival. According to author Catherine A. Cerney,

> The quilt is the key symbol of the [contemporary] quilt subculture. It "summarizes" quilt tradition by synthesizing the life experiences of nineteenth-century women and relating these as values to modern society. By virtue of its form, the quilt represents the contributions of a group of women to the home life of a historic America, expresses the priority that women have given to family and social relatedness, and evokes powerful emotions from quilter and nonquilter, from women and men.[9]

It makes sense that one of the main motivations for forming quilting groups is that these groups function as a setting for symbolic communication. In quilting groups women have an opportunity to show their artistic achievements and learn techniques of quilting while sharing food, friendship, and news. They also find an opportunity to affirm their values publicly, joining with others in creating shared definitions of themselves as women.

The Busy Bee Homemakers Club of Dalton is true to its name. Started in 1937 as the Busy Bee Club and undergoing a few name changes over the years, this group has made more than 1,500 quilts, most of which have been given to the needy or raffled off for various charities. During the 1930s members collected signatures to petition for electricity in southern Whitfield County. In 1941 they raised funds to build a clubhouse by selling aprons, bedspreads, and quilts and holding rummage sales. Over the years they have sewn other items for hospitals and the Red Cross. A report for 1955 lists the activities and items of the year, which included 200 visits to the sick, 55 get-well cards, 65 trays of food, 22 hours worked at the hospital, 50 flowers, 58 groceries and other items to the needy, 64 pieces of clothing, 19 quilts, 4 sheets, and 43 birthday cards from the club. They still gather every Wednesday to quilt in the same clubhouse (over the years updated with running water and air conditioning), occasionally earning extra income by taking in quilt tops from nonmembers for quilting.

The Busy Bees are not unique in any of these respects. Several other clubs—some started by county extension services as home demonstration clubs, some by groups of neighbors—share a similar history. Other sewing groups thus far identified include the Rosebud Women's Club of Gwinnett County (organized 1932); the Pine Needle Quilters of Lilburn, Gwinnett County (organized 1951 and not affiliated with the Pine Needle Sewing Club of New Lois); and the Luxomni Quilters, near Lilburn, Gwinnett County (organized 1948). Like the Busy Bees, each of these groups has sewn and raised funds for charity and has built a clubhouse by seeking donated materials and labor and by raising funds. They have sold everything from newspapers to doughnuts and have sponsored baseball games, plays, and rummage sales to raise money; they have sewn for soldiers, invalids, cancer and tuberculosis patients; and they have donated to various causes. In addition, they have supported fellow members in distress, emotionally and at times financially.

Club minutes and personal recollections of members show that, in addition to giving time to community needs, they worked on the upkeep of their clubhouses. The effort involved in raising money to build, outfit, and maintain a clubhouse suggests their motivation to have a space of their own rather than meet in members' homes. This motivation might be explained by the convenience in the clubhouse of having the quilting frame accessible at all times. In a sense, however, the building itself affirms the solidarity of the group and its firm feeling of place within the commu-

Figure 10.2. Sampler. Carole Thorpe (b. 1945), formerly of Lilburn (Gwinnett County), now of Hampton (Henry County) 1984. 105" x 103". Cotton hand pieced by fellowship group members; hand quilted by Carole Thorpe. Collection of the maker. [GQP 8171]

An example of a fellowship and quilting group was the friendship group that twelve members of the Gwinnett Quilters' Guild formed in 1983. The members in turn helped each other complete blocks for a quilt. Each member decided what kind of quilt she would like and purchased the fabric. Names were drawn monthly to determine the order in which the quilts would be made. The woman whose name was drawn distributed fabric and provided a pattern, and each member made a block for her. Once she received the finished blocks from the other members, it was up to her to assemble and finish the quilt.

*Janice Morrill*

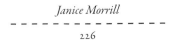

Busy Bee members Irene Ragan and Opal Defore at work in their clubhouse in Dalton, putting a quilt in the frame, 1995. Photo by Anita Weinraub.

nity. In addition, the members' clubhouse efforts and responsibilities express in a tangible way both their inclination to fill their spare time not with idle pleasure but with productive tasks, and their enjoyment in sharing productive work with like-minded women. In this respect, club membership is an expression of personal identity.

Over the years, the Busy Bees, the Rosebuds, the Pine Needle Quilters, and the Luxomni Quilters have clearly done much more than get together over a quilting frame. These women have essentially taken their roles as homemakers and caregivers into more public settings. By setting up a home away from home (albeit to be used but once a week), they have brought their personal skills and values into the social setting of the club while also positively impacting the broader community.

Their industriousness and their assistance to others in the group and within the community are striking. Their activities demonstrate concern for others and their willingness to serve. For these groups a quilt is, like their clubhouse, a physical expression of their hard work. Author Joyce Ice describes how the term *work* is used often to evaluate quilting; there is frequent, positive acknowledgment that a great deal of time and effort goes into the creation of a quilt.[10] These particular sewing clubs—and others who quilt for neighbors and the needy—perpetuate and honor the historical reciprocal work relationships of farming families.

Frugality, hard work, and neighborliness—the giving of time to others—all express the values of southern farming communities, values that are rooted in the subsistence lifestyle that is the heritage of the South. This is not to suggest that these values are exclusively southern, only that they are decidedly southern, among rural Southerners in particular. In the modern marketplace, quilts are also commodities. Quilters can sell or raffle them and put the money to good purpose. This makes the quilt even more valuable to the task-minded club as a means of contributing to society.

Since a quilt is literally a piecing together of fragments into a whole, some say it expresses the social bonds between those working together on the quilt and—if the quilt is given as a gift—between the makers and recipient.[11] Quiltmaking not only forms connections between members of a quilting group but also binds the quilters to the community at large. Quilts can be given as commemorative gifts or raffled and the proceeds donated to community causes. Both strategies are used not only by well-established clubs such as the Busy Bees, the Rosebud Club, and the Pine Needle Sewing Club of Berrien County but also by the more recently formed quilting guilds of Georgia.

As part of the quilting revival, more than seventy quilting guilds have been organized in Georgia since the late 1970s. Guilds differ from sewing or quilting clubs in that their focus is on sharing information and techniques. Georgia quilting guilds hold business meetings and sponsor programs rather than working together on quilts (although many guilds orga-

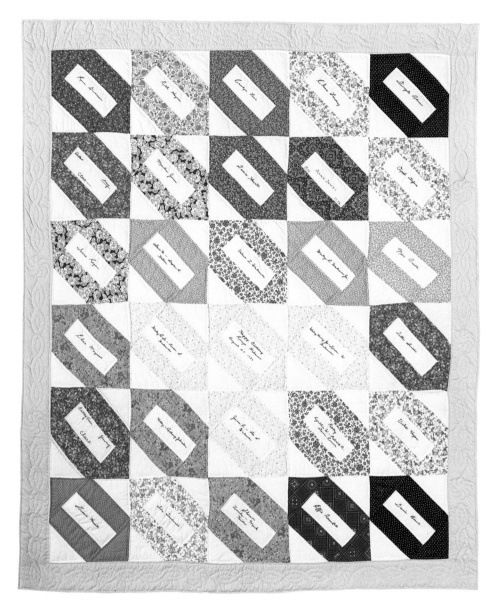

Figure 10.3. Friendship Quilt. Made by members of the Busy Bee Homemakers Club, Dalton (Whitfield County), 1994. 68" x 80". Cotton blocks assembled by machine by Romye Waldraven; hand quilted by Irene Ragan. Collection of Romye Waldraven. [GQP 8162]

The Busy Bees make gifts to one another as well as to the community. One of their traditions is to present each member with enough friendship blocks to make a quilt on the occasion of her eightieth birthday. The blocks in this quilt were presented to member Romye Clark Walraven. Another quilt made by a member of the Busy Bees can be seen at figure 5.10.

Figure 10.4. The Rosebud Women's Club of Grayson (Gwinnett County), quilting at a local fair, ca. 1992.

nize subgroups for weekly quiltings; the "bee" groups of the East Cobb Guild, which has more than two hundred members, are organized by zip code). Guild members declare their enthusiasm about quilting and their dedication to their quilting groups in a variety of ways, from sponsoring shows to wearing pieced name tags bearing their club insignia along with assorted pins from quilt associations, meetings, and shows attended.

Unlike the members of the Busy Bees, Pine Needles, and Rosebuds, these quilting guild members are not usually neighbors, and guild membership encompasses a wider range of backgrounds and age groups than the typical community sewing club. Still, guilds promote a sense of community by organizing holiday parties, gift exchanges, family picnics, and other events that encourage friendship. They also reach out as a group to the larger community.

The Gwinnett Quilters Guild, for example, contributed from its treasury to the family of a local slain police officer, and gave to the widow a wall hanging bearing signatures of fellow officers. Over 75 percent of the guilds surveyed indicated that they perform similar types of community service, often using proceeds

from quilt raffles. The tradition of the quilting group as a gift-giving agent engaged in community service has held in its new incarnation as a guild. In the modern South and elsewhere, the definition of *community* has expanded well beyond the immediate neighborhood, and quilters' contributions affirm these new definitions.

No better example of this process can be found than the 1996 Olympic Gift Quilts. Quiltmakers throughout Georgia responded with enthusiasm to the call for quilts to welcome the Olympic nations. For these Georgians, participating in this project extended the legacy of quilting groups, as it was an expression of their identities as southerners. The Georgia Quilt Project, originators of the Olympic Gift Quilts, put forward the project as a gesture of "southern hospitality." Indeed, the giving of quilts to Olympic athletes and organizing committees expressed much about southern values. These quilts conveyed the same sentiments of hard work, frugality, and neighborliness that cause quilting and sewing groups to flourish in Georgia. (See more on the Olympic Gift Quilts in the next chapter.)

A dynamic new guild in metropolitan Atlanta is the Brown Sugar Stitchers. In the winter of 2000, Nancy Franklin and Jocelyn Carter began efforts to bring together area quilters at the Wesley Chapel–William C. Brown Library in southern DeKalb County. As word spread, an enthusiastic group of stitchers coalesced and held its first show the following May. Today the group's fifty members range in age from the twenties to the seventies and are a self-described "diverse group of African American quilters." Like other guilds, the Brown Sugar Stitchers conduct monthly meetings with programs, classes, and challenges. Its members are also community minded; among its public service activities is the annual donation of quilts to

## Signature Quilt

This signature quilt was made as a fund-raiser in the late nineteenth century by Mrs. Margaret Culberson, mother of Hubert Culberson, who was the first pastor of Park Street United Methodist Church in Atlanta. Women of the church sold spaces on the quilt at ten cents each in support of a new church building and then had the names of the sponsors inscribed on the quilt. The 810 names on the quilt read like a who's who of early Atlanta and include Mayor John B. Goodwin, State Treasurer Daniel N. Speer, Governor Henry D. McDaniel, and other elected officials. Among the prominent Atlantans are John Collier (lawyer, judge, and resident of the area since 1823), Jonathan Norcross (merchant and resident since 1844), John S. Candler (lawyer and judge), Evan P. Howell (editor of the *Constitution*), Er Lawshé (jeweler), the founders of Rich's Department Store (brothers Morris, Emanuel, and Daniel Rich), and Laura Haygood (Girls' High School principal and foreign missionary). The identities of two parties—Old Man Bennett and Snowball Jones—remain unknown. Jeff Pierce, a bookkeeper for Atlanta real-estate developer George W. Adair, inscribed the names.

Signature Quilt. Margaret Culberson (dates unknown), ca. 1895. 80" x 72". Hand-pieced and -quilted cotton, machine bound. Atlanta History Center collection, 1978. 137.M1. Photo courtesy of the Atlanta History Center.

Detail of Signature Quilt showing the name of Joel Chandler Harris, author of the Uncle Remus stories.

Figure 10.5. Butterflies, Petals, and Petticoats. Yellow Daisy Quilters' Guild, Stone Mountain (DeKalb County), 1992. 90" x 116". Machine-pieced, hand-appliquéd, hand-quilted cotton. Private collection. [GQP 7954]

Thirty-seven members of the Yellow Daisy Quilters' Guild made blocks for this fund-raiser quilt, and about twenty-five members worked on the hand quilting.

Renee Allen, 2005. Photo by France Dorman.

Hallelujah. Renee Allen (b. 1959), Ellenwood (DeKalb County), 2005. 45" x 46". Hand-appliquéd and hand-quilted cotton. Collection of the maker. [GQP 8656]. Photo by France Dorman.

## Renee Allen

A member of the Brown Sugar Stitchers, quiltmaker Renee says her fellow guild members help inspire her. Although most depictions of churches portray the altar, in this wall hanging Renee has chosen to "turn this around" and show the congregation. As she says, "The spirit of the Lord is everywhere; it is the people who give a church life." The figures are not static but in motion, and the multicolored background lends even more vibrancy to the piece. Hand-painted windows, flowers, and beads embellish the quilt.

Although a lifelong sewer, Renee didn't take up quilting until 2000 as a way to relax and as a form of creative expression. Self-taught, she gets her designs from her imagination and from personal experiences. She works primarily in appliqué. She named this work Hallelujah because that is the highest form of praise.

Originally from Philadelphia, Renee now resides in DeKalb County, where she teaches career technology at the Open Campus high school.

Jan Brashears, ca. 1998.

Figure 10.6. Xel-Ha. Jan Brashears (b. 1942), Canton (Cherokee County), formerly of Atlanta (DeKalb County), 1994. 48" x 53". Machine-pieced, hand-embellished, machine-quilted cotton. Collection of the maker. [GQP 8175]

Jan likes to use traditional blocks in new ways. This wall hanging features an off-center Feathered Star, several other Ohio Star blocks, and Seminole patchwork. This piece was inspired by a vacation in Mexico. Xel-Ha is a barrier reef off the Yucatán peninsula, where salt and fresh water commingle. Jan is a former member of the Art Cloth Network and the Surface Design Association.

the Carrie Steele-Pitts Home, a child-caring agency in Atlanta.[12] The activities of the Brown Sugar Stitchers enable members to find satisfaction in their individual accomplishments while building community ties through their charitable efforts.

For all of these groups, from the traditional sewing circles to the contemporary guilds, quiltmaking is a way of both reaching in—solidifying bonds with other women and one's identity as a woman—and reaching out. While Georgia's quilters continue to use quilts to serve the community, there has also been a change in focus. The mission of community service is not as essential to contemporary quilting guilds, for example, as it is to the Busy Bees and Rosebuds. For guild members, friendship and community service are aspects of their group activities, but greater emphasis is on the individual and her product. Says Jan Brashears of Atlanta: "My membership in several guilds exposes me to other people and their techniques. It keeps me up-to-date with what's happening outside my realm of activity and provides fellowship, for the lack of a better word, with those who care and understand my artistry."[13] Techniques and designs are much discussed at guild meetings, and guild newsletters announce challenges (competitions using prescribed fabrics), workshops, lectures, and quilt shows. Since the 1970s such activities have brought quilting into greater prominence and have spawned specialty shops featuring quilting fabrics and supplies. As Georgia quilter and quilt researcher Holly Anderson points out, guilds are largely responsible for bringing this traditional craft into the contemporary art world.

Comparing the quilting guilds of the early twenty-first century with the quilting and sewing clubs of the mid-twentieth century, a difference in focus is obvious. For many contemporary guild members, the quilt is largely an artistic product—an end in itself. By contrast, for the earlier, rural quilting groups such as the Busy Bees and the Pine Needles, quilts were primarily useful items—they served as bedcoverings, for fundraisers, and as gifts for the needy and for loved ones.[14] Although some of the quilts such groups produced were stunning in their beauty and workmanship, quilting was more about social relationships and meeting the needs of the community than about producing a work of art. As Wilma Cornelius of the Pine Needle Sewing Club wrote, "We've sewed ourselves through a Depression and a World War, through the droughts and floods of this farm community, and through the pleasure-filled lives of children, grandchildren, and great-grandchildren."[15] For such women, quilts have provided good tools for achieving practical and social ends. Through quilting, these women have found opportunities for communication, sharing their industriousness and community-wide caring, and thus expressing their heritage as Southerners and as women.

# 11. The Olympic Gift Quilts

## Georgia Quiltmakers Welcome the World

**ANITA ZALESKI WEINRAUB**

- - - - - - - - - - - - - - - - - - - - - - - - - - - - - - - - -

*Native Americans presented blankets as gifts only to honored friends,*
*those whose deeds were admired or whose position was esteemed.*
*In that tradition, I present this quilt to you, your Centennial*
*Olympic Games 1996 team and your country.*

—from inscription on reverse of Olympic Gift Quilt Lone Star:
That's Not What You Are, made by Sally Schuyler, Atlanta

"Look into the faces of these athletes. . . . Look into their faces and you will see the possibilities . . . for if we believe, there is nothing we cannot achieve . . . and if we dream, all things are possible." William Porter "Billy" Payne, chairman and CEO of the Atlanta Committee for the Olympic Games (ACOG), spoke these moving words during the opening ceremony of the Centennial Olympic Games in Atlanta on July 19, 1996. Georgia quilters, however, had already met and looked into the faces of athletes and officials from 197 countries during the Team Welcome Ceremonies in Atlanta's Olympic Village in the days just prior to the opening ceremony. A handmade Georgia quilt was made for each participating country's flag bearer as well as for the head of each country's delegation—gestures of welcome, goodwill, and friendship. The quiltmakers of Georgia conceived and implemented a dramatic and appropriate celebration of the Olympic Games, which were being held in the South for the first time. In describing this Olympic Gift of Quilts, Billy Payne stated that these quilts would convey to the recipients the "sincerity of our welcome and give them a special prized possession, an expression, in fact, of who we are."

Making quilts to commemorate and celebrate events is nothing new to quiltmakers. The GQP documented quilts celebrating the 1876 Centennial, the 1976 Bicentennial, both world wars (V for Victory quilts), and the 1990 Gulf War. Quilts commemorating local or personal events were also presented at Quilt History Days—presentation quilts to an eligible bachelor or departing pastor or loved one, and many, many quilts made for a wedding or the birth of a child. Quilts commemorating the jubilee or centennial years of churches, municipalities, and even a park were also documented.

In addition to commemorating and celebrating a

Figure 11.1. The delegation from American Samoa poses with the quilt that was presented to its flag bearer (at the far right). Photo by Anita Z. Weinraub.

global event, the Olympic quilts, as they came to be called, were also presented as gifts. It would be interesting indeed to determine what percentage of quilts over the centuries have been made as gifts. Many, if not most, commemorative quilts are also gifts—certainly all baby quilts, presentation quilts, and many wedding quilts are gifts.

Quiltmakers have also historically made quilts as gifts to strangers in need. *New York Beauties*, the book resulting from the research of the New York State Quilt Project, reports that the women of New York made more than 26,000 quilts for soldiers during the Civil War.[1] At present, most quilting groups in Georgia and around the country make quilts for battered women or abused children shelters, for Ronald McDonald houses, for at-risk babies, for visually impaired children, and as fund-raisers (raffle quilts) to support a myriad of causes (see the previous chapter). Quiltmakers have a long tradition of using their needle skills to help others.

However, never before had a gift of quilts been organized quite like the GQP's Olympic Gift of Quilts—quilts made to celebrate a peacetime event, given as gestures of welcome to unknown participants from around the world. Never before had a gift of quilts been distributed worldwide. Never before had an Olympic Games embraced the symbolism inherent in a quilt and chosen the quilt as a design motif to represent its games. Yet all of this and more occurred in Atlanta, Georgia, during the summer of 1996.

The GQP conceived the idea of a gift of quilts soon after the closing ceremony of the Barcelona Summer Olympic Games in 1992 and put together a proposal for ACOG. Preliminary discussions and planning of the Olympic Gift of Quilts took place that autumn.

The host city customarily presents a small gift to each of the chefs de mission heading each country's Olympic delegation, but the idea of presenting handmade quilts was a dramatic escalation of that tradition. By presenting a second quilt to each country's flag bearer—the athlete chosen by the teams to represent their country—individual athletes would also be recognized regardless of their subsequent performance in the games. It was determined by lottery which countries would receive which quilts.

No restrictions were placed on quilt design other than to specify overall size as fifty-four by seventy inches—a large lap or "personal" size—and to prohibit use of the official Olympic symbols (rings, torch, mascot, etc.). Any construction technique was permitted (piecing, appliqué, etc.; by hand or machine), and quilting was to be either by hand or machine (no tied quilts). Because cotton is a Georgia specialty as well as the traditional medium of quiltmakers, guidelines suggested that quilts be made from all cotton. Quiltmakers were required to sign each quilt they made, and some included a personal message with their label. Sewn on the reverse of each quilt was also a distinctive label especially designed by ACOG for this purpose.

When the Olympic Gift Quilt program was announced in January 1993, it was met with immediate

enthusiasm by Georgia's quiltmakers and by the media. Pledges to make quilts flooded the GQP's mailbox. A month after the formal announcement, the first quilts were submitted. All 396 quilts were completed by August 1995, in time to be photographed for inclusion in a book on the Olympic quilt project. From January through May 1996, more than 68,000 people viewed the quilts at the Atlanta History Center in an exhibition dedicated to Georgia's Olympic Gift Quilts.[2] Two special Olympic Gift Quilts, as well as the Quilt of Leaves (see below), were also part of the exhibit: one was given to International Olympic Committee President Juan Antonio Samaranch for the permanent collection of the Olympic Museum in Lausanne, Switzerland, and one was given to Billy Payne. The seventeen weeks of the Atlanta History Center's exhibition was the only time the quilts were ever together in one place—after the Olympic Games, our Georgia quilts traveled to all parts of the globe.

The Olympic quiltmakers were honored in many ways. A special pin was created and issued to them by ACOG. This pin could not be purchased; it had to be earned. One quiltmaker turned down an offer of six hundred dollars for her pin from a pin collector at Centennial Park in Atlanta. A commemorative photograph was taken of the quiltmakers at the state capitol in Atlanta (fig. 11.4). The Atlanta History Center selected three Olympic quilts to be reproduced at half size by their makers; these replicas became part of the center's Shaping Traditions: Folk Arts in a Changing South permanent exhibit. The Atlanta History Center is the repository for the Atlanta Committee for the Olympic Games Collection and for the signature Centennial Olympic Games exhibition that opened on the tenth anniversary of the 1996 Summer Olympics.

One of the greatest honors came when ACOG developed the design motif, called the Look of the

Figure 11.2. This label was stitched onto the back of each Olympic quilt.

Figure 11.3. Nicos Kartakoullis, chef de mission of Cyprus, accepts his quilt, Georgia Pines, from Susie Dumas and Teresa Duley, representatives of the group that made the quilt, the Skipped Stitches of the Heart of Georgia Quilt Guild of Macon. Photo by Anita Z. Weinraub.

Games, for the 1996 games. The name of the "look" of the 1996 Centennial Olympic Games was A Quilt of Leaves. The motif, an askew patchwork of squares with superimposed leaves representing Atlanta's greenery, appeared everywhere during the 1996 games: on banners throughout the city and at every venue, on tickets, hurdles, kiosks, and volunteers' uniforms. The symbolism inherent in a quilt motif—small pieces or patchwork of cultures coming together to create a stronger whole—gave greater depth and meaning to the look. The Olympic committee commissioned the GQP to create a quilt of this design. GQP volunteers Barbara Abrelat (now Dorn) and Sammie Simpson created the special piece (fig. 11.7). Abrelat did the color placement and pieced and appliquéd the top, and Simpson did the hand quilting. The Look of the Games was revealed to the world at a press conference in July 1994 by unveiling the Quilt of Leaves.

The quilts reflected the diversity and creative vision of the quilts being made in Georgia then and now. Star motifs appeared in many of them; red, white, and blue were popular color choices; and many quilts incorporated symbolism. Although the Olympic rings and other specific symbology were prohibited, quiltmakers incorporated the colors of the Olympic rings. Traditional quilt patterns were popular, especially Log Cabin and Trip around the World. Names given to the quilts expressed the emotional exuberance and well-wishing of the makers. Names included Olympic Stars, Garden of Dreams, Go for the Gold, Fields of Dreams, Golden Dreams, When You Wish Upon a Star, Shoot for the Stars, Simply . . . Congratulations, and Friendship Album. Some names made reference to Georgia, such as When Cotton Was King, Georgia Pines and Kudzu Vines, Windows over Georgia, Dogwood Dreams, and Georgia on My Mind. The quiltmakers were as diverse as their quilts—all races, representing all walks of life and times of life, men and women, groups, individuals, beginning quilters and experienced needleworkers.

All of the Olympic quilts were documented by the GQP. The majority of makers indicated that they chose to contribute to this gift of quilts because they wanted to participate in some small way in the Olympic Games. Barbara Abrelat expressed this well: "I'm not an athlete. I don't have time to volunteer. I don't speak a foreign language. But this is a way for me to participate." A quilter from Ellenwood (DeKalb County) inscribed a personal message on the reverse of her quilt: "Reach for the Stars is the name of this quilt. I've been quilting for four years. When I heard about the Olympic quilt donation, I just had to be in on the fun. I hope you enjoy it as much as I enjoyed making it for you. Atlanta is proud to be your host. Your friend, Marty Ruppert."

Some quiltmakers, including Peggy Littrell of Raleigh, North Carolina (formerly of Stone Mountain, DeKalb County), saved scraps from their quilts and made a miniature of the same design to keep as a memento. The Carrie Bibelhauser–Effie Hall sister duo went one step further. Carrie, of Louisville, Kentucky (but then living in Norcross, Gwinnett County), and Effie, of Charlotte, North Carolina, met for weekend sessions to create Kaleidoscope, their first collaborative effort (fig. 11.8). They were so taken with the result that they couldn't bear to give it away; in the tradition of the modern quiltmaker, they made a beeline back to the fabric store and made two duplicate quilts.

Margaret LaBenne of Hendersonville, North Carolina, formerly of Tucker (Gwinnett County), made one of the first Olympic quilts submitted. She was so enthusiastic about the gift of quilts that she couldn't stop making them, eventually making eight, some with friends and some on her own. Part of an annual quilting retreat to Hilton Head Island, South Carolina, with similarly impassioned friends was spent making one Olympic quilt after another; the Jacob's Ladder quilt (fig. 11.9) presented to Grenada was made with traded fabrics from that trip. Marge's other quilts were awarded to American Samoa, Burkina Faso, the Central African Republic, Ghana, St. Lucia, Sweden, and the Virgin Islands.

Some of the personal labels quiltmakers added to the reverse of the quilts touch upon symbolism and offer messages of global friendship. Carrie and Effie, the sisters noted earlier, wrote on the reverse of their gift quilt, "This quilt would not have been possible without the Olympic spirit of perseverance and cooperation. We like to think that our efforts, in a small way, resemble those of the many athletes and nations around the globe that have come together to make these Olympic Games a reality." Kathy Hefner of Peachtree City (Fayette County) inscribed on the back of her Dogwoods around the World Quilt, which was presented to the chef de mission of Bolivia: "Dogwood blossoms are a

symbol of the city of Atlanta. The pattern of this quilt is Trip around the World. Your trip to the 1996 Olympics may have been from across the country or across the globe. When you return home, I hope you will take with you many memories of your stay in Atlanta and the warmth of friendships forged by competition and camaraderie. This quilt is made for you as a token of my friendship. As you travel back to your home, a piece of me will make a 'trip around the world' with you."

A particularly eloquent sentiment was expressed by Priscilla Casciolini of Grayson (Gwinnett County), formerly of Stone Mountain (DeKalb County), on the reverse of her Lone Star Sampler quilt: "This gift of an American Sampler quilt honors the pioneers of the American frontier and the Olympic athletes of the world who have followed their impossible dreams and won their places in history."

Figure 11.4. Olympic quiltmakers gathered at the state capitol in Atlanta for a commemorative photo in August 1996. Members of the Georgia Quilt Project board hold the banner at the bottom. Several of the Olympic quilts appear in the photo.

*The Olympic Gift Quilts*

Figure 11.5. City of Gold. Original design by Barbara Abrelat (now Dorn, b. 1944), Canton (Cherokee County), formerly of Decatur (DeKalb County), 1994. 52" x 70". Machine-pieced and -quilted cotton. Collection of the Olympic Museum in Lausanne, Switzerland. [GQP 9015]

The phoenix is a traditional symbol for the City of Atlanta. In Barbara's piece, its wings are spread, welcoming the Olympic participants.

Figure 11.6. Georgia on My Mind. Margaret Jenkins (1935–2000), N. Augusta (Aiken County), South Carolina, 1995. 52" x 68". Machine-pieced, hand- and machine-appliquéd, machine-embroidered, machine-quilted cotton. This quilt was one of three also made in half size for the Atlanta History Center. [GQP 9346]

One huge, glorious, gigantic Georgia peach is what Margaret wanted the recipient to take back to his or her country. Athletes exercise at the bottom with the Atlanta skyline as a backdrop. Margaret machine embroidered the cities and years of all the modern summer Olympic Games in the border. The quilting world suffered a loss when Margaret succumbed to breast cancer in 2000.

Barbara Abrelat personally presented her quilt to the head of the International Olympic Committee, Juan Antonio Samaranch, in 1996. Photo by Anita Z. Weinraub.

Margaret Jenkins was on hand to witness the presentation of her quilt to John Coates, the chef de mission of Australia, who presented it to Liane Tooth, Australia's beloved women's hockey gold medalist. Margaret's hand-painted T-shirt matches her quilt. Photo by Anita Z. Weinraub.

Figure 11.7. Quilt of Leaves. Barbara Abrelat (now Dorn, b. 1944), Canton (Cherokee County), formerly of Decatur (DeKalb County), and Sammie Simpson (b. 1941), Murphy, North Carolina, formerly of Alpharetta (Fulton County), 1994. 69" x 70¾". Machine-pieced, hand-appliquéd, hand-quilted cotton. Centennial Olympic Games Collection at the Atlanta History Center. [GQP 8137]

Barbara Abrelat determined the color placement and created the quilt top; Sammie Simpson hand quilted the top of this piece for the Georgia Quilt Project as a commission from ACOG. This motif appeared everywhere in Atlanta during the 1996 Centennial Olympic Games.

Barbara Dorn (formerly Abrelat) (*left*), 2005 and Sammie Simpson (*right*), ca. 1995.

Sisters Carrie Bibelhauser (*left*) and Effie Hall (*right*) in 2003.

Figure 11.8. Kaleidoscope. Carrie Spurlin Bibelhauser (b. 1949), Lousville, Kentucky, formerly of Norcross (Gwinnett County), and Effie Spurlin Hall (b. 1952), Charlotte, N.C., 1994. 49" x 69". Machine-pieced and -quilted cotton. The quilt was given to the chef de mission of Israel. [GQP 9102]

Carrie said: "Even though we are sisters, we approach quiltmaking in totally different ways. Effie thinks the quilt through from beginning to end before she starts working on it while I see a design or fabric I like and jump right in without a lot of planning or calculations. This is our first collaboration. Effie did all of the designing and cutting while I sat at the sewing machine furiously sewing pieces together as fast as she could hand them to me."

Marge LaBenne was on hand at several of the team welcome ceremonies to see her quilts presented and to meet the recipients. Here she chats with members of the delegation from Ghana, who received another of her quilts. Photo by Anita Z. Weinraub.

Figure 11.9. Jacob's Ladder. Margaret LaBenne (b. 1952), Hendersonville, N.C., formerly of Tucker (Gwinnett County), 1995. 54" x 72". Cotton. Machine pieced by Marge LaBenne; machine quilted by Sandra Haynes, Roswell (Fulton County). Given to the chef de mission of Grenada. [GQP 9367]

Bonnie Finne, ca. 1996.

Figure 11.10. Seasons. Original design based on the traditional Maple Leaf pattern, Bonnie Finne (b. 1942), Atlanta (Fulton County), 1995. 54" x 70". Machine-pieced, hand-appliquéd, hand-quilted cotton. Given to the chef de mission of Canada. [GQP 9339]

Bonnie wanted to represent the colors of the landscape in Atlanta as the seasons progress from winter (upper left) through spring, summer, fall and back to winter (lower right). Bonnie was inspired by a picture of a cape made by Susan Deal in an article in *Wearable Art* magazine. It employed the technique of using the Maple Leaf pattern with adjacent blocks flowing together in a kind of tessellated pattern. Bonnie used about 130 different fabrics in the quilt, both purchased fabrics and scraps. She has sewn since childhood, made theatrical costumes, and worked as a technical artist at the Advance and Vogue pattern companies. She now has her own economic consulting firm.

Figure 11.11. We Come. Original design, Shirley Erickson (b. 1934), Athens (Clarke County), 1995. 54" x 70". Machine-pieced, hand-appliquéd, hand-quilted cotton. The quilt was presented to the chef de mission of Korea. [GQP 9378]

The colors used in this quilt are those of the Olympic rings, and the stick figures represent Olympic events. The background diamonds represent all of the athletes who train so hard for the Olympics. On the back, Shirley inscribed an original poem that begins "We come together from near and distant lands."

Cindy Richards and Great Britain's chef de mission at the presentation of her quilt. Photo by Anita Z. Weinraub.

Shirley Erickson in 1996 with two fans given to her by the Korean delegation. Photo by Anita Z. Weinraub.

Figure 11.12. Go for the Gold—A Heart of Gold. Original design, Cindy Rounds Richards (b. 1957), Snellville (Gwinnett County), formerly of Decatur (DeKalb County), 1995. Machine-pieced and machine-quilted cotton. This quilt was presented to the chef de mission of Great Britain; a half-size version is in the permanent folklife collection at the Atlanta History Center. [GQP 9390]

One of the most talked-about Olympic quilts was this one, composed entirely of 1½" squares of fabric in the watercolor style. Cindy created a beautiful golden heart on an awards podium. Just barely visible in the machine-quilting stitches is an athlete (modeled after her daughter, Megan, a gymnast) standing on the "gold" platform and holding a bouquet of flowers. Cindy collected floral fabrics during vacations to Seattle and Utah and pondered the design for about a year before beginning the quilt.

Inscribed on the back of her quilt is "Go for the Gold—A Heart of Gold," an original poem by Cindy. Cindy noted: "I feel strongly that each of us needs to seek out and develop the talents God gave to us. The physical talents of the Olympians are easy to recognize as being finely honed. Spiritual talents often go unnoticed and unapplauded. Kindness, service, loving our fellow man regardless of age, beauty, economic status, gender, race, religion, or color; self-discipline, slow to anger, soft words, etc."

Figure 11.13. Panorama of the stage at a team welcome ceremony, Atlanta's Olympic Village, July 1996. Wall hangings made by Barbara Abrelat (now Dorn), part of a series depicting athletes, filled the spaces between gift quilts.

*Anita Zaleski Weinraub*

As word spread of Georgia quiltmakers' magnanimous gesture of welcome to visitors from around the world, quilts and quiltmaking received widespread recognition. Georgia's quiltmakers were invited to create a "quilters' corner" at the Uniform Distribution Center (UDC) in Decatur, where from May through July 1996 over a million pieces of clothing and accessories were distributed to more than fifty thousand Olympic volunteers and staff. Marge LaBenne coordinated quilters to staff the corner daily for the three months, greet volunteers and staff from all over the world, share works in progress, and invite onlookers to take a stitch or two around the frame. Quilts were hung around the walls of the UDC next to Olympic banners. Many good things came to quiltmakers and to the art of quiltmaking as a result of the Olympic Gift of Quilts.

Unprecedented in Olympic Games history— though not likely to be repeated in the post–September 11 era—quiltmakers were welcomed into the international zone of the Olympic Village to witness the presentation of their quilts. More than two hundred

Olympic quiltmakers accepted ACOG's invitation to come to the Olympic Village when their quilts were presented at a traditional ceremony welcoming each country's delegation. The Team Welcome Ceremonies took place over a ten-day period and were scheduled only after a country's delegation had arrived in the village, so coordination was something of a logistics nightmare. However, working closely with the Village Protocol Department and its capable director, Mark Irwin, quiltmakers were issued VIP day passes and treated as honored guests. The Team Welcome Ceremonies took place in a small outdoor amphitheater. Quilts were hung prior to the ceremony and formed the backdrop of the ceremony itself. At the appointed time they were taken down, folded, and handed to Olympic Village Mayor Russ Chandler or one of the deputy mayors to present.

Many quiltmakers said that their greatest thrill, however, was the informal reception following the ceremony and the opportunity to meet the recipients of their quilts. Some teams reciprocated with a small gift to their respective quiltmakers. These included a hand-beaded bag (Nauru), T-shirts and other memorabilia (Saudi Arabia), a gift bag that included an electric razor (Korea), a set of stamps and a beautiful silk scarf in the colors of the national flag (San Marino), a small silver pin in the shape of a llama (Peru), a commemorative medal (Chile), books (Belgium and Bermuda), a length of silk (Tajikistan), and of course the ubiquitous pins, pins, pins.

Some quiltmakers brought additional gifts for their recipients. These ranged from a copy of the Olympic quilt book to survival baskets of Georgia foodstuffs. Jill Schneider of Cumming (Forsyth County) made miniature blocks in the same pattern as her Olympic quilt (American Indian Teepee) and pinned them to the uniforms of each member of Niger's delegation.

Smiles and warm words of welcome and well-wishing for a successful Olympic Games characterized the encounters between quiltmakers and recipients, whether the country was one of the great economic powers of the world, a tiny African nation coming to the Olympic Games for the first time, or a small island nation in the South Pacific. But the connection did not always end there—several quiltmakers were invited to receptions hosted by their recipient country's delegation, and some quiltmakers extended invitations of their own. Jane Glaze of Doraville (DeKalb County) and Carolyn Jeffares of Atlanta were honored guests at an elegant reception hosted by Oman. There they received a book, a carved filigree incense burner, and frankincense, which Oman's Boswellia trees yield. Cindy Richards of Snellville (Gwinnett County) and her husband were received by the British consul in Atlanta prior to the games, where she was presented with a commendation and a small gift. During the games, Richards attended a reception where she met Princess Anne, a former Olympic athlete herself. The Ladies of Southern Heirlooms, whose Sunbonnet Sue quilt was presented to Guam, attended a party at the home of the envoy to Guam, where they sampled traditional food from that country.

Comoros, a small island nation north of Madagascar, participated in the Olympics for the first time in 1996. Determined to provide a true taste of southern hospitality to the seventeen members of the Comoros delegation—none of whom spoke English—Leslie Boss of Atlanta invited them all to her home for a neighborhood barbecue. Putting aside the language barrier was easy, and soon athletes were dancing and singing songs in Swahili on Leslie's deck while enjoying fried chicken, potato salad, and other typically southern fare.

Several of the chefs de mission and their spouses expressed curiosity about how the quilts were made and how the quilting tradition developed in the United States. Madame Moyo, chef de mission of Zambia, was especially interested in quilt construction. When Fatima Shaheed, the wife of the chef de mission of the Maldives and needlework enthusiast, expressed her interest in learning to quilt, representatives of the Piecemakers Quilt Guild of Forsyth County invited her to a member's home for an impromptu quilt show. Shaheed also attended the July 1996 meeting of the East Cobb Quilters' Guild. The program that month was a workshop to construct an Olympic Stars block. Members supplied Shaheed with a sewing machine, fabric, and other supplies, and before the meeting was over she had learned how to make the block and had been presented with a quilt top made of blocks contributed by members. After the meeting, one of the quilters offered to show Shaheed to the nearest fabric store so she could purchase the necessary equipment. We can confirm that there is at least one rotary cutter, mat, and ruler set in the Maldives.

Within a month Georgia quilters "did it again" as quilts were presented to the chefs de mission of each of the 103 nations participating in the 1996 Paralympic Games in Atlanta. Quiltmakers were on hand in

Figure 11.14. Athletes at a Paralympic Welcome Ceremony for the Netherlands in the Paralympic Village, Atlanta, August 1996. The quilt presented to them was made by Debra Steinmann and Girl Scout Troop 1215 of DeKalb County. Photo by Violette Denney.

*The Olympic Gift Quilts*

Figure 11.15. Peace to All. Original design, Ruth A. Altemus (b. 1961), Decatur (DeKalb County), 1995. 55" x 74". Machine-pieced, hand-appliquéd, and hand-quilted cotton. Given to the Paralympic Committee of Australia. [GQP 9527]

Peace, a popular theme of the Olympic and Paralympic quilts, is beautifully interpreted here.

the Paralympic Village to assist with the presentation, coordinated by GQP Vice Chairwoman Holly Anderson along with Paralympic Village officials, and many enthusiastic teams posed with their quilts. The response to the call for quilts for the Paralympic Games was overwhelming, as it had been for the Olympic Games.

With so many quilters participating in the Olympic Gift of Quilts, it is not possible to tell or even know all the stories of goodwill fostered by the quilts and by the interactions of Georgia quiltmakers, Olympians,

and Paralympians. One thank-you letter, from envoy to Syria Ghada Muhanna to Jean Wolfe of Marietta (Cobb County) and Lavonne Timpson of Jonesboro (Clayton County), makers of the quilts given to Syria, suggests that the makers met their hoped-for goals:

As all nations of the world come together in harmony for the Olympic Games, so did the quiltmaker's patches. The richness of the whole is far greater than that of the parts. It is the personal graciousness of the people of Georgia that has made these Centennial Games a success. Your generosity and hospitality are magnified by the personal care and effort you have taken to craft this quilt, and thus to make myself, my team and my delegation and indeed all the visitors to this city, feel welcomed that much more warmly. For yourself, for your loved ones, the best in all things and thank you.

The Olympic Gift of Quilts was exciting and fulfilling for Georgia's quiltmakers. As life in Georgia resumed its normal rhythm after the exhilarating summer of 1996, the gift of quilts was causing a stir half a world away in Japan.

Hiromi Kawashima, head of the Nagano Quilt Association, teaches quiltmaking in Nagano, Japan. She has a patchwork school in a department store in Nagano and also travels to small towns throughout the Nagano prefecture to give lessons. After hearing about Georgia's gift of quilts, Kawashima decided to celebrate the 1998 Nagano Winter Olympic Games with quilts. A friend, freelance writer and curator Atsuko Hashiura, spent a day with the GQP in Atlanta to carry back to Kawashima details of our gift of quilts. Then many of Kawashima's two hundred students set to work to create 135 quilts, each in the shape of a kimono, to celebrate Nagano's games. Quilters all over Japan were asked to send Japanese fabric to Nagano, resulting in more than four hundred packages of fabric to be used in the making of the quilts. Each quilt was of a different design, a collaborative effort between *sensei* (teacher) and *seito* (student). Quilts were presented to each of the seventy-two countries participating in the Nagano Olympic Games and each of the thirty-two countries participating in the Paralympic Games. The remaining quilts were presented to Olympic officials, to Nagano torch-lighter Midori Ito (1988 figure-skating silver medalist), and one each to GQP Chairwoman Anita Weinraub and Vice Chairwoman Holly Anderson.

Invited to Japan by Brother Industries, maker of Brother sewing machines, Anita and Holly attended a quilt ceremony at the Zenko-ji Temple in Nagano on January 25, 1998, where Anita presented a quilt from the quiltmakers of Georgia to Deputy Director General of the Nagano Olympic Committee Takaichi Mikosako. This quilt was designed for the Nagano Games by Barbara Abrelat. Barbara also pieced the top of the Nagano quilt, Carolyn Kyle of Decatur did the hand appliqué work, and Sammie Simpson hand quilted it. Linda Camp of Ellerslie made two half-size versions of the same design. One was presented to Hiromi Kawashima; the other to President Yoshihiro Yasui of Brother Industries. Holly and Anita took 165 wall hangings (twenty-four inches square) as gifts from the quiltmakers of Georgia to the quiltmakers of Nagano. Many tears came and speeches were made on the cold, crisp morning of the quilt ceremony as we realized how very small a place the world can be and how people of different cultures, continents, and races can be linked by their mutual love for two pieces of cloth with some stuffing between and their mutual desire for world peace, which is at the core of each Olympic Games.

Expanding on Georgia's idea of making quilts for country representatives at the Olympics, Brother

Figure 11.16. My Kimono. Original design, anonymous, Nagano Prefecture, Japan. 39" x 43". Hand-appliquéd, hand-embroidered, hand-quilted cotton, silks, and blends. Collection of Anita Z. Weinraub. Photo by France Dorman. [GQP 8655]

This quilt is filled with symbols of Japan. From the cherry blossom to the Temari balls and lanterns to the boy and girl representing the Children's Day holiday, each motif was carefully planned and exquisitely executed. The maker is a master of *ochie* appliqué, a technique where fabric is contoured around a stiff foundation. The words "From Nagano to Georgia" are embroidered in gold on the lower right. The quilt was presented to Anita at a party in her honor the evening before the Zenko-ji ceremony.

Figure 11.17. From Atlanta to Nagano. Original design by Barbara Abrelat (now Dorn, b. 1944) of Canton (Cherokee County), formerly of Decatur (DeKalb County). 54" x 70". Pieced by Barbara Abrelat; hand appliquéd by Carolyn Kyle of Decatur (DeKalb County); hand quilted by Linda Camp of Ellerslie (Harris County), 1997. Photo by Jacque Sanderson.

This quilt incorporates elements from the Atlanta and Nagano Olympic Games: the vibrant palette of the Quilt of Leaves and the soft pastel palette used in Nagano's Look of the Games. Appliquéd snowflakes contrast with the "hot" Atlanta sunshine.

Industries sponsored a contest in *Patchwork Quilt Tsushin* (a Japanese quilting magazine) asking readers to make twenty-five-centimeter-square (about eight-inch-square) miniquilts to give to athletes. Japanese quilters responded generously, submitting more than 2,300 miniquilts—enough to give one to each athlete when they visited the Brother booth in the Olympic Village. In this way, quilters throughout Japan were able to express their support and enthusiasm for the Nagano Games.

Also present at the quilt ceremony at Zenko-ji Temple was Margaret Wright, representing Australian quiltmakers. Wright carried back to Australia ideas about the Georgia and Nagano Olympic Gift Quilts and helped organize an Internet quilt sale that benefited the 2000 Sydney Paralympic Games.

The idea that originated in Georgia and continued in Japan and Australia is still alive. Utah quilters created a number of quilts that were displayed during the 2002 Salt Lake City Winter Olympics. Although there was no quilt involvement in the 2004 Athens Summer Olympics or the 2006 Torino Winter Olympics, Georgia quiltmakers remain hopeful that the tradition they started in Atlanta for the 1996 games will be taken up at future games.

The GQP continues not only to record quilt history but to make it, as it did at the 1996 Olympics. Although it has successfully recorded information about the quilts and quiltmakers of Georgia through its documentation effort, the project's story does not end with the last Quilt History Day. Quilting continues across the state of Georgia; the stories continue and quilt history continues to be made, one stitch and one quilt at a time.

Figure 11.18. Quilt Ceremony, Zenko-ji Temple, Nagano, Japan, January 25, 1998. Miniquilts from all over Japan are displayed on banners in the colors of the Olympic rings. Photo courtesy of Brother Industries.

Figure 11.19. Prize-winning miniquilt, only eight inches square, made by Yohko Kobayashi of Tokyo, now part of the permanent collection of Brother Industries. Photo courtesy of Brother Industries.

# APPENDIX A

## Statistical Summary of Documented Quilts

### MARGIE ROGERS

*Introduction*

The information in this appendix is derived from summaries of our original documentation records. Only certain significant data was extracted—the complete records are being input into a database, and programs are being developed to allow the information to be accessed by researchers and the public. These statistics include data on 8,057 of the 8,136 quilts documented at Quilt History Days.

The Georgia Quilt Project (GQP) actually documented over 9,000 quilts: the original 8,136 plus the Olympic Gift Quilts, Birdhouse Artfest quilts and wall hangings, and gift wall hangings taken to Japan in 1998, as well as a few other quilts documented after the Quilt History Days had taken place. Every effort has been made to present accurate information, but some errors are inevitable.

The GQP documented quilts from any origin or date. This differed from some state projects, which for various reasons limited their documentation to quilts known to be from that state and/or quilts made before a certain cutoff date, usually eliminating the modern era. Our feeling was that all quilts residing in Georgia were worthy of documentation and study, and that including recently made quilts would allow us to collect detailed information—often from the maker—that would be of value to future quilt historians. We also hope that eventually our information can be shared with other state documentation projects.

Our data did not indicate a significant shift of the percentage of the quiltmaking population from rural to urban areas until the 1970s and 1980s. It did seem to indicate that fewer quilts had been made in the 1950s and 1960s than before that time.

We documented 256 quilts made by African Americans among the 8,057 reflected in this appendix. This represents 3.16 percent of the total number of quilts in our sample. African American–made quilts were documented at twenty-seven of the forty-four documentation sites. The oldest, although not dated and relying solely on the history provided in a note attached to the quilt, was made by a slave ca. 1810. Nearly 5 percent of the African American–made quilts documented were believed to be original designs compared to about 3 percent of our total 8,057 quilts.

Male quilters made sixty-five quilts, 0.8 percent of our total. Of those quilts, 17 percent were believed to be original designs. Forty-nine of the sixty-five quilts were made in 1981 or later. The earliest documented quilt made by a man (according to his daughter) was made by an African American ca. 1906.

Quilts made from kits numbered 132 of the 8,057 quilts; of these, seventy-six were made in Georgia.

An enormous thank-you is due Judie Glaze in appreciation of the long hours she spent at the keyboard inputting data so that these core statistics could be shared.

## All Quilts

### Sorted by Date

GQP volunteers received training in quilt dating before the Quilt History Days were held. Nationally known experts Barbara Brackman, Laurel Horton, and Bets Ramsey taught seminars to almost one hundred volunteers during two information-filled days.

Documenters would consider the fabrics, batting, style, pattern, technique, and other characteristics, as well as the information given by the owner, when dating a quilt. Generally, quilts would be given a "circa" date, allowing ten years before or after. Unless a quilt is inscribed with a date, quilt dating is educated guessing, not an exact science. A specific date was chosen when the completion date was on the quilt or when the stated reason for making the quilt (birth, marriage, etc.) suggested a date that coincided with the appearance of the quilt (in the documenter's opinion). Please note that the information below appears in decades with the exception of the Civil War decade, which has been divided. Of the 8,057 quilts, 1,494 had a date inscribed on them, 1,676 were signed by the maker, and 1,317 were both dated and signed.

| Date | Number of Quilts | Percentage of Total |
|------|------------------|---------------------|
| 1800–1810 | 5 | 0.01% |
| 1811–1820 | 6 | 0.01% |
| 1821–1830 | 5 | 0.01% |
| 1831–1840 | 25 | 0.31% |
| 1841–1850 | 86 | 1.06% |
| 1851–1860 | 118 | 1.46% |
| 1861–1865 | 35 | 0.43% |
| 1866–1870 | 97 | 1.20% |
| 1871–1880 | 210 | 2.61% |
| 1881–1890 | 354 | 4.39% |
| 1891–1900 | 385 | 4.78% |
| 1901–1910 | 200 | 2.48% |
| 1911–1920 | 351 | 4.36% |
| 1921–1930 | 1,020 | 12.66% |
| 1931–1940 | 932 | 11.57% |
| 1941–1950 | 420 | 5.21% |
| 1951–1960 | 283 | 3.51% |
| 1961–1970 | 244 | 3.02% |
| 1971–1980 | 561 | 6.96% |
| 1981–1990 | 2,176 | 27.01% |
| 1991–1993 | 518 | 6.42% |
| no date recorded | 26 | 0.32% |

### Construction Techniques

Many techniques were used to construct quilts. Some quilts involved more than one or two techniques.

| Technique | Number of Quilts |
|-----------|------------------|
| Pieced | 5,275 |
| Appliquéd | 1,092 |
| Both pieced and appliquéd | 902 |
| Crazy | 307 |
| Embroidered (but not Crazy) | 235 |
| Cathedral Window | 117 |
| Whole cloth | 115 |
| Yo-yo | 44 |
| Painted | 33 |
| Stenciled | 12 |
| Photos on cloth | 3 |
| Needle punch / tufted | 2 |

**Patterns**

Below are many of the patterns or patterns grouped by motif and their frequency.

| | |
|---|---|
| STARS | 746* |
| *Lone Star* | 135 |
| *Lemoyne Star* | 118 |
| *Ohio Star* | 32 |
| ONE PATCH | 675* |
| *Grandmother's Flower Garden* | 276 |
| FLORAL DESIGNS PIECED AND/OR APPLIQUÉD | 632* |
| *Tulips* | 142 |
| *Roses* | 128 |
| Crazy Quilts | 307 |
| Log Cabin | 265 |
| Samplers | 262 |
| WEDDING RING / DOUBLE WEDDING RING AND VARIATIONS | 280* |
| *Double Wedding Ring* | 249 |
| *Wedding Ring* | 21 |
| *Indian Wedding Ring* | 9 |
| *Triple Wedding Ring* | 1 |
| Original Designs | 246 |
| Dresden Plate | 216 |
| Nine Patch | 208 |
| Dutch Doll / Sunbonnet Sue / Overall Sam | 208 |
| String pieced (including 23 String Stars already listed under Stars) | 197 |
| Step around the Mountain / Trip around the World / Boston Common | 187 |

* Includes subtypes listed below

| | |
|---|---|
| Fan | 150 |
| Basket | 145 |
| Irish Chain | 142 |
| Commemorative / historic recognition | 100 |
| Butterfly | 98 |
| Bowtie | 93 |
| Drunkard's Path | 70 |
| Four Patch | 64 |
| Animals | 63 |
| Pinwheels | 59 |
| Diamond in Square | 54 |
| Friendship / Signature / Fundraiser | 51 |
| Churn Dash | 48 |
| Colonial Lady | 42 |
| Bear Paw | 40 |
| Album | 40 |
| Flying Geese | 37 |
| Mariner's Compass | 36 |
| Pine Tree or Pine Burr | 35 |
| Jacob's Ladder | 32 |
| Oak designs | 32 |
| Rail Fence | 32 |
| Snowball | 32 |
| Maple Leaf | 31 |
| Heart | 28 |
| Rocky Mountain Road / New York Beauty | 26 |
| Spider Web | 25 |
| Monkey Wrench | 24 |
| Ocean Waves | 24 |
| Shoo Fly | 22 |
| Princess Feather | 15 |
| Baltimore Album (not included under Album) | 11 |

## Quilt Origins by State and Country

Interviewers recorded the origin of each quilt for which that information was known. Unfortunately, some errors may have been made and possibly overlooked because incorrect state abbreviations may have been used. Quilts were documented from all but four states—Hawaii, Maine, Montana, and Nevada.

Thirty-nine quilts made in other countries were also recorded. Of the quilts documented, 71.9 percent were known to have been made in Georgia, 20.4 percent in another known state, 7.1 percent in an unknown state (but not Georgia), and .005 percent in another country. No information was recorded about the remaining 5.5 percent.

| State | Number of Quilts | State | Number of Quilts |
|---|---|---|---|
| Alabama | 263 | Montana | 0 |
| Alaska | 8 | Nebraska | 10 |
| Arizona | 3 | Nevada | 0 |
| Arkansas | 34 | New Hampshire | 2 |
| California | 27 | New Jersey | 11 |
| Colorado | 12 | New Mexico | 6 |
| Connecticut | 4 | New York | 45 |
| Delaware | 15 | North Carolina | 121 |
| District of Columbia | 3 | North Dakota | 7 |
| Florida | 97 | Ohio | 65 |
| Georgia | 5,796 | Oklahoma | 37 |
| Hawaii | 0 | Oregon | 3 |
| Idaho | 3 | Pennsylvania | 84 |
| Illinois | 53 | Rhode Island | 1 |
| Indiana | 59 | South Carolina | 64 |
| Iowa | 41 | South Dakota | 5 |
| Kansas | 16 | Tennessee | 141 |
| Kentucky | 48 | Texas | 68 |
| Louisiana | 24 | Utah | 2 |
| Maine | 0 | Vermont | 3 |
| Maryland | 10 | Virginia | 38 |
| Massachusetts | 18 | Washington | 6 |
| Michigan | 24 | West Virginia | 28 |
| Minnesota | 14 | Wisconsin | 14 |
| Mississippi | 31 | Wyoming | 1 |
| Missouri | 77 | Unknown | 576 |

| Country | Number of Quilts |
|---|---|
| Africa (specific country unknown) | 1 |
| Belgium | 1 |
| Canada | 9 |
| China | 5 |
| England | 2 |
| Germany | 1 |
| Ireland | 2 |
| Japan | 8 |
| Liberia | 4 |
| Mexico | 1 |
| Philippines | 3 |
| Poland | 1 |
| Tunisia | 1 |

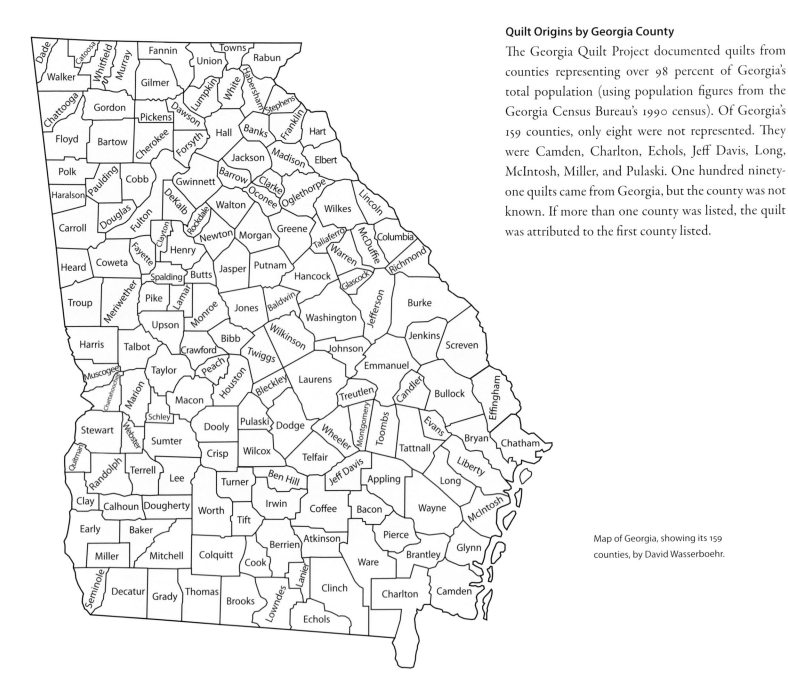

## Quilt Origins by Georgia County

The Georgia Quilt Project documented quilts from counties representing over 98 percent of Georgia's total population (using population figures from the Georgia Census Bureau's 1990 census). Of Georgia's 159 counties, only eight were not represented. They were Camden, Charlton, Echols, Jeff Davis, Long, McIntosh, Miller, and Pulaski. One hundred ninety-one quilts came from Georgia, but the county was not known. If more than one county was listed, the quilt was attributed to the first county listed.

Map of Georgia, showing its 159 counties, by David Wasserboehr.

| County | Number of Quilts |
|---|---|
| Appling | 4 |
| Atkinson | 31 |
| Bacon | 7 |
| Baker | 3 |
| Baldwin | 64 |
| Banks | 6 |
| Barrow | 28 |
| Bartow | 138 |
| Ben Hill | 15 |
| Berrien | 36 |
| Bibb | 209 |
| Bleckley | 1 |
| Brantley | 36 |
| Brooks | 25 |
| Bryan | 6 |
| Bullock | 84 |
| Burke | 8 |
| Butts | 17 |
| Calhoun | 5 |
| Camden | 0 |
| Candler | 5 |
| Carroll | 217 |
| Catoosa | 50 |
| Charlton | 0 |
| Chatham | 80 |
| Chattahoochee | 3 |
| Chattooga | 99 |
| Cherokee | 33 |
| Clarke | 43 |
| Clay | 3 |
| Clayton | 127 |
| Clinch | 1 |
| Cobb | 135 |
| Coffee | 7 |
| Colquitt | 123 |
| Columbia | 26 |
| Cook | 3 |
| Coweta | 14 |
| Crawford | 4 |
| Crisp | 3 |
| Dade | 4 |
| Dawson | 11 |
| Decatur | 4 |
| DeKalb | 238 |
| Dodge | 5 |
| Dooly | 14 |
| Dougherty | 63 |
| Douglas | 21 |
| Early | 5 |
| Echols | 0 |
| Effingham | 9 |
| Elbert | 22 |
| Emmanuel | 30 |
| Evans | 12 |
| Fannin | 50 |
| Fayette | 34 |
| Floyd | 47 |
| Forsyth | 33 |
| Franklin | 43 |
| Fulton | 206 |
| Gilmer | 12 |
| Glascock | 8 |
| Glynn | 35 |
| Gordon | 12 |
| Grady | 26 |
| Greene | 11 |
| Gwinnett | 216 |
| Habersham | 34 |
| Hall | 76 |
| Hancock | 12 |
| Haralson | 22 |
| Harris | 27 |
| Hart | 21 |
| Heard | 27 |
| Henry | 55 |
| Houston | 35 |
| Irwin | 11 |
| Jackson | 30 |
| Jasper | 12 |
| Jeff Davis | 0 |
| Jefferson | 81 |
| Jenkins | 2 |
| Johnson | 2 |
| Jones | 80 |
| Lamar | 6 |
| Lanier | 8 |
| Laurens | 27 |
| Lee | 6 |
| Liberty | 2 |
| Lincoln | 6 |
| Long | 0 |
| Lowndes | 109 |
| Lumpkin | 32 |
| Macon | 14 |
| Madison | 24 |
| Marion | 16 |
| McDuffie | 7 |
| McIntosh | 0 |
| Meriwether | 32 |
| Miller | 0 |
| Mitchell | 27 |
| Monroe | 41 |
| Montgomery | 5 |
| Morgan | 23 |
| Murray | 71 |
| Muscogee | 158 |
| Newton | 34 |
| Oconee | 27 |
| Oglethorpe | 32 |
| Paulding | 32 |
| Peach | 14 |
| Pickens | 7 |
| Pierce | 4 |
| Pike | 30 |
| Polk | 62 |
| Pulaski | 0 |
| Putnam | 12 |
| Quitman | 7 |
| Rabun | 13 |
| Randolph | 7 |
| Richmond | 51 |
| Rockdale | 27 |
| Schley | 3 |
| Screven | 8 |
| Seminole | 1 |
| Spalding | 122 |
| Stephens | 71 |
| Stewart | 18 |
| Sumter | 44 |
| Talbot | 20 |
| Taliaferro | 12 |
| Tattnall | 8 |
| Taylor | 9 |
| Telfair | 18 |
| Terrell | 8 |
| Thomas | 65 |
| Tift | 91 |
| Toombs | 9 |
| Towns | 30 |
| Treutlen | 20 |
| Troup | 118 |
| Turner | 20 |
| Twiggs | 3 |
| Union | 47 |
| Upson | 18 |
| Walker | 90 |
| Walton | 103 |
| Ware | 7 |
| Warren | 11 |
| Washington | 15 |
| Wayne | 9 |
| Webster | 17 |
| Wheeler | 1 |
| White | 14 |
| Whitfield | 77 |
| Wilcox | 1 |
| Wilkes | 69 |
| Wilkinson | 28 |
| Worth | 30 |
| Unknown | 191 |

## Family Occupations

Unfortunately, the quilt owner's questionnaire was often misunderstood, and as a result, the reply to the "family occupation" question was frequently "retired" or "homemaker." The following statistics reflect the occupations listed in information we did receive.

### Common Occupations

| | |
|---|---|
| Farm / rural (including 24 mentioning plantations) | 1,824 |
| Blue collar | 1,001 |
| White collar | 854 |
| Small business / merchant | 553 |
| Professional | 498 |
| Government / civil service | 320 |
| Military | 161 |
| Clergy / missionary | 112 |
| Mill related | 112 |

### Interesting or Unusual Occupations

| | |
|---|---|
| Boarding house worker* | 2 |
| Carriage maker* | 2 |
| Coal miner | 1 |
| Harness maker | 1 |
| Herb doctor | 1 |
| Kaolin-mine related* | 2 |
| Logging camp cook | 1 |
| Moonshiner | 1 |
| Mule trader | 7 |
| Piano maker* | 2 |
| Potter | 1 |
| Riverboat captain | 1 |
| Saddlemaker | 1 |
| Seminole plantation legislator | 1 |
| Wagonmaker and preacher | 1 |
| Watchmaker | 1 |

*It is unknown whether the people who selected these occupations came from separate families or if the same family brought more than one quilt to be documented.

## African American Quilts

The above statistics include African American quilts documented by the GQP. Due to the special interest in African American quilts, summaries of dates for 256 of the 260 quilts known to have been made by African Americans are provided below (the remaining four quilts were documented after this database was compiled). Of the 256 African American–made quilts, thirty-four were dated. One was dated 1881 but was owned by a white family who asserted that it was made by former slaves on the family plantation. The next dated quilts were made in 1908 and 1910, both still family owned. One quilt each from the years 1940, 1946, 1958, and 1970 were documented. Three dated quilts from 1971–80, seventeen from 1981–90, and seven from 1991 to the present complete the number of dated quilts. Below are the dates attributed to all 256 quilts by the documenters.

**By Date of Origin**

| Date | Number of Quilts | Date | Number of Quilts | Date | Number of Quilts |
|------|------|------|------|------|------|
| 1810 | 1 | 1930 | 23 | 1969 | 1 |
| 1811 | 1 | 1935 | 1 | 1970 | 13 |
| 1850 | 2 | 1937 | 1 | 1972 | 1 |
| 1855 | 1 | 1939 | 2 | 1976 | 4 |
| 1860 | 3 | 1940 | 14 | 1977 | 1 |
| 1865 | 1 | 1942 | 1 | 1978 | 2 |
| 1870 | 2 | 1943 | 3 | 1980 | 11 |
| 1875 | 1 | 1945 | 3 | 1981 | 2 |
| 1880 | 2 | 1946 | 2 | 1982 | 3 |
| 1881 | 1 | 1947 | 2 | 1984 | 2 |
| 1890 | 1 | 1949 | 1 | 1985 | 7 |
| 1900 | 3 | 1950 | 3 | 1986 | 5 |
| 1908 | 1 | 1952 | 3 | 1987 | 7 |
| 1910 | 4 | 1955 | 2 | 1988 | 17 |
| 1912 | 1 | 1956 | 1 | 1989 | 15 |
| 1915 | 2 | 1958 | 2 | 1990 | 12 |
| 1920 | 4 | 1960 | 11 | 1991 | 22 |
| 1924 | 1 | 1964 | 3 | 1992 | 6 |
| 1925 | 4 | 1965 | 2 | 1993 | 1 |
| 1928 | 3 | 1967 | 1 | Unknown | 4 |

# *Quilt Owner's Questionnaire*

ID#: _____   init: _____   date: _____

## Quiltmaker's History:

Name _____

County _____   Birthdate _____   Birthplace _____

Religion _____

Where lived most of life _____   Date and place of death _____

Quiltmaker's occupation _____   Spouse's name _____   Occupation _____

Number, names and sex of children _____

Mother's name and birthplace _____

Father's name and birthplace _____

How did quiltmaker learn to make quilts and when? _____

_____

Is quiltmaker a native of Georgia? _____   If not, how/why did he/she come here? _____

_____

What is the ancestry of the quiltmaker's family? _____

Why did the quiltmaker quilt? (Circle)     Income     Pleasure     Church     Gifts     Necessity     Other

Did the quiltmaker make other quilts? _____   If so, how many, and where are they? _____

Did he/she participate in group quilting activities? _____

Did he/she grow up in an URBAN or RURAL environment? _____

Education of quilter _____

Where did she get her patterns? _____

Where did she get her quilting designs? _____

What were her fabric sources? _____

Anything else we should know about quilter? _____

_____

**Quilt History:**

Quilt name used by maker _____ _____ By owner _____ ____

Did the quiltmaker (Circle)    design    piece    appliqué    quilt    tie    the quilt?

If you know of other people who worked on this quilt please give names and what role they played: _____

Why was the quilt made? (Circle)    Dowry    Income    Gift    Personal Use    Fundraising    Other

Was the quilt made for a special occasion? (Circle)    Birth    Death    Marriage    Dowry    Historical Event    Anniversary

Other (Specify) _____

_____

Where was the quilt made?    City _____    County _____    State _____

When was the quilt made? _____    How old was the quilter at the time? _____

When was the quilt brought to Georgia? _____    Anything else we should know about this quilt, stories, customs? _____

_____

_____

Has this quilt been exhibited or displayed?    Explain _____

Has this quilt been repaired or restored?    By whom? _____

Has this quilt won prizes? _____    Dates and events _____

Do you know if any of the following exist? (Circle)    Quiltmaker's diary    Letters    Photos    Scrapbook    Pattern    Sewing tools

Will    Award ribbons or pins    Family bible records    Newspaper clippings    Photo of quilt    Patterns for quilt/quilting    Other    None exist

Please give any other details you would like to share _____

_____

_____

_____

_____

Has this quilt or any other quilt made by this quiltmaker been registered in a quilt documentation project in another state? If so, where?

_____

Do you know of any other quilts or quiltmakers that should be included in this Project? Yes _____    No _____

May we contact you later for this information? Yes _____    No _____

## Quilt: Physical Description

Maker _____     ID# _____

Location of QHD _____     Negative# _____

Date of Examination _____     Slide# _____

Size _____ x _____     Documentor Initials _____

### 1. PATTERN

Name _____

Source of name _____

DATE QUILT WAS MADE _____

Is the date on quilt? Where? _____

_____

Any restoration/conservation? _____

### 2. TYPE

_____ TOP ONLY          _____ Bed size

_____ Crib              _____ Wall hanging

_____ Other _____

_____ Something unusual about this quilt? _____

_____

Where? _____

### 3. TECHNIQUE OF TOP CONSTRUCTION

_____ Pieced _____ Hand _____ Machine

_____ English piecing; paper still in? _____

_____ String; paper still in? _____

_____ Appliqué     _____ Hand     _____ Machine

                   _____ Reverse  _____ Stuffed

                   _____ Blind    _____ Buttonhole

_____ Whole cloth

_____ Quilt-as-you-go

_____ Embroidery

_____ Stencilled

_____ Other _____

### 4. DESIGN

_____ Blocks; size of blocks _____

_____ Crazy       _____ Charm      _____ Commercial kit

_____ One patch   _____ Strip      _____ Novelty

_____ Pictorial   _____ Album      _____ Wedding ring, circles

_____ Sampler     _____ Medallion  _____ Other _____

### 5. SET

_____ Sashing

_____ Straight              _____ On Point

_____ Alternating blocks    _____ Other

### 6. FABRIC (Top)

_____ Cotton    _____ Velvet      _____ Feed Sack

_____ Wool      _____ Synthetics  _____ Other _____

_____ Silk      _____ Blends      _____

_____ Linen     _____ Chintz      _____ Cannot determine

Patterns

_____ Solids    _____ Checks

_____ Prints    _____ Plaids

_____ Stripes   _____ Printed Patchwork ("cheater")

**7. PREDOMINANT COLORS (Top)**

| | | | | | |
|---|---|---|---|---|---|
| _____ Very Dark | _____ Black | _____ Lavender | _____ Pink | _____ Orange | _____ MULTI |
| _____ Pastels | _____ Blue | _____ Maroon | _____ Purple | _____ Yellow | _____ White |
| _____ Very Bright | _____ Brown | _____ Navy | _____ Red | _____ Other_____ |
| _____ Medium | _____ Green | _____ Gray | _____ Tan | | |

**8. SASHING – Construction       Width of sashing _____**

_____ Hand or _____ Machine

| | | CORNERSTONES | SASHING FABRIC |
|---|---|---|---|
| _____ none | _____ Horizontal | _____ None | _____ Same as blocks |
| | _____ Vertical | _____ Same as sashing | _____ Solid color |
| _____ Pieced | _____ Diagonal | _____ Different from | _____ Other _____ |
| _____ Appliquéd | _____ Streak of lightning | _____ Pieced _____ | |
| _____ Other | _____ Garden Maze | _____ Appliquéd | |
| | _____ Other _____ | | |

**9. BORDER       Width _____**

| | | FABRIC | CONSTRUCTION |
|---|---|---|---|
| _____ None | _____ Plain | _____ Solid | _____ Mitered |
| _____ Single | _____ Pieced | _____ Print | _____ Butted |
| _____ Double | _____ Appliquéd | _____ Same as sashing | _____ Cornerstone |
| _____ Triple | | _____ Combination | _____ Hand or _____ Machine |
| _____ Quadruple | | | |

SAME ON       _____ Two sides       _____ Three sides       _____ All sides

**10. BACKING**

Color _____

| | FIBER | PATTERN | |
|---|---|---|---|
| _____ One piece | | | |
| _____ Two piece | _____ Cotton | _____ Solid | _____ Check |
| _____ Many pieces | _____ Wool | _____ Print | _____ Stripe |
| _____ Patched | _____ Silk | _____ Plaid | _____ Other _____ |
| _____ Designed | _____ Linen | _____ Feed Sack | |
| _____ Hand _____ Machine | _____ Other _____ _____ | | |

**11. BINDING**

COLOR _____

| | | | |
|---|---|---|---|
| _____ Print | _____ Back to Front | _____ Applied | _____ Machine |
| _____ Solid | _____ Front to Back | _____ Bias | _____ Hand |
| | _____ Top and Backing | _____ Straight | |
| | _____ Folded In (knife edge) | _____ Commercial Tape | _____ Woven Tape |

## 12. EDGE OF QUILT

SHAPE

_____ Straight

_____ Scalloped

_____ Other _____

_____

TECHNIQUE

_____ Piped          _____ Prairie Points          _____ Fringe

_____ Lace           _____ Ruffle                  _____ Other _____

## 13. BATTING

_____ None

_____ Very thick

_____ Very thin

_____ Cannot determine (not visible)

FIBER

_____ Cotton              _____ Old quilt

_____ Wool

_____ Poly                _____ Flannel sheet

_____ Other _____

## 14. QUILTING

Color of thread _____

_____ Hand          STITCHES

_____ Machine       _____ # of top stitches per inch    _____ Even

_____ Tied                                             _____ Uneven

BODY

___ Echo          ___ Wreaths                ___ In the ditch

___ Outline       ___ Diagonal lines         ___ Grid

___ Stipple       ___ Pictorial              ___ Straight lines

___ Parallel lines    ___ Diamonds/Crosshatch

___ Clamshell/fan     ___ Other _____

___ Trapunto          ___ Designs _____

___ Stuffed                    (Short description please)

BORDERS, SASHING, ETC.

Choose from above _____

_____

## 15. CONDITION

_____ Excellent     _____ Fair       _____ Unwashed        _____ Faded      _____ Fragile

_____ Very Good     _____ Poor       _____ Moderate Use    _____ Stained    _____ Repaired

_____ Good                           _____ Worn            _____ Soiled     _____ Damaged

## 16. DECORATION

_____ Signature     _____ Date       _____ Embroidery

_____ Painted       _____ Fringe     _____ Ribbons

_____ Images        _____ Stencil    _____ Other _____

Where decoration is located: _____

# Listing of Quilt History Days Held

ANITA ZALESKI WEINRAUB

| Location (County) | Sponsor | Date | Number of quilts documented |
|---|---|---|---|
| **1990** | | | |
| Atlanta (DeKalb) | Chamblee Star Quilters | Jan. 24 | 54 |
| Tifton (Tift) | Georgia Agrirama | Mar. 16–17 | 226 |
| Summerville (Chattooga) | Cloudland Quilters | April 13 | 147 |
| Griffin (Spalding) | Mary Ross / Griffin Tech | April 26–27 | 295 |
| St. Simons Island (Glynn) | Museum of Coastal History | May 11 | 132 |
| Macon (Bibb) | Heart of Georgia Quilt Guild | May 18–19 | 211 |
| Andersonville (Sumter) | Andersonville Fair | May 26 | 54 |
| Marietta (Cobb) | East Cobb Quilt Guild | June 7–8 | 80 |
| Cassville (Bartow) | Noble Hill-Wheeler Memorial Foundation | June 23 | 52 |
| Cartersville (Bartow) | Etowah Creative Arts Council | June 30, July 1 | 181 |
| Dahlonega (Lumpkin) | North Georgia College | July 13–14 | 164 |
| Columbus (Muscogee) | Columbus Museum | Aug. 10–11 | 455 |
| Athens (Clarke) | Cotton Patch Quilters | Sep. 7–8 | 264 |
| Young Harris (Union) | Misty Mountain Quilters | Sep. 14 | 174 |
| Social Circle (Walton) | Alice Hughes | Oct. 8, 11 | 253 |
| Soperton (Treutlen) | Treutlen County Historical Society | Oct. 26–27 | 58 |
| Dalton (Whitfield) | Whitfield-Murray Historical Society | Nov. 9–10 | 208 |
| Carrollton (Carroll) | West Georgia Quilters Guild | Dec. 8–9 | 269 |

| Location (County) | Sponsor | Date | Number of quilts documented |
|---|---|---|---|
| **1991** | | | |
| Albany (Dougherty) | Thronateeska Heritage Foundation | Jan. 11–12 | 199 |
| LaGrange (Troup) | Troup County Archives | Jan. 25–26 | 230 |
| Lawrenceville (Gwinnett) | Donna Black | Feb. 22–23 | 232 |
| Moultrie (Colquitt) | Ellen Payne Odum Genealogical Library | March 8–9 | 226 |
| Louisville (Jefferson) | Louisville High School | March 25 | 76 |
| Atlanta (Fulton) | Apex Museum / Atlanta Life Insurance | April 5 | 18 |
| Rossville (Walker) | Walker County Historical Society | April 20 | 117 |
| Valdosta (Lowndes) | Withlacoochee Quilt Guild | May 10–11 | 168 |
| Tifton (Tift) | Georgia Agrirama | May 17 | 77 |
| Thomasville (Thomas) | Lapham-Patterson House | May 18 | 111 |
| Jonesboro (Fayette) | Tara Quilt Guild of Clayton County | July 12–13 | 299 |
| Blue Ridge (Fannin) | Blue Ridge Art Association | Sep. 8 | 83 |
| Cedartown (Polk) | Homemaker's Council | Sep. 28 | 122 |
| Nahunta (Brantley) | Nahunta Regional Library | Oct. 3 | 61 |
| Brunswick (Glynn) | Museum of Coastal History / Jekyll Island Museum | Oct. 5 | 95 |
| Milledgeville (Baldwin) | Milledgeville / Baldwin County Allied Arts | Oct. 24–25 | 199 |
| Augusta (Richmond) | Pieceful Hearts Quilters | Nov. 8–9 | 216 |
| **1992** | | | |
| Juliette (Monroe) | Jarrell Plantation Historic Site | Jan. 23–24 | 163 |
| Savannah (Chatham) | Savannah History Museum | Feb. 22–23 | 144 |
| Atlanta (Fulton) | Atlanta History Center | March 6–7 | 156 |
| Gainesville (Hall) | Hall County Quilt Guild | March 27–28 | 238 |
| Atlanta (Fulton) | Emmaus House | April 10–11 | 120 |
| Washington (Wilkes) | Washington County Historical Society | May 1–2 | 150 |
| Marietta (Cobb) | Cobb Landmarks and Historical Society | July 17–18 | 277 |
| Toccoa (Stephens) | Currahee Quilters | Sep. 25–26 | 218 |
| Statesboro (Bulloch) | Statesboro Regional Library | Oct. 2–3 | 249 |
| **1993** | | | |
| Stone Mountain (DeKalb) | Yellow Daisy / Gwinnett Quilters | Jan. 12–14 | 409 |

In addition to the above public events, several practice and/or special events were held in Atlanta, Social Circle, Macon, Cartersville, Roswell, Dalton, and Doraville. The total number of quilts documented during these sessions was 218.

The total number of quilts documented during Quilt History Days was 8,136!

Additional quilts—for instance, the more than four hundred Olympic Gift Quilts, small quilts made to benefit Habitat for Humanity, and so on—were documented after the Quilt History Days ended, bringing the total number of quilts documented to more than 9,500.

# *Sources*

------------------------------

## Chapter 1. Darlene R. Roth, "A Background for Quilting in Georgia"

### SOURCES

Bryan, Thomas Conn. *Confederate Georgia*. Athens: University of Georgia Press, 1953.

Burr, Virginia Ingraham, ed. *The Secret Eye: the Journal of Ella Gertrude Clanton Thomas*. Chapel Hill: University of North Carolina Press, 1990. Information on Ella Thomas from telephone conversation between Anita Weinraub and Virginia Burr, March 1995.

Coleman, Kenneth. *Georgia History in Outline*. Athens: University of Georgia Press, 1960.

———, ed. *A History of Georgia*. Athens: University of Georgia Press, 1977.

Flanigan, James C. *History of Gwinnett County, Georgia*. 2 vols. Hapeville: James C. Flanigan, 1943, 1959.

Garrett, Franklin. *Atlanta and Environs*. New York: Lewis, 1954.

Hornsby, Alton, Jr. *Chronology of African American History*. Detroit: Gale Research, 1991.

Martin, Clarence. "A Glimpse of the Past: the History of Bulloch Hall and Roswell, Georgia." Roswell: Historic Roswell Inc., n.d.

Martin, Harold H. *Georgia: A History*. New York: W. W. Norton, 1977.

Mason, Herman "Skip," Jr. *African American Life in DeKalb County, 1823–1970*. Charleston, S.C.: Arcadia, 1998.

McMichael, Lois, comp. *History of Butts County, Georgia*. Atlanta: Cherokee, 1978.

Roth, Darlene R. *Greater Atlanta: A Shared Destiny*. Carlsbad, Calif.: Heritage Media, 2000.

———. *Matronage: Patterns of Women's Organizations in Atlanta, 1890–1940*. New York: Carlson, 1994.

Roth, Darlene R., et al. *Georgia: A Woman's Place* (historic context study and narrative). Atlanta: Historic Preservation Division, Georgia Department of Natural Resources, 2005.

Roth, Darlene R., and Louise Shaw. *Atlanta Women: From Myth to Modern Times*. Atlanta: Atlanta Historical Society, 1980.

Sherwood, Adiel. *A Gazetteer of the State of Georgia*. 1827. Reprint, Athens: University of Georgia Press, 1939.

Temple, Sara Blackwell Gober. *The First Hundred Years: A Short History of Cobb County, Georgia*. Atlanta: Walker Brown, 1935.

White, George. *Statistics of the State of Georgia*. Savannah: W. Thorne Williams, 1849.

White, Otis. "A Tale of Two Georgians." *Georgia Trend* (April 1986), 46–50.

## Chapter 2. Irene McLaren, "Early Quilts"

### NOTES

I acknowledge with gratitude the people who were especially helpful in making available their time and information: Olivia Allison, Owens-Thomas House, Savannah; Stephen Bohlin, Juliette Low Birthplace, Savannah; John H. Christian, Bryan-Lang Historical Library, Woodbine, Georgia;

Mary King at the Chieftans Museum, Rome, Georgia; Tania Sammons, Telfair Academy of Arts and Sciences Inc., Savannah; and the staff at the Georgia Historical Society, Savannah, who were endlessly patient explaining to me where to find particular information. Many thanks to Judy Scholz, descendant of Mary Elizabeth Clayton Miller Taylor, and her husband, Herbert Scholz, who provided many of the details that give life to her story.

A special thanks to Alice Hughes who, despite many demands on her time, was always available with advice, encouragement, and guidance.

1. Of the 244 early quilts, 3 are dated but not signed, 7 are signed but not dated, and 16 are both signed and dated. Two additional quilts, both of which are signed and dated by one of the known early quiltmakers, subsequently came to light while researching this chapter, although they were not documented by the GQP. Of the 21 quilts bearing dates, only 12 were known to be from Georgia. Of these 12, only 3 (all by the same quiltmaker) were from a coastal county (Chatham), the rest from Carroll, Wilkes, Gordon, Twiggs, Sumter, and Webster counties. Of the remaining 9 quilts, 2 were of unknown origin, 3 were from out of state but the owner did not know from which state, and 1 each were from Virginia, South Carolina, Tennessee, and New York.

2. Documented designs for quilts of this period were as follows: 8 Irish Chain, 7 Tulip, 5 Sunburst, 5 Mariner's Compass, 5 New York Beauty, 4 Log Cabin, 4 One-Patch; 37 rose or floral, 9 album or wreath, and 3 original design.

3. Appling County was subdivided into several counties over its long history, and at the time of Kirkland's death he was living in Coffee County. The location of his farm is now present-day Atkinson County.

4. The information about the Timothy Kirkland estate was provided by Sue Kirkland McCranie, descendant of Timothy Kirkland and devoted volunteer of the GQP. Sue and her husband, Shasta, spent many long days helping at many of the Quilt History Days, Sue as a documentor and Shasta as a photography assistant. In addition, Sue provided valuable research assistance and advice for several chapters of this book.

5. William's daughter, Miss May Harp, owned the quilt until her death at age 109 in 1998. Nancilu Burdick, quilt historian and author, first alerted the GQP to its existence. Thanks to her and to the efforts of Carolyn Cary of the Fayette County Historical Society, the GQP was able to locate and document this exceptional piece.

SOURCES

Brackman, Barbara. *Clues in the Calico.* Sedona, Ariz.: EPM Publications, 1989.

Capps, Clifford S., and Eugenia Burney. *Colonial Georgia.* Nashville: Thomas Nelson, 1972.

Clinton, Catherine. *The Plantation Mistress: Woman's World in the Old South.* New York: Pantheon, 1982.

*Columbian Museum*, December 1796.

Finley, Ruth E. *Old Patchwork Quilts.* Newton Centre, Mass.: Charles T. Branford, 1929.

Georgia Historical Society Archives, Savannah.

*Georgian*, April 1839.

Jones, Charles C. *History of Georgia.* Vol. 1. Boston: Houghton Mifflin, 1883.

King, Spencer B., Jr. *Darien: The Death and Rebirth of a Southern Town.* Macon, Ga.: Mercer University Press, 1981.

Lane, Mills. *The People of Georgia: An Illustrated History.* Savannah: Beehive Press, 1975.

McCullar, Bernice. *This Is Your Georgia.* Montgomery, Ala.: Viewpoint, 1972.

*Morning News*, April 1889.

Orlofsky, Patsy, and Myron Orlofsky. *Quilts in America.* New York: McGraw-Hill, 1974.

Pettit, Florence H. *America's Printed and Painted Fabrics.* New York: Hastings House, 1970.

Rehmel, Judy. *The Quilt I.D. Book: 4,000 Illustrated and Indexed Patterns.* New York: Prentice Hall, 1986.

*Savannah*, December 1816, February 1829.

*Savannah Republican*, January 1865.

Smith, Julia Floyd. *Slavery and Rice Culture in Low Country Georgia, 1750–1860.* Knoxville: University of Tennessee Press, 1985.

U.S. Bureau of the Census. Census records for Georgia, 1820 through 1880.

## Chapter 3. Julia Anderson Bush, "Tattered Veterans and Genteel Beauties: Survivors of the War between the States"

NOTES

1. Quoted in Harold Martin, *Georgia: A History* (New York: Norton, 1977), 107.

2. Jim Miles, *To the Sea* (Nashville: Rutledge Hill Press, 1989), 53.

3. On raffle items, see Bryding Adams Henley, "Alabama

Gunboat Quilts," *Uncoverings 1987*, ed. Laurel Horton and Sally Garoutte (San Francisco: American Quilt Study Group, 1989). In preparing this chapter, I decided to include only those quilts that weathered the Civil War, were made during the war, or have a memorial theme relating to the war. The many other quilts made by wives and widows of war veterans that were documented during the GQP are not included in this chapter because many of these were made well into the late nineteenth century and have no relationship to the war. An exception is the fine Baltimore Album–style quilt, which was made in 1870 but has an appropriate connection to the war.

4. Company D, Sixteenth Georgia Regiment, was also called the Sallie Twiggs Regiment.

5. This style of quilt began to appear in the Baltimore area in the mid-1840s. It is a finely appliquéd, sampler style (each block different) quilt, often with embroidered and/or inked embellishments. Urns, floral wreath, bouquets, birds, and other botanical motifs are common. These quilts were frequently made by groups of women, each woman contributing a block, sometimes signing her name or initials. The popularity of these quilts seemed to wane after about 1860, suggesting that the patterns for the blocks were prepared by one or more individual designers and then sold to the makers (see Jennifer F. Goldsborough, "An Album of Baltimore Album Quilt Studies," *Uncoverings 1994*). Today, this style of quilt enjoys a resurgence, and many of today's quiltmakers consider their Baltimore Album to be their masterwork.

## Chapter 4. Patricia Phillips Marshall, "King Cotton"

NOTES

1. *Albany Patriot* 5, no. 2 (21 Apr. 1849): 2; *Worth County Local* 4, no. 31 (17 Nov. 1888): 2.

2. On extent of cotton growing in Georgia, see George B. Crawford, "Cotton, Land, and Sustenance: Toward the Limits of Abundance in Late Antebellum Georgia," *Georgia Historical Quarterly* 72, no. 2 (summer 1988): 215–47; on introduction of Sea Island cotton, see James C. Bonner, *A History of Georgia Agriculture, 1732–1860* (Athens: University of Georgia Press, 1964), 51; on color range, see Robert H. Baird, *The American Cotton Spinner and Managers and Carders Guide* (Philadelphia: A. Hart, 1852), 237, and Paul H. Nystrom, *Textiles* (New York: D. Appleton Century, 1933), 41.

3. On Sea Island cotton, see Herbert R. Maurersberger, ed., *Matthews' Textile Fibers: Their Physical, Microscopic, and Chemical Properties* (New York: John Wiley, 1954), 112; on rice and indigo, see Bonner, *History of Georgia Agriculture*, 47–48.

4. Dr. Isabel B. Wingate, ed., *Fairchild's Dictionary of Textiles* (New York: Fairchild, 1967), 514; Nystrom, *Textiles*, 41; Nancy Bradfield, *900 Years of English Costume: From the Eleventh to the Twentieth Century*, rev. ed. (New York: Crescent Books, 1938, 1987), 131.

5. For prices, see M. B. Hammond, *The Cotton Industry: An Essay in American Economic History* (New York: Macmillan, 1897), 19. For use in cotton goods, see Bonner, *History of Georgia Agriculture*, 49; Nystrom, *Textiles*, 42; Wingate, *Fairchild's Dictionary*, 613.

6. Bonner, *History of Georgia Agriculture*, 52.

7. For amount of cotton, see Hammond, *Cotton Industry*, 23; for production increases with Whitney's gin, see Bonner, *History of Georgia Agriculture*, 52–53.

8. Bonner, *History of Georgia Agriculture*, 53.

9. Ibid., 53–54.

10. On effect of new inventions on demand, see Hammond, *Cotton Industry*, 12–16; for 1850s production, see Crawford, "Cotton, Land, and Sustenance," 240–47.

11. On development, see Ralph Betts Flanders, *Plantation Slavery in Georgia* (Chapel Hill: University of North Carolina Press, 1933), 62; on yeoman farms, see Steven Hahn, *The Roots of Southern Populism: Yeoman Farmers and the Transformation of the Georgia Upcountry, 1850–1890* (New York: Oxford University Press, 1983), 29; on concentration of slaves, see Flanders, *Plantation Slavery*, 63, and Thomas W. Hadler and Howard A. Shretter, *Atlas of Georgia* (Athens: Institute of Community and Area Development, University of Georgia, 1986), 84.

12. For 1920s prices, see Bonner, *History of Georgia Agriculture*, 56; on increased production in Georgia, see Willard Range, *A Century of Georgia Agriculture, 1850–1950* (Athens: University of Georgia Press, 1954), 14, and Flanders, *Plantation Slavery*, 66; for production figures, see Tenth Census of the United States of America, 1880, *Report of the Productions of Agriculture* (Washington, D.C.: 1883), 18.

13. On spacing, see Bonner, *History of Georgia Agriculture*, 51–52; for more on western movement, see Range, *A Century of Georgia Agriculture*, 18.

14. On guano, see Bonner, *History of Georgia Agriculture*, 188; on mechanical fertilizer, see D. A. Tompkins, *Cotton and Cotton Oil* (Charlotte: D. A. Tompkins, 1901), 135.

15. The John McDuffie estate inventory, Wilcox County, Georgia, 1896, lists not only a Dow Law planter but also a guano distributor. For planting process, see Tompkins, *Cotton*, 135, 149.

16. Tompkins, *Cotton*, 150; Charles Joyner, *Remember Me: Slave Life in Coastal Georgia* (Atlanta: Georgia Humanities Council, 1989), 8; Pete Daniels, *Breaking the Land: The Transformation of Cotton, Tobacco, and Rice Cultures since 1880* (Urbana: University of Illinois Press, 1985), 4; Tompkins, *Cotton*, 154.

17. Quotation in Joyner, *Remember Me*, 8; Collier's statistics in Flanders, *Plantation Slavery*, 84–85; Daniels, *Breaking the Land*, 4.

18. Statistics from 1876 in Hammond, *Cotton Industry*, 129; school closings in *Berrien County Pioneer*, 5 and 19 Sep. 1890; *Douglas Breeze*, 10 Jan. 1896, 2.

19. *Worth County Local* 2, no. 20 (9 Sep. 1887), 3.

20. Tompkins, *Cotton*, 162.

21. J. L. Herring, *Saturday Night Sketches* (Tifton: Sunny South Press, 1978), 143–45.

22. GQP documentation form 2090.

23. Production increase in *Georgia Historical and Industrial* (Atlanta: Franklin Printing and Publishing Co. for the Department of Agriculture, 1901), 352; local accounts in *Worth County Local* 4, no. 19 (25 Aug. 1888) and no. 25 (6 Oct. 1888); James Hancock Estate Inventory, Worth County, 14 Jan. 1891; Thomas Warren Estate Inventory, Wilcox County, 30 Nov. 1891.

24. Herring, *Saturday Night Sketches*, 221.

25. *Worth County Local* 2, no. 32 (27 Nov. 1886); 4, no. 38 (5 Jan. 1889), no. 36 (22 Dec. 1888), and no. 39 (12 Jan. 1889); value of products in Range, *Century of Georgia Agriculture*, 116–17.

26. Frederick Law Olmsted in *The Cotton Kingdom*, ed. by Arthur M. Schlesinger (New York: Alfred A. Knopf, 1953), 206; Bottoms quoted in Nancilu B. Burdick, *Legacy: The Story of Talula Gilbert Bottoms and Her Quilts* (Nashville: Rutledge Hill Press, 1988), 43. Bottoms's childhood occurred during the difficult period of Southern Reconstruction. Although sewing machines were readily available, she does not remember them because of the poverty her rural family experienced after the Civil War.

27. Estate and inventory records cited in Hahn, *Roots of Southern Populism*, 30; estate inventory of Timothy Kirkland, Coffee County, 13 Dec. 1864; estate inventories of Elizabeth Johnson, Wilcox County, 19 Sep. 1891, and Sarah P. Hancock,

Wilcox County, 28 May 1895; *Tifton Gazette* 4, no. 46 (26 Feb. 1892); *Worth County Local* 5, no. 1 (4 Apr. 1889).

28. Bottoms quoted in Burdick, *Legacy*, 36; *Worth County Local* 5, no. 6 (25 May 1889), 2.

29. GQP documentation forms 1979, 2125, 2126, 2128.

30. *Homespun to Factory Made: Woolen Textiles in America, 1776–1876* (North Andover: Merrimack Valley Textile Museum, 1977), 16.

31. Virginia G. Hower, *Weaving, Spinning, and Dyeing* (Englewood Cliffs: Prentice-Hall, 1976), 33; Herring, *Saturday Night Sketches*, 74.

32. *Homespun to Factory Made*, 22; Burdick, *Legacy*, 82; Herring, *Saturday Night Sketches*, 76–77.

33. Edward F. Worst, *Foot-Power Loom Weaving* (Milwaukee: Bruce Publishing, 1924), 20; *Homespun to Factory*, 36.

34. Although some sewing machines were used during the Civil War, the mass production of machines did not occur until afterwards. In a survey of estate inventories of South Georgia counties, sewing machines did not consistently appear until the late nineteenth century. See research files at the Georgia Agrirama, State Museum of Agriculture and Living History Site, Tifton, Georgia.

35. Lu Ann Jones, *Mama Learned Us to Work: Farm Women in the New South* (Chapel Hill: University of North Carolina Press, 2002), 8–9.

36. Annabell's father died when she was nine years old; her mother moved to Texas, leaving her to be reared by neighbors. GQP documentation form 1255.

37. Range, *Century of Georgia Agriculture*, 173, 172, 174; Gilbert C. Fite, *Cotton Fields No More: Southern Agriculture 1865–1980* (Lexington: University Press of Kentucky, 1984), 188, 194.

38. Fite, *Cotton Fields No More*, 180–225.


## Chapter 5. Vista Anne Mahan, "Textiles: Who Made Them and Who Used Them"

### NOTES

1. Lynn Patterson, letter to the author, 14 June 1994. When Patterson brought her quilt to the Quilt History Day in Toccoa, she also brought a three-page narrative to attach to the documentation forms. I wrote to Patterson for more details of this story.

2. Kenneth Coleman, ed., *A History of Georgia*, 2nd ed. (Athens: University of Georgia Press, 1991), 19.

3. Ibid., 107.

4. Marjorie W. Young, ed., *Textile Leaders of the South* (Anderson, S.C.: James R. Young, 1963), 439.

5. Jack Beatty, "Lowell Weaves a Spell," *National Geographic Traveler* 2, no. 3 (autumn 1985): 120, 122.

6. Benita Eisler, ed., *The Lowell Offering: Writings by New England Mill Women (1840–1845)* (Philadelphia: J. B. Lippincott, 1977), 24.

7. Thomas Dublin, *Women at Work: The Transformation of Work and Community in Lowell, Massachusetts, 1826–1860* (New York: Columbia University Press, 1979), 132–33.

8. Ibid., 9.

9. Young, *Textile Leaders*, 440.

10. Coleman, *History of Georgia*, 162.

11. Young, *Textile Leaders*, 455–57.

12. Robert S. Baker, *Chattooga: The Story of a County and Its People* (Roswell, Ga.: W. H. Wolfe Associates, 1988), 31.

13. Young, *Textile Leaders*, 441.

14. Baker, *Chattooga*, 427–30.

15. Coleman, *History of Georgia*, 156; on steamboats, see Amanda Johnson, *Georgia as Colony and State* (Atlanta: Cherokee, 1970), 234.

16. Glenda Major and Forrest Clark Johnson III, *Treasures of Troup County: A Pictorial History* (LaGrange, Ga.: Troup County Historical Society, 1993), 145.

17. Coleman, *History of Georgia*, 158–59.

18. Ibid., 170; Young, *Textile Leaders*, 441, 443; Coleman, *History of Georgia*, 234.

19. Young, *Textile Leaders*, 455; Baker, *Chattooga*, 438.

20. Baker, *Chattooga*, 444; Coleman, *History of Georgia*, 236.

21. Mildred Gwin Andrews, *The Men and the Mills: A History of the Southern Textile Industry* (Macon, Ga.: Mercer University Press, 1987), 1–4.

22. Dublin, *Women at Work*, 22.

23. Ibid., 61–64.

24. Lynn Patterson, letter to author, 14 June 1994; Emily Collette, letter to author, 4 Aug. 1994.

25. Jacquelyn Dowd Hall et al., *Like a Family: The Making of a Southern Cotton Mill World* (Chapel Hill: University of North Carolina Press, 1987), 33.

26. Merle Travis, "Sixteen Tons," sung by Tennessee Ernie Ford, 1955, CAPITOL 3262; Douglas Flamming, *Creating the Modern South: Millhands and Managers in Dalton, Georgia, 1884–1984* (Chapel Hill: University of North Carolina Press, 1992), 91.

27. Ralph Bankey, interview with author, July 1994; Frank James Norman supplied information contained in Emily Collette's letter to author, 6 Aug. 1994.

28. Gavin Wright, *Old South, New South: Revolutions in the Southern Economy* (New York: Basic Books, 1986), 122.

29. Flamming, *Creating the Modern South*, 190–91.

30. Ibid., 190.

31. Ibid., 207, 229.

32. Ibid., 239–42.

33. Baker, *Chattooga*, 656.

34. Flamming, *Creating the Modern South*, 244–45.

35. Maria Neder Douglas, *A Handmade Life: Ida Whaley Chance of Dalton* (Athens, Ga.: Agee, 1988), 1–2.

36. Flamming, *Creating the Modern South*, 236.

37. Ibid., 278.

38. Elaine Taylor, *I've Had a Millionaire's Fun: The Mose Taylor Story* (Dalton, Ga.: Painter and Taylor, 1982), 86; Flamming, *Creating the Modern South*, 279.

39. Flamming, *Creating the Modern South*, 311.

40. Beatty, "Lowell Weaves a Spell," 124.

41. Scott Thomas, interview with author, 1 Feb. 2005.

42. Bets Ramsey, letter to the author, July 1994.

43. Some information on Trion is from Baker, *Chattooga*, 428–29. Other information is from interviews with Ralph Bankey, Jeanne Bille, and Catherine Hurtt, summer 1994.

## Chapter 6. Anita Zaleski Weinraub, "African American Quiltmaking in Georgia"

### NOTES

I would like to thank all the quiltmakers and owners interviewed for this chapter for their cooperation, friendship, and willingness to share personal data. In addition, heartfelt thank-yous are due to Madeline Hawley for her research assistance and to the late Janice Morrill for her editorial advice.

1. Of all of the state quilt documentation projects conducted throughout the country, only Michigan documented more quilts than Georgia. Most of Michigan's quilts, however, were made in the last quarter of the twentieth century. On abundant African American quilts, telephone conversation on 25 September 1998 with Roland L. Freeman, independent quilt documenter, photographer, and author of *A Communion of the Spirits: African-American Quilters, Preservers, and Their Stories* (Nashville: Rutledge Hill Press, 1996).

2. Cuesta Benberry, *Always There: The African-American Presence in American Quilts* (Louisville: Kentucky Quilt Project, 1992), 23.

3. Ibid., 24.

4. Ronald Killion and Charles Waller, eds. *Slavery Time When I Was Chillun Down on Marster's Plantation* (Savannah: Beehive Press, 1973), ix, 12.

5. Ibid., 6.

6. Manuscript 916, Ex-Slave Interviews, Hargrett Rare Book and Manuscript Library, University of Georgia, Nancy Boudry interview, 5.

7. Killion and Waller, *Slavery Time*, 83.

8. *Noble Hill–Wheeler Memorial Center*, brochure (Noble Hill–Wheeler State Historic Site, 1989).

9. Alexa Benson Henderson, *Atlanta Life Insurance Company* (Tuscaloosa: University of Alabama Press, 1990), 3–19, xi.

10. The Madison-Morgan Cultural Center undertook a documentation of Morgan County quilts in May of 1989. The GQP provided several of the volunteers at this daylong documentation, giving the project a preview of what was in store for it when its own Quilt History Days would begin in January 1990. Information from 1860 census from telephone conversation with Georgia Department of Archives and History, May 1995.

11. For more information about this foundation, visit www.clarafordfoundation.blogspot.com. To see Clara Ford's quilts, visit www.clarafordgallery.blogspot.com.

## Chapter 7. Catherine L. Holmes, "The Darling Offspring of Her Brain: The Quilts of Harriett Powers"

### NOTES

1. Jennie Smith, "A Biblical Quilt." Smith wrote this seventeen-page account of the quilt, possibly for publication, before the Atlanta Cotton States and International Exposition opened in September 1895. Georgia counties were invited to participate in late 1894, so Smith probably wrote the account in 1895. The anonymity of the Athens fair's entries is mentioned in "A Talented Young Artist," Athens *Banner-Watchman*, 16 Nov. 1886, 1. Harriett Powers's full name can be found in Clarke County State of Georgia Returns and Mixed Records Book AA 1868–1884, 33.

2. Alice Walker, *In Search of Our Mothers' Gardens: Wom-*

anist Prose by Alice Walker* (New York: Harcourt Brace Jovanovich, 1983), 239.

3. Grace Glueck, "The Art-Minded Have a Field Day," *New York Times*, 17 Feb. 1990, 15.

4. Throughout this chapter I use the spelling of "Harriett" as found on her gravestone. Harriett Powers's full name can be found in Clarke County State of Georgia Returns and Mixed Records Book AA 1868–1884, 33. Books containing information about Harriett Powers include Gladys-Marie Fry, *Stitched from the Soul: Slave Quilts from the Ante-Bellum South* (New York: Dutton Studio Books and the Museum of American Folk Art, 1990), 84–91; John Michael Vlach, *The Afro-American Tradition in Decorative Arts* (Athens: University of Georgia Press, 1990), 44–54; Mary E. Lyons, *Stitching Stars: The Story Quilts of Harriet Powers* (New York: Scribner's, 1997); and Regenia A. Perry, *Harriet Powers's Bible Quilts* (New York: Rizzoli, 1994). A description of the Lester property can be found in the 1840 Madison County Tax Roll, Grove Hill District. Nancy Lester's father, Humphrey Hendrick, and John Lester's father, Thomas Lester, appear in the 1782 Census of Pittsylvania County (from the Records of the Circuit Court of Pittsylvania County, Virginia) and the 1800 Oglethorpe County Georgia Census.

5. Oglethorpe County Will Book A 1793–1807, Will of Thomas Lester, 175, 176; Oglethorpe County Deed Book J, Will of Humphrey Hendrick, 124, 125; Madison County Miscellaneous Bonds 1794–1890, 340; Madison County Georgia Minutes of the Court of Ordinary Book A 1812–1832, 141; Madison County Georgia Bond Book, 42; Madison County Georgia Marriage Index Book A, 111; 1840 Federal Census of Walton County, Ga.; Oglethorpe County Deed Book E 1806–1809, 56, 109. Nancy Lester appeared as head of household in the 1840, 1850, and 1860 Federal Censuses of Madison County, Ga. Madison County documents can be found in the Probate Court located in the Madison County Government Complex in Danielsville, Ga. Oglethorpe County documents can be found in Oglethorpe County Courthouse in Lexington, Ga.

6. Harriet's son Alonzo Powers was interviewed in 1939 by Ina B. Hawkes for the Folklore Project of the Federal Writers' Project for the U.S. Works Progress Administration (WPA). All descriptions and quotes that follow come from this interview, "Reminiscences of a Negro Preacher," which can be found on the Library of Congress website at http://lcweb2.loc.gov/ammen/wpaintro/wpahome.html. Alonzo Powers's interview may also be found in Al Hester, ed., *Athens Mem-*

ories: *The WPA Federal Writers' Project Interviews* (Athens: Green Berry Press, 2001), 1–12.

7. Alonzo Powers, WPA interview.

8. The ages of Harriett's mother and the two girls belonging to the Lesters can be traced in the 1840, 1850, and 1860 Federal Censuses and Slave Schedules of Madison County, Ga.

9. John Blassingame, *Slave Community: Plantation Life in the Antebellum South* (New York: Oxford University Press 1972), 164; 1870 Federal Census for Madison County, Ga.

10. Nancy Lester is recorded as illiterate in the 1840 Federal Census for Madison County, Ga. Harriett Powers is recorded as illiterate in the 1880 Federal Census for Clark County, Ga. Albert J. Raboteau, *Slave Religion: The "Invisible Institution" in the Antebellum South* (New York: Oxford University Press, 1978).

11. 1880 Federal Census, Clarke County; Alonzo Powers, WPA interview.

12. Clarke County State of Georgia Returns and Mixed Records Book AA 1868–1884, 33.

13. Powers quoted in Lucine Finch, "A Sermon in Patchwork," originally published in *Outlook Magazine*, 28 Oct. 1914. Republished in Kristen Frederickson and Sarah E. Webb, eds., *Singular Women: Writing the Artist* (Berkeley: University of California Press, 2003), 96, 98. Descriptions for each square of this quilt were transcribed in a letter by Jennie Smith (ca. 1891, Smithsonian National Museum of American History) and are reprinted in Perry's *Bible Quilts*, 5.

14. On avoidance of symmetry, see Robert Farris Thompson, *Flash of the Spirit: African and Afro-American Art and Philosophy* (New York: Vintage Books, 1984), 218–22. John Michael Vlach documents similarities between Powers's quilts and various African textiles in *Afro-American Tradition in Decorative Arts*, 44–54. On blending of African influences in U.S. slave culture, see Michael A. Gomez, *Exchanging Our Country Marks: The Transformation of African Identities in the Colonial and Antebellum South* (Chapel Hill: University of North Carolina Press, 1998). The birthplaces of Harriet and Armsted Powers and their parents are indicated in the 1900 Federal Census for Clarke County, Ga.

15. *Athens Weekly Banner-Watchman*, 11 Nov. 1886, 1.

16. *Athens Weekly Banner-Watchman*, 16 Nov. 1886, 1; Fry, *Stitched from the Soul*, 86.

17. Deed Record KK, Clarke County, Office of County Court, Athens, Ga., 1891.

18. Fry, *Stitched from the Soul*, 86.

19. Reprinted in *Parson's Weekly Blade*, 21 Nov. 1895, 1.

20. "The Colored Race at Atlanta," *Broad Ax* (Salt Lake City, Utah), 7 Dec. 1895, 1.

21. Ibid. This is the only known description of the Bible Quilt by someone who saw it at the Atlanta exposition.

22. Fry, *Stitched from the Soul*, 86.

23. On forest fire, see Timothy Dwight, quoted in *Connecticut Historical Collections*, compiled by John Warner Barber (Storrs, Conn.: Bibliopola, 1999), 403; on Leonid meteor shower, see Samuel Rogers, *Toils and Struggles of the Olden Times* (n.p.: Standard Publishing Co., 1880); Ellen Gould Harmon White, *The Spirit of Prophecy: The Great Controversy between Christ and His Angels and Satan and His Angels* (n.p.: Seventh-Day Adventist Pub. Association, 1870), 304, 308.

24. Alonzo Powers, WPA interview.

25. Finch, "Sermon in Patchwork," 99.

## Chapter 8. Martha H. Mulinix, "Cover: Everyday Quilts"

**NOTES**

1. R. E. Mulinix is the husband of the author.

2. Asa Mulinix is the author's grandson.

## Chapter 9. Anita Zaleski Weinraub, "There's Something about Feed Sacks . . ."

**NOTES**

Anita Weinraub began collecting feed sacks in the mid-1980s to make quilts with a Depression Era look. The going rate was then about twenty-five cents for two sacks! Eventually amassing a collection of more than two thousand sacks, she loaned several to the Smithsonian National Museum of American History for its 1991–92 exhibit, Feed Bags as Fashion.

The epigraph to this chapter is quoted from *Georgia Quilts: Stitches and Stories*, Georgia Public Television, 1998.

1. Ricky Clark, George W. Knepper, and Ellice Ronsheim, *Quilts in Community: Ohio's Traditions* (Nashville: Rutledge Hill Press, 1991), 94. No home-sewn sacks were discovered during Georgia's documentation, however.

2. Owners of nineteenth-century quilts often stated that natural dyes (walnut hulls, red clay, pokeberries, etc.) were

used to dye the sack. Rit was the commercial dye most often mentioned by owners or makers of twentieth-century quilts.

3. The earliest sack sizes corresponded to the amounts held by the earlier way of packaging or transporting goods, the barrel. Thus a quarter barrel corresponded to a forty-nine-pound sack, a half barrel to a ninety-eight-pound sack. Standardization of sack sizes began in the twentieth century and continued during World War II with increased regulation.

4. John Steele Gordon, "The Chicken Story," *American Heritage*, September 1996, 52.

5. Dr. Beth Thorne and Dr. Joanna Nesselroad, Fairmont State College, presentation on feed sacks at the American Quilt Study Group's Annual Seminar in Charleston, W.Va., 17 Oct. 1998.

6. One of the class members, Opal Fowler Reece, responded to a GQP query published in the *Farmers and Consumers Bulletin* soliciting feed-sack recollections from readers.

7. The twister room was where the cording that went into tires was made, initially from cotton, then rayon, nylon, and eventually glass.

## Chapter 10. Janice Morrill, "Georgia's Quilting Groups: Shared in the Making, Shared in the Giving"

### NOTES

Susan Neill, chief curator of the Atlanta History Center, provided updates to the original manuscript of this chapter after the 2003 death of Janice Morrill.

1. Findings are based on the following primary sources: written survey of thirty-four Georgia quilting guilds conducted in 1994 by Holly Anderson; personal interviews with guild and club members (mostly unrecorded) conducted by Holly Anderson, Anita Weinraub, and other GQP volunteers during 1994–95; club minutes; telephone interviews and correspondence received by GQP personnel in response to requests for information in the *Market Bulletin*. The membership of the clubs described in this chapter is Anglo-American unless otherwise noted, and the guilds that responded to the survey are predominantly though not exclusively white. Based on initial investigation, it appears that the patterns and purposes of group quilting described herein apply to black quilters of Georgia in many respects as well. This is discussed more fully below.

2. Rebecca Wuertemberger (quoting from her mother, Mamie Dugan), letter to GQP, 10 May 1995. Nancy Barnes of Macon recalls quiltings of this same type at her grandmother's house in Pike County during the 1930s (telephone interview with Anita Z. Weinraub, 9 March 1995).

3. Jewel Edwards of Statesboro, Bulloch County, Ga., telephone interview conducted by Janice Morrill, 9 June 1995; Annie Howard of Putnam County, personal interviews conducted by Anita Z. Weinraub, 1995.

4. Mrs. Lonnie Rogers of Ephesus, Ga., letter to GQP, received May 1995.

5. Wilma Cornelius, tape-recorded interview conducted by GQP volunteer Sue McCranie, 8 May 1995.

6. *Berrien Press* (Nashville, Ga.), 1976.

7. John A. Burrison, "The Cat in the Quilt: Social Dimensions of a Folk Art," in *Patterns: A Celebration of Georgia's Quilting Traditions*, exhibition catalog from Madison-Morgan Cultural Center, Madison, Ga., 8 Sept.–28 Oct. 1990, 6–11.

8. On history of quiltmaking, see Laurel Horton, "Quiltmaking Traditions in Georgia," in *Patterns* (see note 7), 12–13; Pat Ferrero et al., *Hearts and Hands: The Influence of Women and Quilts on American Society* (San Francisco: Quilt Digest Press, 1987), 28.

9. Catherine A. Cerney, "A Quilt Guild: Its Role in the Elaboration of Female Identity," *Uncoverings* 1991: 46.

10. Joyce Ice, "Women's Aesthetics and the Quilting Process," in *Feminist Theory and the Study of Folklore*, ed. Susan Tower Hollis et al. (Urbana: University of Illinois Press, 1993), 166–77.

11. See Gayle R. Davis, "Kansas Quilting Groups: Surviving the Pressures of Change," in *Kansas Quilts and Quilters*, ed. Barbara Brackman et al. (Lawrence: University Press of Kansas, 1993), 177–88; Joyce Ice, "Splendid Companionship and Practical Assistance," in *Quilted Together: Women, Quilts, & Communities*, ed. Joyce Ice et al. (Delhi, N.Y.: Delaware County Historical Association, 1989), 15; also Cerney, "Quilt Guild," 45.

12. On Brown Sugar Stitchers: Maxine Moore of Lawrenceville, Gwinnett County, Ga., telephone interview conducted by Susan Neill, 2 May 2005; Brown Sugar Stitchers Web site, www.quiltsites.com/brownsugarstitchers.htm. Known as the "mother of orphans," Carrie Steele Logan was born into slavery and orphaned as a young child. Her empathy for Atlanta's abandoned children compelled her in 1888 to take orphans into her own home, write her autobiography,

and sell her house to raise money for a larger orphanage—a three-story brick building dedicated in 1892. Today the Carrie Steele-Pitts Home continues Mrs. Logan's legacy (see www.csph.org).

13. Jan Brashears, interview conducted by Holly Anderson of GQP, 1995.

14. More than thirty years of club minutes recording the activities of the Busy Bees and more than thirty-two years of the Pine Needle Sewing Club's minutes reveal little attention to quilts per se. While quilting has been mentioned as an activity, no discussion of quilts themselves is found (no description of patterns or fabric, for example), and quilt displays or competitions are never mentioned. (While Pine Needle Sewing Club minutes do not discuss quilt patterns or colors, in two *Berrien Press* articles, reporting on meetings of 20 May 1976 and 17 July 1976, quilt colors and designs are described.) For the Busy Bee Home Demonstration Club, monthly demonstrations by club members have included gift making, craft projects, and needlework such as crewel and embroidery, but no quilting-related subjects! The Busy Bee Club did organize competitions among its members, but not of quilts or other needle arts. There were several contests in flower arranging and awards given for "dress revues."

15. Wilma Cornelius of New Lois, Ga., letter to GQP, 20 April 1995.

## Chapter 11. Anita Zaleski Weinraub, "The Olympic Gift Quilts: Georgia Quiltmakers Welcome the World"

### NOTES

1. Jacqueline M. Atkins and Phyllis A. Tepper, *New York Beauties: Quilts from the Empire State* (New York: Dutton Studio Books in association with the Museum of American Folk Art, 1992).

2. Carol Logan Newbill, *The Olympic Games Gift Quilts: America's Welcome to the World* (Birmingham, Ala.: Oxmoor House, 1996). The Atlanta History Center exhibition was titled Olympic Games Quilts: Georgia's Welcome to the World.

# *About the Contributors*

--------------------------------------------------

**Julia Anderson Bush**

Judy Bush is a lover of things old who made her first quilt block while sitting on her grandmother's front porch when she was twelve years old. She is a talented quiltmaker and popular lecturer whose specialty is miniature quilts. A descendant of Confederate soldiers, this native Georgian has brought an unerring eye and personal perspective to our book.

**Catherine L. Holmes**

Catherine Holmes is a writer, quilter, and graduate student at the University of Georgia. She lives in Athens with her husband, David Berle; daughter, Chloe; sons, Orion and Gabriel; and stepdaughter, Hannah. She is currently working on a book about Harriett Powers.

**Vista Anne Mahan**

Vista Anne Mahan was a volunteer worker for state documentation projects in Georgia and Tennessee. Her original research, "Quilts Used as Backdrops in Old Photographs," has been published in *Uncoverings 1991*, *Lady's Circle Patchwork Quilts*, *Georgia Journal*, and a Japanese magazine, *Patchwork Quilt Tsushin*.

She is a member of the American Quilt Study Group, Georgia Quilt Council, Chattanooga Quilters' Guild, and Choo Choo Quilters (former president). She is a magna cum laude graduate of the University of Tennessee at Chattanooga and the laboratory coordinator and instructor in anatomy and physiology at Chattanooga State Technical Community College. She and her husband, Charles, have traveled extensively throughout the United States, Canada, New Zealand, and Australia and have made many trips to Europe to study art history. They live in Rising Fawn, Georgia.

**Patricia Phillips Marshall**

Pat Marshall is curator of furnishings and decorative arts at the North Carolina Museum of History. She was formerly the coordinator of Curatorial and Research Services at the Georgia Agrirama in Tifton. In addition to serving on the GQP board, Pat was a regional coordinator for the GQP and organized several of the Quilt History Days held in South Georgia. She has curated many exhibitions and written many articles for a variety of publications. She is currently at work on a book about Thomas Day, a free African American cabinetmaker of the nineteenth century.

## Irene McLaren

A Florida resident since 1946, Irene McLaren spent her summers in Hiawassee, Geogia, from 1982 until 1996. Her interest in old quilts and early quiltmaking led her to take classes in quilt history and documentation from such experts as Barbara Brackman, Katy Christopherson, Suellen Meyer, and Julie Silber. She has worked as a documenter and in other capacities for quilt projects in North Carolina, Florida, and Georgia. A quilt judge, certified by the National Quilting Association Inc. in 1985, she is a member of the teaching team for the NQA-sponsored three-day Short Course on Quilt Judging. She is a teacher, lecturer, and writer, as well as an award-winning quiltmaker. Her publishing credits include *The Professional Quilter*, *Patchwork Patter*, and *Country Quilts*.

## Janice Morrill

A graduate of the University of California–Los Angeles (BA, anthropology) and the University of North Carolina–Chapel Hill (MA, folklore), Janice Morrill was a folklorist, project manager, and exhibit coordinator. She wrote and edited promotional materials, text for exhibits, and numerous articles. She was published in a wide array of publications, including specialized interpretive and informative materials, books, journals, and newspapers. As a folklorist she conducted research and produced text for exhibits that were rich with cultural history, several of which received national recognition for their excellence. Janice died in October 2003.

## Martha H. Mulinix

Martha H. Mulinix was born in the mountains of North Georgia to a self-sufficient family that made quilts for bedcovers. Seven years at Berry Schools instilled an appreciation for the simple way of life that a utility quilt represents. A graduate of Berry High School and Berry College, Martha holds master's and professional degrees in education from the University of Georgia. A former public-school teacher and counselor, she has become known as Bartow County's Quilting Lady. In 1986 Martha was awarded the Bartow Cultural Heritage Award, presented annually by the Etowah Creative Arts Council to a local artist chosen for his or her long-term impact on the arts.

## Darlene R. Roth

Darlene Roth has a doctorate in American studies from George Washington University. She pioneered in the field of public history in Atlanta for more than two decades, working in historic preservation, public interpretation, and museums and writing books and articles on local history. She now makes her home in Cottage Grove, Oregon, where she writes, consults, and pursues new endeavors.

## Anita Zaleski Weinraub

Anita Weinraub has been chairwoman of the GQP since its formation in 1989. She holds BS (conservation) and MBA (finance) degrees from the University of Michigan and studied for three years at the University of Valencia in Spain. She is a member of the American Quilt Study Group, the Georgia Quilt Council, and the Gwinnett Quilters' Guild. She has published many articles on quiltmaking and quilt history, both nationally and internationally (U.K., Japan, Australia), especially on the Olympic quilts. Anita has curated four quilt exhibits at the Atlanta History Center. She lives with her mother and daughter in Atlanta.

# A Tribute to Bill Weinraub, 1948–1997

Bill Weinraub, 1990.

A devoted volunteer photographer, husband, and father who attended seventy-odd Quilt History Days across the width and breadth of Georgia, Bill Weinraub also unstintingly provided other assistance to the GQP from its inception. He snapped more than forty thousand 35mm exposures of quilts during GQP's Quilt History Days, as well as completing the medium-format photography for this book and for *The Olympic Games Gift Quilts: America's Welcome to the World*. Bill's untimely death in 1997 was a great loss not only to his family but to the world of quilt photography.

At our last public Quilt History Day in Stone Mountain in January 1993, the idea was hatched to recognize Bill for his efforts on behalf of the GQP—what more fitting than a quilt? Since Bill had become somewhat of a pimiento cheese sandwich connoisseur over the course of seventy-odd Quilt History Day lunches, volunteers settled on creating a pimiento cheese quilt for him. Photography volunteers and others from around the state made eight-inch blocks with the theme of pimiento cheese. Others were asked to sign their names and cities on pieces of muslin provided—these signatures became the border. Say Cheese is not only a colorful expression of appreciation to a volunteer who truly went above and beyond on behalf of the GQP but also the only known pimiento cheese quilt in existence.

Say Cheese. Original design made by volunteers of the GQP for photographer William C. L. Weinraub, 1994. 81" x 91". Machine- and hand-pieced, hand-appliquéd, hand-quilted cottons; polyester and synthetic embellishments. Collection of Anita Z. Weinraub. [GQP 8138]

# Index

------------------------------------------------